TED AXELROD

JIM AXELROD
In the Long Run

Jim Axelrod, a national correspondent
for CBS News, previously served as
chief White House correspondent.

IN THE LONG RUN

In the Long Run

A Father,
a Son, *and*
Unintentional
Lessons in
Happiness

JIM AXELROD

FARRAR, STRAUS AND GIROUX | NEW YORK

FARRAR, STRAUS AND GIROUX
18 West 18th Street, New York 10011

Printed in the United States of America
Published in 2011 by Farrar, Straus and Giroux
First paperback edition, 2012

The Library of Congress has cataloged the hardcover edition as follows:
Axelrod, Jim, 1963–
    In the long run : a father, a son, and unintentional lessons in happiness /
Jim Axelrod.— 1st ed.
        p.   cm.
    ISBN 978-0-374-19211-2 (alk. paper)
    1. Axelrod, Jim, 1963–   2. Television journalists—United States—Biography.
3. Fathers and sons.   4. Marathon running—Biography.   5. Runners (Sports)—
Biography.   6. New York City Marathon.   I. Title.

PN4874.A875A3 2011
070.92—dc22
[B]

                                                                  2010047717

Paperback ISBN: 978-0-8090-5752-8

Designed by Abby Kagan

www.fsgbooks.com

P1

FOR CHRISTINA
*who is always waiting with love
at the finish line*

Happiness is as a butterfly, which, when pursued, is always beyond our grasp, but which, if you will sit down quietly, may alight upon you.

—NATHANIEL HAWTHORNE

All men should try to learn before they die what they are running from, and to, and why.

—FORTUNE COOKIE

CONTENTS

IN THE LONG RUN

My BlackBerry started buzzing on my right hip just as the crowd got its first glimpse of Barack Obama. I'd put it on vibrate, since I knew I'd never hear the ringtone once Obama appeared on the floor of the Toyota Center in Houston. The roar was immediate as he glided into the arena from a corner tunnel, and grew louder still as each of his loping strides carried him into fuller view of the crowd. By the time he jogged gracefully up the stairs to take the stage, I couldn't hear a word of the instructions my cameraman was yelling at me from four feet away.

I was standing on the media riser—a plywood platform set six feet off the arena's concrete floor, atop rickety scaffolding concealed by rectangles of rough royal-blue fabric. A dozen TV reporters were crammed together, each provided with a four-foot-wide broadcasting space marked off by electrical tape.

As chief White House correspondent for CBS News, I'd been assigned to cover Hillary Clinton during the Democratic primary campaign. I'd loved getting the assignment, seeing it at the outset as just the kind of validation I'd been looking for from a new set of bosses. In the last year of his increasingly unpopular presidency, George W.

Bush wasn't going to generate enough interest to get me on the evening news regularly. Lame ducks never did. So the White House was not the place to be.

When the assignments for the campaign had been doled out three months earlier, Obama was intriguing but still a long shot. Clinton was clearly the plum. Covering her positioned me not just for a short-term supply of lead stories but also for another few years on the biggest beat in TV news if she went all the way.

But since then, Obama's strong performance had raised the possibility that I hadn't landed the plum after all. I'd grown eager to see him live on the campaign trail. The breathless descriptions I'd been reading of the raw emotion Obama generated in the crowds hadn't set any standards for journalistic objectivity, but the reporters who wrote them hadn't oversold.

Standing in front of the camera making my last-minute preparations before I went on, I looked to my left and saw an African American man in his mid-thirties hoist a boy onto his shoulders so the kid could get a better look. The man's face was pulled tight in a severe smile, astonished to be sure but cautious as well, as if he wasn't quite sure he could trust what he was seeing. The expression on the face of the five-year-old was simpler: innocent, undiluted joy. Even if the boy didn't fully understand the meaning of the moment, he was on his daddy's shoulders. That alone was apparently reason enough for his ear-to-ear grin.

Houston might have seemed like an odd place for Obama to be on February 19, 2008, given that it was primary day in Wisconsin, but he was already looking ahead to the Texas primary in two weeks. I checked my watch, which I kept on New York time no matter where I was to stay synchronized with CBS headquarters in Manhattan. It was 9:15. At the bottom of the hour, I would update my report with a live shot for the West Coast feed of the *CBS Evening News*.

If, as some grizzled cameraman once told me, TV news is "hours of boredom, moments of terror," the live shot is the moment of terror. Not only can your whole day go to hell in an instant; your whole career can. There's a gazillion ways to screw up the shot—technical screwups, editorial screwups, going blank just when you're supposed to speak to seven million people—and every member of the live-shot team spends the last fifteen minutes checking and rechecking potential trouble spots to prevent TV tragedy.

On the media riser in Houston, Rob the cameraman and Giovanni the sound tech checked cables and lights while Chloe the producer linked up with the control room in New York. Inside the TV truck parked just outside the Toyota Center, the satellite operator made sure we had a steady broadcasting signal. As the correspondent, my obsession, naturally, was with myself. In my fifteen-minute run-up to the live shot, I flitted from applying a new layer of powder on my forehead to checking my tie knot, from smoothing the wrinkles in my suit jacket to making sure my earpiece fit snugly. Then I took a moment out of tending to the cosmetic touches and barked at the ever-calm Chloe to double-check the facts of what I was about to report.

Most of my two-minute story was a preproduced video spot running roughly a minute and a half and providing an overview of what was at stake in the Wisconsin race. That gave me fifteen seconds to introduce the spot live and fifteen seconds on the back end to add a final thought. The whole idea was to provide a way for me to update my story if anything had changed from the 6:30 East Coast broadcast. Good thing, because a few minutes after 9:00, we received word that Obama had been declared the winner in Wisconsin. Harry Smith, substituting for Katie Couric in New York, would handle that headline in his toss to me. My job was to seamlessly weave a reaction to Obama's win into my live intro.

Blowing the live shot would ruin the rest of the night and most of the next day, until I had another chance at one. Forget a thick Rolodex of sources or a finely honed ability to bang out sharp, urgent copy under deadline pressure; network news reporters are judged first and foremost by their ability to flawlessly deliver a four-sentence live introduction to a pretaped story with an insouciant air of command to millions of viewers. In the minds of the executives who run the network news operations, a single "um" or "uh" can undermine a reporter's credibility. And God save the correspondent who actually breaks eye contact with the camera to look down at his notes.

Over the years, I'd wrestled the live-shot demons to the ground. Somewhere between a live bungee jump on the local news in Syracuse and a live battlefield report under missile fire the night the war in Iraq started, I'd reached an accommodation with the pressure. Like learning to play the piano, speak French, or hit a nine iron, it was all a matter of repetition. In Syracuse, Raleigh, Miami, Dallas, Skopje, Brussels, Riga, and Amman, I'd figured out how to cleanly negotiate all the dangers and threats a live shot could present. I wasn't Edward R. Murrow, but I rarely flubbed. I still got butterflies when a director's gruff voice would urgently cue me, but hundreds of successfully negotiated live shots over the years had liberated me from the thought of a spectacular flameout recirculated in perpetuity on YouTube.

Or at least I thought it had. In the last few weeks, I'd grown less able to ignore the thoughts of failure. CBS News, my professional home for the past dozen years, had been through a violent shake-up. My new bosses were unfamiliar with my rock-solid live reports from the Iraqi battlefields. Not only were all the executives long gone who'd watched me go live flawlessly for ten minutes at a time, under fire, in the triple-digit heat of the Iraqi desert without a single "um," but so was Dan Rather, whose favor I'd earned and protection I'd enjoyed. Lately there'd been hints that my Clinton coverage had caused my stock to fall with the new executive team, but I wasn't sure. It could've easily been my paranoia, honed, like every TV reporter's, to museum-grade quality. Then came a meeting with my boss, CBS News president Sean McManus, which confirmed my suspicions with brutal clarity.

Most network news correspondents worked on three- or four-year contracts. The executives negotiated your next deal based on how often you'd been on the air during the last one. The system had been good to me over the years. I'd pushed for and received high-profile assignments—Afghanistan, Iraq, the Kerry campaign—to guarantee me an ever-increasing supply of exposure and airtime that I was able to redeem for big raises at the end of each of my three-year deals. But less than two weeks earlier, for the first time in my career at CBS, I'd pushed for a shot at a big job coming open and had the door resolutely slammed shut. Waiting on that riser, I felt some extra pressure. I needed to nail the live shot to see if I could wedge that closed door back open just enough to let a sliver of light through.

I could feel a film of sweat on my palms. Since that meeting with Sean, I'd been shaky going live, like a professional golfer suddenly unable to make a three-foot putt after twenty years of sinking them without a second thought. In golf it's called "the yips," a dreaded condition indicating that after years of battling the pressure, your nerves are shot. I was fighting a sinking suspicion that I'd contracted the broadcasting yips.

Which explains why at 9:28 New York time, I was standing on that platform in Houston, attempting to shut out eighteen thousand delirious voices chanting "Yes we can" by reciting the new copy I'd just dashed off about Obama's win. I needed to set it in my frontal lobe. I'd have one chance, and the slightest sense of panic could throw me off and cause me to go blank. Like a supplicant quietly chanting a prayer to ward off evil, I rehearsed my first line over and over, hoping to ensure a smooth start to my live shot when it was for real.

"Right now Barack Obama is riding a surge of momentum that the Clinton campaign would do anything to stop." I paused and took a deep breath, like I was between sets of bench presses. "Right now Barack Obama is riding a surge of momentum that the Clinton campaign would do anything to stop." I stopped and collected myself again. "Right now Barack Obama is riding a surge of momentum that the Clinton campaign would do anything to stop."

I couldn't decide where to put the emphasis: "a *surge* of momentum" or "a surge of *momentum*." I kept repeating it both ways, hoping one would sound better than the other to my ear. What the fuck was wrong with me? Forty-five years old, two Ivy League degrees, the chief White House correspondent for CBS News, and I was paralyzed with indecision about which of two words my bosses would want me to hit hardest.

The buzz I felt on my hip as Obama took the stage snapped me out of the inane debate I was conducting with myself. I pulled my

BlackBerry from its holster. I had no time to check the e-mail beyond the basics—sender, subject heading—just to make sure no one was forwarding any last-second development that would change my story. A quick look told me it could wait:

> *From*: Moughalian, Dave
> *Sent*: Tuesday, February 19, 2008 9:48 PM
> *To*: Axelrod, Jim
> *Subject*: pretty cool

It was from my buddy Dave, who had a habit of sending me e-mails just before broadcast time, usually to vent some impassioned hatred of George W. Bush. I loved Dave, an in-it-for-life friend since we'd been ten years old, but his timing often sucked.

We'd grown up three blocks apart, ran track together, dated the beautiful Parisi sisters in high school, and were roommates for a year after college. His mother was my high school English teacher, a wise and enchanting Armenian who immigrated to America when she was thirty-two and proceeded to teach a generation of kids in our small New Jersey town how to write. In a soft voice dipped in honey and rose water, Mrs. Moughalian had drilled into us a three-word guiding principle: Show, don't tell.

Ever since I'd met him on the first day of fifth grade, Dave had been a calming presence in my life. He took in the chaos of my parents' home—four kids; a demented Hungarian sheepdog with a thick, matted white coat and ceaseless, paint-peeling bark; and my force-of-nature father—like a kid watching a pack of agitated chimps at the zoo. He was curious and intrigued, drawn to something in the overflowing passion of the Axelrod family. Perhaps it made him feel better about the stark stillness in his own home. My father spun through our house like an F-5 tornado. Dave's father, an engineer who was often gone for months at a time on business, would return to brood deeply about his lost old-country life amid stacks of metallurgy journals. I'd always thought Dave needed the roar of the circus to balance the soft voices of the library.

Once I saw Dave's name on my BlackBerry screen, I knew I could wait until after the live shot to open the e-mail, and I returned to preparing for my imminent moment of terror. In my earpiece I heard the music that signaled the start of the broadcast. I reviewed my newly tweaked live top one more time, took a deep breath, and waited for the toss from Harry Smith.

"Jim Axelrod joins us now from Houston. Jim, a big night for Barack Obama . . ." I took it from there. All the prep work paid off. I nailed the shot, integrating the new information without a single "um" and emphasizing "surge." The control room cleared me, and I was done for the day. I unhooked my earpiece and microphone, careful to keep an impassive expression fixed on my face. I wanted to project a business-as-usual demeanor to mask the elation produced by my clean kill. Relief oozed warmly through my system. There was no better salve for the welts raised during that meeting with Sean twelve days earlier than the hope that I could still turn it all around.

I looked down at my BlackBerry again. There was nothing from New York. On the one hand, that was good news; no rockets launched about some screwup. On the other hand, while I didn't expect any "attaboys" for a job well done—a mistake-free live shot was what they were paying me to deliver, after all—I worried that the bosses had all gone home after the East Coast feed and missed my folding in the new information without breaking a sweat. I needed my new bosses to see what the old ones always had and begin to thicken the ice that had started to feel remarkably thin beneath me.

I might've been done for the day, but Obama wasn't. While he raised the roof delivering his stump speech, I walked off the arena floor and into an outer lobby, looking for a corner that might shield enough of the noise so I could call my wife. I checked in with Stina twice a day, bare minimum, once when she woke up and again just before she went to bed, and tried to catch her several other times so I could talk to our three kids as well. I could tell from the four rings before she picked up, and her sleepy voice once she did, that she'd fallen asleep reading to Bobby, our four-year-old.

"Hi, honey," she said, her voice trailing off. She sounded so worn-out. Sure she was tired of raising three kids alone, with me gone for months at a time, but this was more than fatigue. She was worried. This had nothing to do with her husband's new bosses and a change in his professional standing. In the eight years since my father died, she'd watched me head off to cover two wars, suffer enough post-traumatic stress to require several months of therapy, then allow my unrestrained ambition to lead me to an intensely demanding job at the White House. Until his death we'd been walking a path together, holding hands. Then suddenly I'd dropped hers and veered off into some thick woods, chasing something I couldn't catch. The easy joy Stina had always found as a wife and mother had started to leach from her home.

"That's okay, Stina," I told her. "Back to sleep. I'll talk to you in the morning. Love you." I hung up feeling hollow and detached. The balancing act I'd worked out long ago between my scampering up the career ladder and remaining connected to my wife and kids had started to feel badly outdated.

Wandering back into the arena, I climbed the stairs up to the media riser, pulled out my BlackBerry, and scrolled down to Dave's e-mail. I hit Open and saw a chart:

YEAR	FIRST NAME	LAST NAME	AGE	TIME
1980	ROB ERT	AXE LRO D	44	3:42:43
1981	ROB ERT	AXE LRO D	45	3:39:53
1982	ROB ERT	AXE LRO D	46	3:29:58

It took a moment for me to realize what I was looking at, and just a split second more for my nose to wrinkle and my eyes to fill. Dave, who loved to tool around on the Web, panning for whatever nuggets he could find from our pasts, had found my father's race times for the three New York City Marathons he'd run in the early 1980s.

The tears were no surprise. I'm a world-class weeper. Since she was five, my daughter, Emma, has proudly declared, "My dad cries more than most men." Funerals and weddings are for amateurs. I've lost it at the end of *Charlotte's Web*. But nothing brings the tears more reliably than thinking about my dad.

His was one of those deaths that left everyone shaking their heads and scared the hell out of the men in the neighborhood. Never mind the three marathons he'd run in his forties. He'd eaten right and hadn't been much of a drinker. His parents had been ninety-one and eighty-nine at his funeral. And my mom was a health-food nut who'd made my dad the first guy on the block to mix wheat germ into his yogurt. He bubbled over with vigor. If they could've figured out a way to harness his energy, he could've lit Cleveland for a decade. All that, and he'd died at the age of sixty-three in January 2000, following a nine-year battle with prostate cancer.

I put the BlackBerry back in its holster and watched Obama finish his stump speech. "Yes we can. Yes we can. Yes we can, Houston." The electrified crowd didn't want to go anywhere, but after ten minutes, they realized he wasn't coming back onstage. The houselights went up, and the arena began to clear.

Wanting to look at my dad's race times again, I climbed down off the riser and found a dull-brown metal folding chair, collapsed and leaning against a wall. I grabbed it, unfolded it, and sat down, rocking slightly back and forth with my BlackBerry extended at arm's length to accommodate my rapidly deteriorating vision, which I'd been refusing to acknowledge.

"Okay, let's see here, he ran 3:39:53 when he was forty-five."

I was whispering to myself, lips barely moving, as I went from column to column, performing calculations.

"He ran 3:39:53 when he was forty-five," I repeated, digesting what I was seeing. My mind raced to the next set of numbers. "Then

3:29:58, when he was forty-six." That stopped me for half a second. I remembered my dad telling me, when I was a kid and he was in the middle of his marathon years, that breaking 3:30 was a big deal. Going sub-3:30 meant running a little more than twenty-six miles at eight minutes per mile, an impressive pace.

"He broke 3:30 when he was forty-six," I continued to myself.

I sat and rocked for half a minute more, thinking of the framed photograph hanging in the front hallway of our home in the Washington, D.C., suburb of Chevy Chase, Maryland. There was my father, enraptured, crossing the finish line of one of those marathons, his arms thrusting straight up in triumph. I could use some of that. His body may have been exhausted, but his eyes were dancing. A running magazine had published it, clearly looking to inspire.

"I'd need at least a year."

I'd never run a marathon, but I'd watched my dad as he planned his training, beginning a year before the race. I knew the kind of dedication required just to finish a marathon, never mind to run one in eight-minute miles. The old man was already in top shape when he did it, having run steadily for four years before he took on the challenge. I didn't even pause—

"I could do this."

—which was slightly delusional, given that I was in the worst shape of my life, flabby in every imaginable way. Without much of a fight, I'd surrendered to the grind of the campaign trail, dismissing the thought of exercise as an indulgence the long hours didn't permit. At that moment, leaning forward in that brown metal chair, elbows on my knees, BlackBerry in my hands, belly drooping over my belt and sagging toward the floor, I couldn't run around the block.

"It might be just what I need."

I knew the New York City Marathon was always run in late October or early November. In other words, right around Election Day. No way, especially if Hillary won the nomination. But 2009 was a definite possibility. I'd be forty-six years old. My dad's age when he ran his last New York City Marathon would be my age running my first.

"Twenty-one months. I could do that."

I tried to slow myself down to take full measure of what I was contemplating. But I couldn't. My very next thought was on me in a heartbeat. It wasn't a choice. It was instinct. There was nothing conscious about it.

"I bet I can run it faster than he did."

When it comes to childhood memories, especially the earliest ones, it's hard to be sure whether you are recalling an event as you remember it unfolding, or whether you've heard someone else's account so many times you've adopted it as your own. When it comes to my first memory of my father, I don't have any doubt—it is mine, all mine.

In the summer of 1965, my parents took my sister and me to the New York World's Fair. We were approaching the end of the Walt Disney exhibit It's a Small World, the one where a little boat floated through displays of hundreds of dolls from different parts of the world. As our boat pulled up to the deck where riders disembarked, my father hopped out, bent down, and lifted me out.

I would have been two and a half at the time—which raises the fair question of whether this is actually my memory. But every time I've taken my own kids to Disney World, where It's a Small World is still a must-do attraction, I go to get into the boat and have a flash of my father's strong hands, surprisingly beefy for an otherwise lean man, slipping under my arms from behind and lifting me clear. He twists me in the air before pulling me close to his chest, warm and safe.

That feeling at Disney never fails to fill me with the same gloomy heaviness that descends every time I'm in a cab heading out to JFK Airport from Manhattan. The route runs by the old World's Fair grounds. There the Unisphere still stands, the twelve-story stainless-steel globe that was the symbol of the 1964–65 fair. It's a perfectly preserved relic of both the technological optimism of the race-to-the-moon mid-sixties and the time in my life when I felt closest to my dad.

You'd think at Disney, suffused with the Small World spirit and thoughts of my father, I'd pull Emma, Will, or Bobby close during the ride. I don't. I've been there three times with my kids. Each trip, no matter how much fun we've had on Space Mountain or Pirates of the Caribbean, when we get to the line for It's a Small World, I grow sullen and silent, consumed by an almost crippling longing.

It's not so much that my dad is gone that creates the yearning. I've had more than a decade to mourn his absence. The longing that leaves me numb and heavy while standing in line at Disney comes from the fact that the man with the strong hands left his two-year-old boy in some fundamental way not long after he pulled him from the boat. Not physically. Nothing that clear. My dad steadily withdrew into his own confusion, overmatched by the responsibilities and implications of the life he'd assembled around him.

It wasn't permanent. He'd be back, cloaked in guilt, earnestly trying to bridge the gaps that had developed during his emotional absence. But driving past the old fairgrounds in Queens, or picking my own kids out of Small World boats in Orlando, I can feel it in my bones. That feeling of being wholly cherished at the World's Fair was so fleeting.

Yes, I was two and a half. But I know exactly what happened. It's not someone else's memory. It's mine. In fact, I'd spend the next thirty-four years I had with my father wondering how to re-create what passed between us in the shadow of the Unisphere that day in the summer of 1965.

———

He was twenty-nine that summer, focused on a wife, two small children, and building his law practice. During the next half-dozen years, he'd double his number of kids and mortgages, and exponentially increase his burdens. When I was two, he had a vision for fatherhood and the capacity to execute it. By the time I was eight, life's pressures had clouded his view and emptied his tank. He began to check out. Sometimes intermittently, with his headphones on while paying bills in the nook off our living room he'd claimed as his own, or later on twelve-mile runs. Other times entirely, leaving my mother twice. But for my first eight years, I lived happily in his gaze, confident I would always hold the attention of this man who seemed to hack out a path with his charisma and passion on which he strolled sure-footedly through the world, tucking me in behind him so I could make my way as well. I was too young to wonder if he was happy, and wouldn't ask that question until years later, when he'd already made it painfully clear that he wasn't.

Even after he started to retreat, he maintained a repertoire of beautiful gestures, cutting the world's most gorgeous apple slices. He'd show up in the den carrying a couple of big, firm Red Delicious apples and the dull brown pocketknife his uncle Stanley brought back for him from World War II.

"Come on, Jimmy, the Yankees are on," he'd say enticingly, turning on the TV, flipping the dial to Channel 11, and stretching out on the blue shag carpet on the floor in front of the black-and-white-checked couch, a sofa cushion folded in half to prop up his head. I'd slide in next to him, lying on my left side, my head nestled on his chest, and listen to Frank Messer and the Scooter call the game.

As he lifted the knife to quarter the apple, he'd twist his torso a touch to the left to accommodate my embrace, not wanting to carve the apple directly over my head. He'd slice it into four sections, then slice each section in half again so there were eight pieces. Next he would effortlessly fashion each piece into a crescent by slicing out the seeds with a smooth stroke of the blade. Then he'd lay one of the crescents flat against his left palm, wrapping his right index finger around the dull edge of the knife blade. Bracing his right thumb against the bottom of the apple crescent, palm stretched, blade cradled in his fingers and poised at the top of the apple slice, he'd gently push the knife down through the flesh of the fruit with surgical precision until the sharp edge came to rest gently on his right thumb.

He was in complete control. He manipulated the blade with such dexterity that I never considered he might cut himself. The right thumb, knife blade, and index finger curled around it formed a small platform for each freshly cut apple slice, so thin they were translucent. He'd move the whole platform over to me to remove the slice, a gesture that signaled his trust that I could get that close to a sharp knife without hurting myself. I'd carefully lift the apple slice from the knife, delicately lay it on my tongue like a small, tart blanket, and pray for extra innings.

During these moments, my dad seemed to be exactly where he wanted to be. Never a flash of temper, always a calm sense of security—whatever might happen to one of his kids, he could fix it. Triage for pinching my finger in the car door was simply a matter of dunking my hand in a cup of ice-cold grape juice he seemed able to conjure on the front lawn where I was screaming in pain. The smile on his face while my index finger turned grape-purple was soothing, strong, and entirely present.

I'd seen it before, on the train home from New York after seeing the circus. Against his better judgment, he'd bought my sister and me special souvenir flashlights, small rectangles of hard plastic, one inch by three inches, each embedded with a small bulb and attached to a loop of plastic cord. Inside the arena, the kids would twirl the flashlights over their heads every time the lights went out, which probably wasn't the smartest idea the circus producers ever had.

We managed to make it through the circus without any bloodshed, but our luck ran out on the way home. Ignoring my dad's instructions not to swing the flashlight outside of the arena, I started twirling it on the train. The bench seat of the Penn Central train car made for much tighter quarters than Madison Square Garden. On the third full loop, I smacked him square in the forehead, drawing blood.

I'd never seen my dad bleed before, a frightening enough sight for any child, but positively terrorizing for one who caused it by ignoring his father's instructions. A number of competing issues suddenly confronted him. While his son had disobeyed him, his son was also freaking out over what he'd done. On top of that, the trickle of blood from the gash opened up by his disobedient, freaked-out son was starting to gather both speed and volume as it ran down his forehead and into his eyebrow. My father sized up the situation and focused on calming me down first. With one hand, he dabbed at the dripping blood with a tissue. But with the other, he reached across the seat to gently touch my shoulder, conveying with that same comforting smile that accompanied the grape juice for my pinched finger his patient understanding that my lesson had been learned.

These were the years he seemed to be fathering by a paternal golden gut, taking me to the circus and teaching me how to ride a bike. His obligations had yet to foster any resentment in him, only purpose.

As soon as he'd taken off the training wheels on our red Schwinn, the one he'd converted to a "boy's bike" as soon as my sister outgrew it by lifting the convertible top tube into a parallel position between the seat and the handlebars, he'd jog alongside me in his desert boots and jeans, sliding his hand under the seat to steady the bicycle. He wouldn't say a thing as I worked the pedals, getting the Schwinn up to full speed before I brought it to a stop by pushing the pedals back in the reverse direction, deploying the bike's simple braking system.

Silently running alongside me, letting me get the feel of balancing the bike for myself, he was so present that I forgot he was there, until one Saturday morning when we were moving along the sidewalks of our neighborhood, past the other new two-story colonials in Echo Woods, a development that had recently sprung from central New Jersey farmland. I was focused on pedaling and balancing, though a small part of me kept track of the red, white, and blue streamers coming from each of the handles, blown almost straight back by the speed I'd managed to pick up by pumping my legs.

Suddenly I heard the booming sound of my dad's voice—"Go,

Jimmy, go!"—coming from well behind me. I didn't dare turn my head to look back, shaky as I was, but I managed to sneak a peak by pushing my chin down hard against my collarbone and glancing quickly past my shoulder. There was my dad, twenty yards back, a big, loopy grin on his face, clapping his hands in front of him and then throwing his straight arms up into the air.

Years later, that gesture, captured by a photographer as my dad crossed the finish line of his first New York Marathon exultant and triumphant, would be engraved in my mind. But on this Saturday morning in the late 1960s, I was the source of his triumph. He'd known exactly how long to stay with me so I'd have enough self-confidence to step outside my safety zone. More important, he'd known exactly when to let me go and prove to myself I could do it on my own.

There was thoughtfulness to his fathering. He wasn't figuring it out on the fly, making random decisions about how he wanted to raise me. This was a man with a plan, which he executed with care and deliberation. Before I'd turned eight, he'd taken me to see Mickey Mantle play at Yankee Stadium, Joe Namath at Shea, and Oscar Robertson at the Garden. He seemed to be checking off boxes on a grand to-do list he'd written as a younger man, hoping that one day he'd have a son and the chance to run down the items one by one. I was this hope come to life, the beneficiary of the list. There was nothing more fortifying for me than mattering to him.

In my favorite white football jersey, red and blue stripes around the shoulder and the number 11 on the front and back, I'd wait in the early evening for him to come home from work. I'd sit at the end of the driveway, a long sloping incline, throwing a baseball hard into the webbing of my mitt and wondering if he'd beat the sunset. On the good days, the lucky days, his dark-green Corvair would turn into the driveway with plenty of daylight left. He'd park it in the garage, disappearing for a second before popping back out of the open garage door, his tan poplin suit jacket hanging over his left forearm. "Hey, big number 11," he'd bellow. "You want to catch some high pops?"

If he was already beginning to feel the pressures that would eventually overwhelm him, I was blissfully unaware as he set down his briefcase on the concrete walkway that led to our back door and drape his jacket over it. He'd walk a few steps over to the grass and motion for me to toss him the ball. He had superpowers, catching it without a mitt, rearing back on his right leg, kicking his extended left leg straight into the air, and reaching so far back with his right arm that the baseball in his hand almost touched the ground behind him. The ball rocketed high into the sky above me. I would call off the imaginary left fielder, "I got it. I got it," and wait while the ball scraped the clouds before falling back to earth.

He always worked Saturday mornings but wouldn't think of missing my Little League games on Saturday afternoon. Years later, I'd grow jealous of teammates on the high school track team whose fathers had become the men who would never miss a meet, but during these golden years, my dad was the one who was always there. He'd even take his turn as an umpire, a job that rotated from father to father as the game wore on.

He approached his turn calling balls and strikes from behind the pitcher with a bit more theatricality than the job required. I was especially self-conscious since I played catcher, and his obnoxiously drawn-out "steeeee-rike one" calls, dripping with glee, raised legitimate questions about a conflict of interest.

Of course I wasn't complaining. Not when, at the end of one game he umpired, a runner on the other team tried to score from third base on a ground ball to short. Our shortstop fielded the ball cleanly and threw it to me at the plate. I caught it and braced for the runner headed for home. The runner lowered his shoulder and ran right over me, knocking me head over heels to the backstop. I kept the ball wedged firmly in the pocket of my catcher's mitt, left and right hands jammed together. I jumped up and showed the ball to my dad, who'd come running toward home plate to see if I'd held on. I thrust the ball triumphantly into the air. The moment he could see it, my father let loose with an unrestrained "Yerrrrrrrrrrrrrrrr OUT!" that would have done any major-league umpire proud. His face was overtaken by a fierce and wild pride.

There's only one problem with having one of life's perfect moments when you're eight. You don't have much to compare it to. You've got no idea it couldn't possibly get any better.

He seemed to draw such pleasure from his purpose, passing along a vision of how to make your way in the world. Waiting in front of our house for a car full of men to come and pick us up for a trip to Yankee Stadium, he gently reviewed the finer points of the proper handshake. "Jimmy, don't forget. Firm grip. Look the man in the eye, tell him your name, and if he asks you how you are, you say 'Fine thank you, how are you?'"

There was nothing like a trip to the stadium. I sat way in the back of the station wagon, behind men named Monroe, Harold, and Leon. When we got there, my dad lifted me through the open rear window, an echo of how he'd pulled me from the boat at the World's Fair half a dozen years earlier, his reveling eyes meeting my own.

Before we went to our seats, before the hot dogs and sodas, before he bought me the program to teach me how to score a game, he suggested we hit the bathroom. I walked into a rancid smell that I wouldn't recognize for a few more years: stale beer and piss. These were not the Yankees' glory years. The stadium was far from packed. The bathroom was nearly empty.

We had our pick of urinals. He walked us down to the end of the row, where there was a pint-sized urinal next to those positioned for grown men. We stood side by side, each taking a leak. My father's face had a look of tender satisfaction. He was taking in the scene, pissing next to his boy, and finding it meaningful. He didn't say much but seemed to be doing some sort of math in his head. He looked down at me and nodded to the urinal he was using. He had a smile, poignant and wistful.

"Next year, Jimmy, you'll use one of these."

But by the next year he was already gone. And he'd taken the smile with him.

I can't say I hadn't been warned. For years, Stina had been making the same prediction: "When your midlife crisis hits, it's going to cripple you, and every man you've ever talked to." She usually said it with an easy laugh, the kind I'd seen plenty of times covering the run-up to hurricanes. The laugh that folks on the Gulf Coast nonchalantly tossed off as they headed to the lumberyard to buy plywood for their windows. A laugh designed to mask the mounting dread of the inevitable.

Now my own hurricane had come ashore. Just like those people on the Gulf Coast, whose stunned faces I'd plastered on the *CBS Evening News* many times as they surveyed the aftermath of some storm, I was astonished at how easy it was to destroy a foundation I'd spent years constructing, swearing I'd built it sturdy enough to withstand the fiercest winds.

Landing in Fort Lauderdale at the end of January to catch up with a Clinton campaign stop, I turned on my BlackBerry to see what I'd missed during the flight. I always felt like a modern-day prospector in those moments, sifting through four dozen e-mails that had accumulated while I'd been in the air to see if there was a nugget or two worth a closer look. This time, I thought I'd struck gold.

The Associated Press was reporting that Bob Schieffer, the grand old man of CBS News, would retire after the fall election. If the AP had it right, I was looking at the kind of opportunity that came along once a generation. Schieffer anchored CBS's Sunday-morning talk show, *Face the Nation*, the network's biggest stage for its premier inside-the-beltway player. The Sunday show anchors were no mere correspondents. They belonged to the elevated caste of movers and shakers, a prominence guaranteeing great seats at the Kennedy Center, look-who-we-saw-getting-coffee-at-the-Starbucks-by-the-zoo status in *The Washington Post*'s style section, and a seven-figure contract.

Using the flywheel to scroll down the screen with my right thumb, I started to slowly read the AP report with great care, hoping to lull my racing heart into a slightly calmer beat. I lost that battle nine sentences in, when I got exactly to the information I was looking for: "There's no obvious successor in place at CBS News. Jim Axelrod and Scott Pelley have both filled in during a rare circumstance when Schieffer was absent."

On the one hand, I wasn't an "obvious successor." On the other, the hand in which I held my half-full glass, mine was one of only two names mentioned, the other belonging to a *60 Minutes* correspondent who was too busy to be interested in the job. It all made perfect sense to me. As the network's chief White House correspondent, a traditional high-profile grooming stop on the climb up the ladder in the world of network news, I figured I was well within my rights to go see the president of CBS News, and pitch myself as Schieffer's replacement.

In fact, if you had injected me with truth serum when I dialed Sean McManus's assistant to make the appointment, the only uncertainty I would've admitted was selling myself short as an up-and-comer. A good part of me wondered if I hadn't already arrived.

Just a few years earlier, CBS had flown me first-class to Los Angeles to be part of a session with the nation's TV critics. The network publicists assigned to come up with a title for the presentation weren't confused about my standing: "Meet the Next Generation of CBS News." I'd carried that phrase close ever since, an imprimatur of sorts. It worked perfectly, just as long as I conveniently forgot that two of the other three members of the "next generation" onstage with me that day were no longer with CBS News, and the management team that designated us "the future" had been entirely replaced in the turbulent wake of the Memogate scandal that cost Dan Rather his job.

Sean's assistant set the meeting for 10:30 a.m. on Thursday, February 7, at CBS News headquarters in midtown Manhattan. Perfect. I'd be in New York that week anyway to cover the results of Super Tuesday, when Hillary Clinton expected to finish off Barack Obama's upstart campaign. A big night for Hillary would guarantee me a ton of airtime and a terrific chance to impress the new management team, the ideal setup for my meeting with Sean.

I was confident. Nights like Super Tuesday had been good to me. On election night in 2004, I'd led off the *CBS Evening News* from Copley Square in Boston, where John Kerry had planned to make his victory speech. I continued to update my reports at least once an hour right through prime time, hanging in until three the following morning. Although it was rainy and raw, with a toe-numbing mist enveloping the triple-decker media riser, I could've stayed there for days, warmed by the thrill of establishing myself. I was an integral part of the team on the defining night for any news organization, a charter member of the "next generation" who was staking his claim and taking his place.

The validation was nice. But the vindication was intoxicating, and I was mainlining it on that riser in Copley Square; a satisfying return on my investment of missed moments—first steps, birthdays, school concerts—that justified the weeks and months I was gone in the Balkans, Haiti, and Iraq. I'd been in New Orleans when my son William, ten weeks old, had been hospitalized with meningitis. I'd been in Afghanistan when a backed-up sewer main filled the basement the day before Emma's sixth birthday party. I'd been in Tallahassee when we moved into a new house in New Jersey, leaving Stina to unpack alone while I chased the hanging chads. But when all was going right—big raises and high-profile assignments—it seemed like a fair trade. At least to me.

I had no reason to think my luck was changing heading into Super Tuesday, though I certainly did coming out. When Chloe and I arrived at the school ballroom in Manhattan's garment district, stuffed with Clinton supporters and reporters eager to see history in the making, everything seemed to be falling into place. It was a perfect night by TV news standards, the drama both natural and palpable, nobody needing to gin up any story lines.

As the returns began pouring in from primaries and caucuses around the country, we started to pitch the producers in the control room at CBS headquarters. They were the gatekeepers, the ones we needed to sell on any observation, insight, or leak from the Clinton camp, convincing them it was compelling enough to come to us for a couple of minutes, instead of any of the dozen other analysts and reporters posted around the country and clamoring to get on television.

Going into the night, I hadn't been worried about elbowing my way onto our broadcast. The airtime that I'd converted into raises and standing over the years had given me a certain sense of security. I knew where I ranked among the dozens of correspondents at all three networks the way a big-league ballplayer knows his batting average. I'd had the third most airtime of all network correspondents in 2006. I was number seven in 2007. I'd forged this quantifiable measure of success into a sturdy base for my identity and career. I was used to being on all the time.

And yet, as Super Tuesday unfolded and CBS News began to broadcast results, I suddenly couldn't get any traction. Not with the quote I wrestled from a high-level Clinton staffer about the growing apprehension behind the scenes in Clinton's camp that her big night wasn't panning out. Nor with a report that Clinton's campaign chairman, Terry McAuliffe, had brazenly called Missouri for Hillary, knowing all too well it was far too early. Nor with an interview of a young African American woman twisted into tears by her decision to support Clinton over Obama. As the night wore on, the urgency of my pitches intensified; nothing did the trick.

"Hey guys," I said into my microphone, pressing but not pleading, "this is Axelrod at the grand ballroom with Hillary. This is Axelrod at the grand ballroom with Hillary." I wanted them to know I had essential information, but I needed to maintain a salesman's eager-to-please affability. I couldn't demand to get on. It had to be their good idea.

"I just spoke to a source inside Hillary's camp. They're making a lot of noise about Massachusetts. Looks like they're crushing Obama even with Kennedy's endorsement. I can talk about New York, but what's really interesting is Connecticut. She's getting beat there. I can explain why—that it's an entirely different kind of Democrat there. They're saying it's egghead lefty types there—not the blue-collars she attracts. I could do two minutes."

"Uh . . . hang on, Jim," came the response, the last thing anyone said to me until I heard the results from Massachusetts, New York, and Connecticut being reported and discussed on the air by the analysts in the studio. There was no other way to spin it: my new bosses clearly didn't want to hear from me as much as my old ones had. In six hours, I got on three times. As each half hour passed, I could feel myself slipping. I'd been home three weeks total in the preceding two and a half months, always with this night in the back of my mind as the payoff, and suddenly everything was derailing.

As I realized what was happening, I felt queasy, a combination of hollowness, nausea, and rage. I was being marginalized. My impulse was to scream. And yet, as if designed to underscore my impotence, I couldn't express even the faintest annoyance. The rules of big-event broadcasting required me to remain in front of the camera all night, lashed to a live microphone, so they could come to me at any moment. Every facial tic could be seen in the control room, every whisper heard. My frustration would be on full display to the very group of new executives I was trying to impress. Which is why I wore the blank, impassive mask of a palace eunuch for six straight hours, despite enough toxic bile bubbling inside me to corrode my gallbladder.

As I listened to Katie Couric sign off and got the all clear from the control room, my anger started to dissipate, replaced by a heavy weariness. Chloe and I packed up and got ready to split. Normally we would have found a place for a couple of drinks, so we could bitch, unwind, and release enough tension to be able to get to sleep. But the Super Tuesday special had run until 2:00 a.m. I had to be up in three hours for our morning broadcast.

I should've had the drink. Sleeping beat drinking, but brooding didn't. Chloe's 5:00 a.m. call, to make sure I hadn't slept through the hotel wake-up, was as unnecessary as the hotel's call had been a few minutes earlier. Stewing in my newly found irrelevance, I hadn't slept a wink. I showered and took a cab to our live-shot location, the roof of the CBS Broadcast Center on West Fifty-seventh Street.

Drained by the disaster of the night before and exhausted by my inability to fall asleep, I'd set a low bar for success, simply wanting an uneventful live shot so I could head back to the hotel and collapse. I relaxed when I saw the cameraman, Henry Bautista, an old pro with a well-deserved reputation for solving problems in the field. His shaggy gray hair parted in the middle and droopy white mustache framed a mouth that seemed stuck in a bemused smile. He'd spent years avoiding snipers in Sarajevo, so knocking out a routine live shot on the roof of the CBS Broadcast Center should've been a piece of cake. Which is why the look of agitation on his face as Chloe announced our two-minute warning confused me.

One look at the soundman explained what was bothering Henry. I'd never seen this guy before, a freelancer. He was paunchy, disheveled, half asleep, and mumbling to himself while moving slowly between his audio mixer and a panel of outlets mounted to a brick wall, disconnecting and reconnecting cables with no particular urgency.

While waiting for someone from the control room to establish contact with me, I suddenly understood what the soundman was trying to do. My earpiece was dead. In two minutes, nearly two million people would hear the anchorman ask me a question, but I wouldn't be one of them. The soundman had one job: connecting the right cables to the right pieces of equipment to ensure the control room could hear me and I could hear the control room. It was a critically important job but not terribly challenging, especially in this case when the soundman was trying to connect me to the control room not from halfway around the world but from the roof of the CBS Broadcast Center. This was the television equivalent of tying your shoe.

The incompetence unfolding in front of me sent me over the edge. I stared at the soundman and growled, "This is unacceptable, this is fucking unacceptable," which was pointless, not to mention inaccurate. I had to accept it. The newscast had already started.

Chloe hopped in as she was trained to do, listening to the show on the phone in her left hand, while she extended her right arm straight out and then up ninety degrees at the elbow. The instant she heard Harry Smith finish the phrase "Jim Axelrod is in New York and joins us now," she urgently snapped her forearm down, her right index finger extended and pointing at me in a gesture that meant "go." I seamlessly picked up with "Good morning, Harry," maintaining the illusion of a couple of guys rehashing Super Tuesday first thing the following morning, despite the fact that one of them couldn't actually hear the other.

The manual cue worked just fine, the live shot went off seamlessly, but the whole episode felt bush league—a final insult to the injury I'd sustained the night before, a last kick-in-the-teeth reminder that I no longer even merited a competent soundman. "Let's get out of here," I told Chloe. "I need to close my eyes for a few hours." Chloe nodded her head in agreement to avoid antagonizing me further. But she knew that any kind of sleep was out of the question until I vented some of my frustration, now at near-lethal levels.

We jumped in a cab and headed back crosstown to our hotel, the New York Helmsley. We pulled up and Chloe hopped out, making a beeline for the doorman, Dennis O'Gorman, who had the answer ready before she asked the question. I suppose Chloe wasn't the first person to have asked him where someone could get a drink at 7:30 in the morning.

"Muldoon's. Forty-fourth and Third. Just a couple of blocks.

One problem." He hesitated for a moment to let us catch up with him. "Doesn't open till eight."

We found a bench at Forty-seventh and Third and sat down to wait in the raw February cold and dirty Manhattan drizzle. Within seconds I could feel the frigid water that had been pooling on the wood slats seep into the seat of my pants. This last, pristine indignity pushed a small smile to the corners of my mouth, a smile of submission. I could hear my father's voice, when confronted with a trivial stroke of bad fortune—the car in front of us grabbing the last space in the lot, the guy in front of us in the bakery getting the last cookie. "Fucked by the fickle finger of fate," he would say almost cheerfully, as the bad luck piled up.

I should've stood to keep my pants from becoming saturated. Instead, I sat there soaking as my mind wandered to the black snake in Afghanistan. I'd been the correspondent on a five-man team dispatched there by CBS right after 9/11. We'd rented a hovel in a medieval village called Jabal al-Saraj, less than a half-hour drive to the Taliban outposts that marked the front lines. The house was primitive; no running water, no electricity. At night, we had to use a flashlight to find our way to the outhouse.

We'd been there about a week when one night our producer, Randall Joyce, burst into the small main room where several of us were sleeping. He'd been in the outhouse when he'd heard something moving. The sound seemed to come from underneath where he'd been squatting. He shined the light downward and saw a pit viper slithering through the shitpile below.

I'd known Afghanistan was going to be dangerous. That was part of the allure of going. Land mines, rocket-propelled grenades, mortar shells—those were serious threats posed every time we left the house. But after that night, my greatest fear was dying from a poisonous bite on my ass during a nighttime trip to the outhouse.

For a network correspondent, two things made for a good war story. First, you had to survive to tell the tale. Second, you had to recount it from a higher position in the food chain than you occupied when it happened. That was the deal. I stared down the black snakes in Afghanistan. My stature rose in New York.

I knew the trajectory wouldn't continue sharply upward forever, but I hadn't planned on it flattening out so abruptly, either. Certainly not without any warning. But here I was, in the middle of a historic campaign, with everything appearing to unfold as it always had before. I'd been handed a high-profile assignment, and with it the chance to climb several more rungs up the ladder. And yet instead of settling deeply into the sleep of the satisfied, knowing I had nailed Super Tuesday, I was sitting on a bench in the freezing rain at eight o'clock in the morning waiting for a bar to open.

Swinging open Muldoon's door cast a ray of dingy light over the cash register, illuminating the phrase CEAD MIL FAILTE (Gaelic for "a hundred thousand welcomes"), spelled out just above it. A boxing poster was tacked to the wall opposite the bar, just a few feet inside, advertising an upcoming fight card in Brooklyn. Next to the poster were framed pictures of Yeats, Brendan Behan, and Flann O'Brien. The air was heavy, almost pulpy with the smell of stale beer, mildew, rust, and the previous night's chili. There was a *New York Post* on a stool, sports section facing up.

Chloe ordered two Bloody Marys. I made my way over to the jukebox, the one inauthentic feature of Muldoon's. The place screamed for a vintage jukebox, beaten and scarred, something a little more back-in-the-day than the sleek black computerized CD player attached to the wall halfway to the back, offering as many selections from Christina Aguilera as from the Clancy Brothers.

I slid a ten-dollar bill into the machine, which bought us twenty-eight songs. I punched in the first five and returned as the bartender set down our drinks. The glasses were tiny, too small for a celery stalk. They were more like plus-size shots. With the ice and slice of lime, they weren't going to last long. We each ordered another before the bartender could get away.

We killed those drinks, and three more rounds in the next hour, while we profiled the other customers who'd been there when we arrived. Either Dennis O'Gorman had it wrong about when Muldoon's opened, or they let the regulars in a few minutes before everyone else. Either way, there they were: the middle-aged banker with his morning screwdriver, a couple of older guys in Starter jackets pounding beers, and an angular young dandy in his mid-thirties wearing a dark-gray skinny-man's suit with narrow lapels and high hems designed to showcase his black pointed shoes that cost more than my monthly mortgage. He'd picked up the *Post* and was having a Scotch.

After my fifth Bloody Mary, I slid off the barstool, stepped outside, and called home. The night before, I'd finished too late to phone Stina and take her through my humiliation. Now there was no answer. I tried her cell but didn't have any luck there, either. I didn't leave any messages, deciding against testing the limits of her understanding by calling her at nine in the morning with some sloppy, slurred sweet talk just as she was walking Bobby into preschool.

Which left me still needing to vent. I thought for a second and dialed my agent, Carol. Compassionate and levelheaded, she was highly skilled at defusing crises, always able to keep her eye on the big picture when her clients were not. She'd talked me down from a thousand ledges over the years.

She listened without saying a word as I took her chapter and verse through my futile efforts to snatch some meaningful airtime the night before, my inability to impress the new management team, and the soundman's incompetence earlier in the morning. In a voice coated by four Bloody Marys, I delivered a rambling dissertation on the concept of marginalization. When I finished, there was silence at the other end of the line.

"So where are you now?" she asked.

I described Muldoon's, right down to Mr. Fancy reading the *Post*, expecting to hear her chuckle.

"Jim, why don't you settle up with the bartender and head back to the hotel," she said evenly instead. "I bet you could use some sleep. Let's talk more after you've had a nap." She wasn't scolding me, but she didn't need to. I got it all by myself. Standing in the drizzle on the sidewalk in front of Muldoon's, a drunken mess, who the hell was I to condescendingly profile anyone?

I turned around, went back inside, and ordered another round.

Chloe tried desperately to find a topic of conversation that would provoke a reaction and distract me from my sullenness: Clinton campaign gossip. Why Will Ferrell wasn't funny and Vince Vaughn was. The beauty of Jon Miller calling an Orioles game on the radio.

It was a valiant effort. But Chloe didn't have three children at home. She wasn't worried about college funds and bat mitzvahs. She hadn't seen other correspondents fall out of favor and let go when their contracts expired.

I knew what the rule book said, the one I'd used to guide me this far, the one I'd borrowed from my father: Head down. Keep the legs pumping. Double down on work.

"Jimmy," he'd explain, "you can't control everything. But here's what you can control. No one can outwork you. Get there early. Stay late. Never say no." The only problem was, my father had never told me what to do when that wasn't enough. Super Tuesday was suggesting I needed a plan B.

It was a quarter past eleven on a Wednesday morning. I was drunk, scared, and so tired I couldn't see straight. I also had the most important meeting of my career in less than twenty-four hours. I paid up, straggled back to the Helmsley, and passed out.

The next morning, I got over to the CBS Broadcast Center at 10:20, giving myself ten minutes to sip some coffee from the cart in the lobby and hit the men's room before heading to Sean's office. As I opened the door to his suite, I checked my watch. It was 10:28. Two minutes early.

His assistant directed me to an anteroom, motioning me to an unpadded chrome-framed chair. I didn't have a clear view into Sean's office from where I was sitting, but his door was open and I could hear just fine. He wasn't talking on the phone, or typing on the computer. The silence, broken by the shuffling of papers every fifteen or twenty seconds, crept over me. I started to suspect what was happening and began to feel slightly unsettled.

Over the past twelve years, I'd sat outside the office of the CBS News president many times, and I'd learned a few things—how to cross your legs, check your watch, and casually leaf through the month-old *Newsweek* on the wood-laminate coffee table. Above all else, I'd come to understand that—after salary—how long you waited was the most precise measure of your value. Those who mattered most waited least.

As the minutes of silence dragged by, I realized my suspicions rooted in Super Tuesday were not some lunatic's paranoia. At 10:42, I heard the phone ring and his assistant say, "Okay, I'll show him in." Twelve minutes. Not terribly long as these things went, but when I'd been an acknowledged member of "the next generation of CBS News," it was rarely half that. I stood up and straightened my tie one last time, drawing the inescapable conclusion: no longer was I someone worth flattering.

I walked into Sean's office trying to project charm and poise. I wanted to be affable and respectful, but if I was going to pitch myself for a job interviewing the nation's most powerful politicians, I needed Sean to see that I wasn't easily intimidated. His desk was twenty feet from the door. I walked nineteen of them as he stood up slowly, moving a few steps out from behind it and clear to the side in order to shake hands.

A slight man with a youthful air, Sean had been the successful president of CBS Sports when he was named president of CBS News as well after the Dan Rather Memogate scandal. He was broadcasting royalty, the son of the legendary sportscaster Jim McKay, the host of *ABC's Wide World of Sports*, and he enjoyed a reputation for attracting and retaining talent. After Tuesday night, I had no idea if that meant me.

I set out to strike him as thorough and well prepared, a preview of the kind of approach I'd bring to *Face the Nation*. I brought a five-page laser-printed proposal with me, spelling out how I'd freshen up the broadcast and attract more of the younger viewers that executives and advertisers coveted.

As we shook hands, I confidently handed him my proposal with its bullet points outlining a sharper setup piece to start the show, a new set with more vibrant colors, and younger, more provocative panelists drawn from outside D.C. Just the sight of the bold black font neatly encased in a silver-green-tinted plastic folder with a sharp red binding filled me with confidence—the document that would change my life.

He took it hesitantly, quickly dropping it on his desk without even leafing through it. But his eyes stayed fixed on the proposal rather than on me as I eagerly launched into the spiel I'd rehearsed to make my case for replacing Schieffer.

"Sean, you told Janet what a great job you thought I did subbing for Bob last summer," I said as we sat down, relaying some positive comments he'd made, passed on to me by the Washington bureau chief. That snapped him to attention. He bristled, annoyed perhaps that something he'd told a manager in confidence was now coming back to him in a way he'd never intended.

He was not about to be tied up with his own words. He raised his hand to cut me off, like a traffic cop irritated by a new driver who was still unclear on the rules of the road.

"Jim, even if Bob does retire, and I'm still not sure he will, I'd need an established star to replace him. I'm talking about someone who can carry that broadcast." He now seemed slightly annoyed.

"I'll be frank," he continued. "I don't mean to be hurtful, Jim, but I don't want to waste anyone's time. There's no way I would consider you."

Getting ready for this meeting, I'd considered the various reactions I might get from Sean. I'd anticipated what I thought was a wide range, from unqualified enthusiasm ("We're on the same page, my man") to polite evasion ("Huh, I really hadn't thought of that"). But outright rejection wasn't a possibility I'd entertained. I sat there, looking at my boss, gripped by an overwhelming feeling of foolishness.

"All they can tell you is no" had been one of my father's favorite refrains when he'd coached me on climbing professional ladders. Truth be told, my dad offered it up, and I wolfed it down, precisely because neither of us expected I'd ever be told no. I'd never given thirty seconds of thought to what I'd do when that happened.

I stood up. A small pool of anger started to ignite but was quickly overcome by a crippling humiliation. I could handle Sean's thinking I wasn't right for the job. But the clear sense of overreach implicit in his reaction suggested something far worse. He thought I was focusing on targets I didn't have the range to hit. That was mortifying.

I would've liked to summon a witty, slightly cutting reply displaying my resilience and plucky resolve. It wasn't in me. Instead, I limply shook his hand and walked out, wholly diminished. I checked my watch: 10:48. I'd been in there for exactly six minutes.

Twelve days later, I was standing on that platform in Houston watching Barack Obama and reading Dave's e-mail. For twelve days, I'd been absorbing the shot to the chops and facing the painful process of recalculating my sense of potential, capacity, and trajectory—of who and what I could be. I knew the posture I was supposed to strike, for myself if for no one else: that I was more than what the CBS News brass said I was. But there was a complicating factor. I wasn't exactly sure that was true.

After a dozen years at CBS News, successfully negotiating every rung of the ladder I'd tried to climb, I wasn't having an identity crisis, was I? That would've been so cliché. But suddenly I'd gone from a guy who loved having someone ask him "So what do you do?" at a cocktail party to living in fear of hearing the nine most dreaded words I could fathom from my ninety-three-year-old great-aunt Ruth: "Jimmy, I haven't seen you on the news lately." Sean's reaction raised a doubt I'd never entertained. Never mind the next generation. Forget *Face the Nation*. What happened if I was dropped by CBS altogether?

I was deeply embarrassed at how badly I'd botched my read of the situation, how flagrantly I'd misjudged my standing. I was ashamed of having bet so much on myself, asking so much of my family, all the while promising Stina a big payoff and getting cleaned out instead. My head was a mess. The only consolation was that it was a perfect match for my body.

The Obama rally came at the tail end of a brutal stretch of travel: a hundred and five stops in fifty-nine cities and towns from Thanksgiving to early March. Pinballing from New York to Santa Fe, Los Angeles to Milwaukee, Selma, Texas, to St. Clairsville, Ohio, left me brittle and casting about for equilibrium. In seventeen weeks, the most time I had spent in one place was four consecutive nights in Des Moines. When four straight nights in Des Moines constitutes stability in your life, you've got issues.

The demanding blur of the road required three coffees in the morning to get going. I told myself the three vodkas at night were to wind down. Chloe and I had a standard operating procedure: no matter what time we arrived at a hotel at night or what time our wake-up calls were coming the next morning, we'd hit the bar for a couple of drinks before calling it a day. Absolut Citron and tonic was our usual but by no means our only. In fact, on those bleak December Saturdays or Sundays when a football game preempted the *CBS Evening News*, leaving us without the routine of producing a story to fill our day, we'd pass the time with a little game of "running the shelf."

All we needed was a bar that lined up all nine flavors of Absolut Vodka on one shelf—Citron, Raspberri, Kurant, Ruby Red, Vanilia, Pears, Apeach, Mandrin, and Peppar. Over three or four hours, we'd systematically proceed down the line of bottles—first ordering Citron and tonic, then Raspberri, then Kurant, all the way down the shelf until we made it through Peppar and tonic. It was a lot of vodka, even for two marooned journalists with a day to kill.

The shelf was about the only kind of running I was doing, and it didn't exactly count as exercise. I'd lamely abandoned any attempt to stay in shape almost immediately upon hitting the road. When I was faced with the choice of getting up an hour earlier to knock out some sit-ups and jog bleary-eyed on a treadmill or rolling over after the wake-up call, rolling over won each time. I was eating every kind of sausage biscuit and dollar-menu cheeseburger that awaited me at the bottom of every exit ramp. For years, I'd thought of myself as five foot ten, a hundred and eighty pounds, including five extra pounds I could easily melt away with a month of jogging three or four times a week. But as I was about to rudely find out, my self-image needed an update. My body was in the same lousy shape as my career.

A week after the Obama rally in Houston, as the Clinton campaign rolled through Ohio, I woke up one morning in the Ritz-Carlton in downtown Cleveland. I stepped out of the shower, doughy and thick, dimpled crescent rolls of fat jiggling over the towel I'd knotted around my waist. I walked to the closet and grabbed a suit from the round metal bar where I'd hung it the night before in the futile hope it would smooth itself of wrinkles once it was liberated from my overstuffed garment bag. If I wasn't getting up early to run, I certainly wasn't getting up early to iron.

I pulled down one of my favorites, a beautiful gray mid-weight with cobalt-blue pinstripes, custom made the year before by a Hong Kong tailor named Daniel Leong. Bill Plante, my colleague at the White House, who had spent forty years at CBS and knew something about fine wine and good suits, had recommended him.

I loved the way Danny embroidered my name in bright-red thread on the left inside pocket. The formal cursive suggested a clubby civility, an arrival at a station I wanted badly to attain. I also appreciated his old-school craftsmanship, plain to see in the small triangle of fabric he always attached next to the strip of the fly where he set the right half of the zipper. It looked like an arrowhead pointing left. In the middle of it Danny had fashioned a small, narrow, oval opening, designed for a button he'd sewn on the opposite side. Out of sight once the pants were buttoned and zipped, the triangle on the right fastened to the button on the left, creating a snugger fit and better line.

Slipping on my pants in Cleveland, I inhaled deeply, pulling the triangle far enough over my bloated gut to line up the buttonhole with the button. Pulling the triangle toward the button, I made a quick move with my right hand, perfected by so much repetition over the years that I no longer thought about it, immobilizing the fabric arrowhead with my index and middle fingers while I pushed the button up and through from underneath the hole with my thumb. I'd done it.

Or at least for a second I had. As I exhaled, I felt the material start to strain. I had just enough time to process what was about to happen before I heard the sickening sound of slowly ripping fabric. Defiantly, the button held in its hole, while the fabric triangle was torn nearly free from the pants, dangling by a few threads from the right side of the fly.

I delicately unfastened the button, then folded the ripped fabric back behind the fly and zipped up my pants. Smoothing out the front of my pants in the mirror, I could feel the flush of embarrassment working its way out from inside my body. I needed to yell. I walked over to the desk, grabbed my phone, and hammered at the numbers with my index finger.

I wanted to explode for the catharsis, but as I stood there waiting for Stina to answer, my lower lip began to quiver, my eyes welling with tears. The battle not to cry flattened my intended snarl into more of a defeated mutter. I knew she'd try to make me feel better and wanted to cut her off before she started.

"Stina," I said when she answered, "there's no other way to look at this. I need you to understand something. You are married to a fat fucking slob."

T he cabdriver slammed his trunk, grabbed the cash I held out for him, and drove off, leaving me standing in front of my house. I had three bags with me: an overstuffed blue duffel, a bulging black garment bag with a perpetually unreliable shoulder strap, and a computer case I'd crammed with so many batteries, power cords, and headphones it felt as if it was lined with lead.

Two sets of steps stood between my front door and me, fifteen in all, and at that moment they looked like Everest. I threw one bag over each shoulder, grabbed the laptop case in my right hand, and started to gingerly hump up the steps like a Sherpa with a heart condition.

It was just before noon on Wednesday, March 5, 2008, two weeks after I'd gotten Dave's e-mail with my father's times. I was fat, broken, and convinced I needed to run a marathon. The primaries in Texas and Ohio had settled nothing between Obama and Clinton. After three and a half months of living on the road, I'd run through the finish line—only to discover they'd moved the damned thing. The campaign would continue for a couple of months more.

With nothing crucial on the calendar for the next few weeks, CBS News executives pulled our teams off the road. They wanted to save some money for a primary season that would extend far past what they'd budgeted to cover it.

I walked into an empty house, working hard to ignore how foreign it felt. Emma and Will were at school. Stina was picking up Bobby from his half day of preschool. Fueled by my self-loathing after the trouser-ripping incident in Cleveland, I dropped my bags and immediately shot upstairs to our bathroom, where we kept the only scale in the house. I stripped down, hopped on, and wanted to throw up. I was staring at three grossly offensive numbers: 2-1-6.

I was astonished. I'd weighed 165 pounds when I graduated college. During the next two decades, I hadn't given my weight much thought and certainly never stepped on a scale. Instead, I'd comfortably surrendered to the idea of putting on a pound every year or two, a natural function of a slowing metabolism. According to that math, I should've weighed 185, tops. The current condition of Danny Leong's custom-tailored pants suggested my calculus had been off. But in a gazillion years, I would've never guessed 31 pounds off.

Any hope that I could pin it on a faulty scale was quickly extinguished the next day, half a block into my first run since I'd read my father's marathon times in Houston. I'd thrown on my blue old-school cotton sweatpants that dated back to the Reagan administration, a gray sweatshirt from a bar in Iowa where I'd run the shelf one lost Sunday three months earlier, and an old pair of Nikes. I walked to the corner, started a slow jog, and quickly realized the scale was in perfect working order. I couldn't say the same of me.

My gut wouldn't stay in synch with the rest of my body. As I ran and pushed forward off my right leg, most of me—my head, shoulders, chest, and legs—moved upward. All of me, in fact, but my stomach. Protruding sloppily over my tightly cinched waistband, my bloated gut headed in the exact opposite direction.

I took in what was happening in slow motion, the way I'd once experienced my car spinning out of control when I hit an ice patch, nearly slamming into the highway guardrail. The brutal laws of physics were at work. As I continued my stride, and my body passed the crest of its arc on the way from right leg to left, all of me started moving down. All of me, again, but my jiggling stomach, which was moving up. Landing on my left foot once more, then pushing off, my body began to rise. Once more my stomach, heavy enough to be governed by its own gravitational pull, started to fall. This continued all the way down the block. I had to confront the cold reality: I was so fat I was oscillating.

Horrified, I pushed on. I'd mapped out a loop through several quiet neighborhoods and a busy downtown business district. They were connected by a peaceful stretch of park. The whole thing measured a little less than six miles. I knew it would be a while before I'd be able to run the entire way, so I figured I'd jog as far as I could each day, then walk the rest of the way home. On this first day, my lungs were good for only a couple hundred yards before they felt as if they were about to burst.

Gasping for air, I lumbered on until I reached the park entrance. Passing the fence post that served as the one-mile marker for my loop, I stopped jogging and started walking. A few steps later I stopped walking and doubled over, with my hands on my knees, hoping I wouldn't pass out. I didn't. On day one of my reclamation project, "not passing out" would have to count as my big achievement.

Yet pooling just beneath the nausea was a familiar feeling of well-being. It was faded but unmistakable. Maybe it was the endorphins, the natural feel-good painkillers the body produces during a run, or perhaps it was just sweating out some of the toxins I'd been storing up from months on the road, but even this first run— out-of-phase midsection and all—carried a teasing reminder of the tranquillity a good run always produced.

Catching my breath, I walked along the asphalt path that meandered through the park, passing soccer and softball fields, a dog run, and an equestrian ring. I stopped for a few minutes at each, watching eight-year-old boys swarm a soccer ball, a couple of golden retrievers and a Border collie catch Frisbees, and adolescent girls in black-velvet-covered helmets negotiate the rails of a three-foot jump on their horses.

There in the park, arms propped on the white fence surrounding the horse ring, I could feel my brain, knotted since Thanksgiving, begin to unkink. I was aware of the girls and their horses, but their images grew fuzzy and indistinct as I stared past them, focusing blankly on nothing in particular. It was just the slightest untangling, the earliest stages of what promised to be a long, delicate process.

Stina was strung out. We were beyond the familiar wear and tear our relationship always developed during my long spells on the road. She was tired of being lonely and raising kids by herself. She was tired of a marriage reduced to a few minutes on the phone during the hectic morning rush, and a few more at night as the two of us, exhausted, ran through a list of children's doctor's appointments and unexpected bills. She was tired of enduring. This was no longer a difficult stage of our marriage. This was our marriage.

An introverted, softhearted redhead who loved Jane Austen and tea at bedtime, Stina had always been enormously flexible and generous when it came to allowing the full measure of my ambition to play out.

When we'd started talking about having kids, her only nonnegotiable was finding a place where she could nest, a comfortable community to anchor us. Instead, we'd moved five times in eight years. We barely made enough to pay rent in Syracuse, let alone be comfortable. She never had time to get comfortable in Raleigh or Miami. She could've had a decade and would've never been comfortable in Dallas. After years of setting up lives in places she had no role in choosing, she'd fallen in love with Montclair, New Jersey, where we'd settled after leaving Dallas so I could work out of CBS News headquarters in New York.

A town of forty thousand, a dozen miles west of Manhattan, Montclair has a liberal, artsy, slightly offbeat vibe and racial diversity that resonated deeply with her. She knew she was home the moment she saw the contingent from La Leche League marching proudly in the Fourth of July parade, fast on the heels of vets in their American Legion hats.

So when I'd floated the idea of moving to Washington after the CBS White House job came open, she was profoundly conflicted. She had every reason to be suspicious of my pitch. She'd heard it all before when I was asking her to make other moves: "If this works out like I think it will, we'll never have to move again. And think about the money, sweetheart. It'd be a nice raise." Each time I'd been half right. The raise, yes. The last move ever, no.

I tailored the Washington pitch with a new wrinkle, hoping to appeal to Stina's top concern to close the deal: "I won't have to travel nearly as much. Most nights I'll report from the White House lawn. I'll be home so much more than now."

On the one hand, she didn't want to stand in the way of the kind of professional opportunity that comes along once in a career. After all, hadn't this been what I'd been dreaming of in Utica, Syracuse, Raleigh, Miami, and Dallas? On the other, she was tired of taking one for the team. The kids had friends in Montclair. Our family finally had roots. Stina wanted to let them burrow as deeply as possible. For the first time in our marriage, her gut was telling her to choose something other than what I wanted.

She ignored it.

On a long drive home one gray winter afternoon, after visiting old friends for a weekend in rural Pennsylvania, she reached across the console and said, "Go for it." For the better part of two days, she'd been listening to my ambition in its pure form, as we kicked around the benefits of taking the job versus the consequences of turning it down. Ultimately, her instinct to say no was trampled by her fear that if she did, she'd do irreparable damage to her marriage to a man who'd never be able to look past his lost opportunity.

I thanked her with an old smile that had always been part of the dance. "Stina, I know this isn't easy," I said, hoping to sound earnest and sympathetic. "I know you are tired of moving. I really think this time it's for good. Thank you, honey. Thank you."

Try as she might to mask it, even as she was giving me the go-ahead her brave face was creased with bewilderment. I chose to read it as the look of a woman confronting the logistics of yet another move. That was a lot easier than wondering if what I'd asked of her was fair.

So as the Clinton campaign extended into the spring of 2008 and my sales pitch about being home more if we moved to Washington was proving to be laughably fraudulent, Stina and I moved ever closer to crisis. Sure, she was angry at the instability my ambition introduced into her life. But that was nothing new. She was far angrier with herself for knowing better and still letting it happen.

On the first Tuesday after I got home in March, we were all curled up on our brown leather sectional sofa, watching *American Idol*. I got up during a commercial break and grabbed three large navel oranges out of the refrigerator to begin the best part of the evening.

With a paring knife, I made one circular cut around the knotted nub at the top of each orange, which gave the navel its name, and another at the bottom. I dug my fingers under the loosened nub and popped it out, and took out whatever was liberated by the matching cut on the bottom. Then I went around the orange making a set of incisions in the peel from top to bottom, an inch and a half or so between each. The peels rolled off cleanly, leaving me with a pristine orange stripped to its flesh in half a dozen cuts. No wasted movement. Not a strand of that bitter, waxy, white sub-peel to be found.

I broke off sections and began passing them around the couch. From the looks of amazement on my kids' faces watching me peel the oranges, you would've thought they were watching Rembrandt paint. It was an orange, not an apple; *American Idol*, not the Yankees, but I was thrilled to be giving my kids what my dad had given me.

I couldn't remember when or how the ritual got started, but I'd held on to it tightly. Peeling oranges during *Idol* had become one of the things the Axelrods did, a glob of the cement that bonded us as a family. At least I liked to think so.

Looking at the five of us arrayed around the couch we'd bought exactly for nights like this, I choked up. I wanted Stina to know I got it—that my being at home on any given Tuesday night had once again become the exception, not the rule. I needed her to know that wasn't what I wanted, either, that her vision was my vision. I looked at her, wanting her to see my eyes moisten, my standard testament to something deeply meaningful. My weak smile, sad and contrite, laid it out clearly and simply for her. "It's me," I was trying to say to her. "I'm still in here. I get it. This is all that matters."

But it was a gesture—and a rather empty one at that—designed to substitute for what I wasn't regularly providing because I simply wasn't there. Stina knew the gesture was as much for me as for her.

For years, she'd answered that particular smile with a certain soft smile back that let me know that she understood. But not this Tuesday night. Perhaps she'd already jumped to Wednesday morning, when I'd be buzzing to get back out on the road and resume the chase, any internal conflict resolved by orange sections and her absolving smile. Not this time. She looked entirely unimpressed, having cataloged all my gestures over the years and refusing to be complicit any longer. Getting choked up over peeling an orange wasn't good enough. Not anymore.

I got it. In fact, looking at my wife, there was no way to miss it. The only thing I wasn't sure about was whether I was looking at Stina's concern or her condemnation. Worse yet, the only response I could summon was to go run around the block.

I ran six times in my first ten days home. Between the running, eating something other than fast food, and not drinking, I started to shed some weight. It was mostly water weight, but when I stepped on the scale again, I'd dropped five pounds. I'd also doubled the distance I was able to run. I could now make it as far as a pair of pay phones that marked two miles.

That would have been fine had I never wanted to go a step farther than two miles. But since a marathon was 26.2 miles, I had a bit of a situation on my hands. Or my legs, to be more accurate. The mind was willing. My left calf and right Achilles tendon were most definitely not.

It happened at the same spot each time. Turning left out of the park, I could see the phones a couple hundred yards away. Like clockwork, I'd start to feel my lower legs tighten and swell. In the next minute, staggering toward the phones, the throbbing muscles encasing my shinbones felt as if they were about to burst right through the skin. Almost incapacitated, I'd hobble a few steps past the phones and stop. After a few minutes the swelling would subside. I'd walk the rest of the way home.

When I'd first contemplated running a marathon, I hadn't counted on this kind of pushback from my body. While this wasn't my first time shocking myself back into shape, I'd never had trouble with my legs. Getting fit had always been more a question of rebuilding my stamina and lung capacity. Doubled over in between the two rusted phones, I realized this reclamation project was entirely different from the others I'd undertaken over the years. Not that I needed any more reminders, but I headed off to our spring break the last week of March keenly aware that the old approaches were no longer working. The problem was, I didn't have new ones to put in their place.

Stina and I loved the tranquillity of North Carolina's Outer Banks. Getting there was no more complicated than stuffing a few pairs of shorts and a couple of T-shirts into a gym bag for each kid, gassing up, and driving five hours, a good chunk of them on two-lane country roads.

Even in the middle of high tourist season, North Carolina's barrier islands had a mellow pace. There was no boardwalk, just mini golf, fudge shops, ice cream stands, crab shacks, and a few tame bars. The off-season added an extra element of desolation and serenity, the perfect setting for taking a deep breath and reconnecting.

We'd rented a house on the beach. Pulling up to it, the only car we saw on the street was ours. It would stay that way for the entire week. Our idea was to sleep late, walk the beach, collect shells, stuff the kids with ice cream, watch *The Princess Bride*, and get me out for a run every day.

The conditions were perfect—sunshine and temperatures in the mid-sixties. The main road from Duck to Corolla, Route 12, had a paved path running alongside it. In tandem, the winding road and the path rolled gently up and down slight elevation changes, passing over several narrow, brackish streams flowing inland from the ocean. Crossing the streams at sunset, I could hear the frogs and birds conduct a compelling end-of-day concert. I might have enjoyed it, if I hadn't been nearly crippled at the time.

I hadn't made it ten minutes into my first run on the first day of vacation before my legs started swelling. The muscles below the knee on both legs felt like balloons filling up with too much water. As I struggled along the path, my lower legs looked stricken with a moderate case of elephantiasis, which would've been fine if it was only a question of appearance. It wasn't. I couldn't move my feet.

The swelling in my shins short-circuited my muscle function everywhere below my calves. My brain was sending the signals, but the nerves were unable to transmit them. All roads south of my swollen shins were blocked. I had no ability to rotate my ankles, which rendered each foot floppy and lame. They were absolutely useless in getting me anywhere I wanted to go at anything beyond a hobble.

I leaned up against a fence to try to stretch and regain some feeling in my feet. No luck. My calves felt as if they were about to explode. There were no cars on the road. No one else was out running. Every house I could see was closed up for the off-season. I hadn't brought my cell phone, so I couldn't call Stina to come get me. And my feet were essentially useless. I was three-quarters of a mile from our house and had absolutely no idea how I'd make it back. If I hadn't hit rock bottom yet, I couldn't imagine I had very far to go.

I tossed aside whatever was left of my pride, bent over, and gripped the underside of each thigh with the corresponding hand. My right hand pushed my right leg forward. My left hand pushed my left leg. Each foot flopped about underneath, physically attached to my body at the ankle but disconnected from my brain by the swollen muscles encasing the shinbone.

Awkwardly, I coaxed enough cooperation from my body to get back to the house. Not that my problem was solved when I limped into the driveway and up to the front door: after all, I still needed to get upstairs.

Like so many beach houses on the North Carolina coast, ours

was designed upside down—the living room, kitchen, TV room, and main deck were all built on the top floor of a three-story house to capture the grandest views of the ocean. Never mind figuring out a way to put one foot in front of the other. That was a piece of cake compared with what I needed to devise now—a method to climb three flights of stairs to where Stina and the kids were hanging out.

As I lifted the ball of my right foot onto the first step to push up to the second step, a sharp bolt of pain shot through my right calf, freezing me in place. The simple stretch of the calf muscle involved in climbing steps—ball of the foot on the step, heel dangling back over the edge before the calf propelled the body up to the next step—was excruciating.

I instinctively turned my body ninety degrees to the right so that instead of facing the staircase, I could climb the steps sideways. Rather than relying on my compromised calves, I was able to distribute my weight more evenly among the larger muscles of my thighs and quadriceps. Leaning forward to grab the banister with both arms, I could lift my left leg up to the next step, and then use my arms for a little extra boost to lift my right leg up to the same step. The sideways climb was slower but far less painful.

Gimping up the steps, I shook my head and chuckled to myself as I suddenly realized the source of the sideways ascension. It was exactly how my grandfather climbed steps when I was a kid. Of course, Pop-Pop Moe was in his late seventies at the time. He also used a cane. And he had an excuse. He couldn't climb stairs normally because his right leg had been crushed in a car accident in 1937. I couldn't climb stairs normally because I'd been on a three-and-a-half-month steak and vodka binge. Not that I needed any more ways to define the extent of my deterioration, but at that moment, my physical role model was my half-crippled grandfather.

Finally I got to the top of the stairs. I waved to Stina as I opened a door and limped out to the expansive third-floor deck. She'd been sipping a glass of wine while working on a jigsaw puzzle at the kitchen table, trying to assemble the pieces that would produce a collage of iconic 1950s images. She'd already completed James Dean and was halfway through Marilyn Monroe when she saw me. Our two older kids were on the floor reading the paperbacks she'd bought for them, and four-year-old Bobby was dousing imaginary flames with the Playmobil firemen she'd packed.

It was my favorite time of day, as the golden light of the late afternoon slowly gave way to the burnt oranges and deep purples of early evening, while the winds settled and the ocean calmed. Everything seemed to slow—shift change for the day.

I collapsed into a white Adirondack chair. The salt air had done a number on the deck, whipping the color out of the wood and softening it into a brown-gray pulp so worn that none of the odd shards were stiff enough to present any sort of danger to the kids' feet. I felt a certain affinity for the deck, so beaten down it was no longer even able to offer up a decent splinter. The whole rotten structure needed to be replaced.

Stina had come outside as soon as she saw me. She approached warily, supportive but unsure what, if anything, the running represented beyond another gesture.

"How are you?" she asked. "I was starting to get worried. You were gone so long."

I apologized, offering a description of my nonfunctioning feet as an explanation. "Honey, I'm a mess," I said, hoping to elicit both sympathy and at least a small chuckle.

I got neither.

"I wish you'd taken your phone," she said. "I would've come and picked you up."

She sat down in the chair next to mine.

"Are you sure you should go running tomorrow?" she continued. After twenty years together, we both knew the answer.

The next day, Sunday, I proactively popped a couple of aspirin to ward off the inflammation in my legs, stretched my calves a few minutes longer than the day before, and headed out to try it again.

A quarter mile into my second run of spring break, as I turned from the road that snaked through our development onto Route 12, I could feel the same muscles that had nearly crippled me starting to swell. I stopped immediately and began to stretch, pushing off against a telephone pole that coated my hands with tar and sap. After stretching, I walked about a quarter mile and started to slowly jog. The muscles strained against their sheaths around my shin, but the incapacitation wasn't nearly as severe as the day before. I had a low standard for improvement—anything more than minimal foot function qualified—but at least I was meeting it. I made it home and up the stairs with no trauma and little drama.

I took Monday off to rest, but was back at it Tuesday. The house we'd rented was three miles from the town center of Duck. This presented the perfect goal. I knew I'd have to walk part of the way, but by week's end, I was determined to get all the way there and all the way back.

I'd driven the route, marking off each mile on the odometer and matching it up to some landmark—the firehouse, the deli, the water tower. Each day, I made it a little bit farther before turning around, alternating five minutes of walking with five of running.

On Friday, the day before we headed back to Washington, I made it to the water tower that marked three miles, turned around, and headed for home. Closing in on completing the full circuit, I stopped alternating between running and walking, and kept jogging. I was about to make it six miles—an indisputable triumph over the curse of the swollen calves—and wanted to be running when I did. But just as I began to allow myself a small measure of satisfaction, the feeling was snatched from me.

Lumbering along half a mile from the house, I sensed someone moving up behind me on my right. The steady beat of footsteps I heard just over my shoulder triggered a long-dormant reflex. I began to accelerate. The instinct may have been buried under thirty extra pounds of flab, but it was in perfect working order. Tattered as it was, I needed to salvage and preserve whatever I could of my self-image.

Then I heard crackling, like the sound of a pickup truck crushing small stones into hard-packed dirt, only softer. I turned to get a look at the guy trying to pass me and see if I could hold him off. Or her. To my surprise, it was a them. And the answer was no, I couldn't.

It was the rubber tires of a stroller producing the crackle as they rolled over the path parallel to the road. I saw the stroller first, the infant in it, then the woman pushing it. I had only a couple of seconds to register her as she went flying by me, a sweep of intensity. She seemed to be in her early thirties, short, dark hair, with a slight, classic runner's build. I focused longingly on her smooth, taut calves flexing into stark, defined relief with each step. Not because she had great legs. Because she had functioning ones.

The stroller threw me. I didn't have any problem getting run down by a woman. But getting run down by a woman and her baby was a bit much. I tried to catch her eye and give her a nod, but I was a moment too late. The new mom was already inching in front of me as I looked in her direction. I still could've briefly established eye contact had she been looking my way, but she'd turned her head the instant I looked up.

I recognized the move. Over the years, I'd thrown a few head snaps just like it myself. Generally they were reserved for anyone I found intriguing in their persistence, but also a little pitiful, like an off-key street musician in a subway station. I might flip a dollar into a ratty saxophone case just for the effort, but I didn't want to look him in the eye as I did it.

For the new mother running me down on Route 12, I was the sax player in the subway. She was snapping her head away before our eyes might meet. Watching her back grow smaller in the distance, it hit me: I was no longer the one throwing the charity glance. I was the guy catching it.

Bob Axelrod spent a good part of the 1970s sitting at a small, square Lucite table in an alcove off his living room. The table was classic seventies mod—a bright royal blue with a pair of slick yellow stripes running across the top, one twice as thick as the other. The stripes gave the table the feel of a race car.

My dad would sit there for hours on weeknights, writing out checks and prepping for trials. We had our stereo in the nook. He'd slide on a pair of bulky headphones, crank up his cassette tapes, and block out the chaos in his home.

Hunched over his checkbook, lost in his music, he was oblivious as I passed by on my way to the TV room. Stretched out on the couch, watching Richie and Fonzie, I'd forget he was there until his booming voice came sweeping around the corner, belting out a Nilsson song only he could hear: "Everybody's talking at me, I don't hear a word they're saying . . ."

Hurtling toward meeting his parents' classic Jewish immigrant expectations, he'd looked up at the age of thirty-five and found himself with four kids, two mortgages, a sometimes turbulent marriage, and no real vision for his life beyond building a successful legal practice that would provide for all of us who depended on him. The real trouble started when he did that—and still couldn't find peace. The more confused he grew, the more intensely he guarded what little space he'd managed to carve out for himself.

Inside the house, the blue Lucite table gave him the arm's length that he needed. Outside was a different story. A gifted charmer, his high-wattage charisma drew people in, which was actually the last place he wanted them. One more item on his overfilled plate could make it crack. He needed a reliable means of escape that stretched longer than the cord on his headphones.

He developed into an accomplished emotional magician with a signature trick: the illusion of intimacy. His relationships were like those homes on Hollywood back lots where the Cleaver family lived, just down the make-believe block from Dr. Welby. Head-on, those houses were idyllic. Moving a few feet either way revealed the fiction. Each home was an impeccably designed, carefully constructed façade. Terrific curb appeal, but just a front.

At a neighborhood bar mitzvah just a few weeks before my own in January 1976, I watched my father work the room. Sizing up Donald, the tall, thin, completely bald father of my friend Willie, he headed over with a captivating grin and outstretched hand.

Donald had gone to Rider College, in Trenton, where my folks had grown up. That gave my father a few different ways to go. They started by comparing memories of Greenfield's luncheonette, one of the popular campus hangouts when Donald had been an undergraduate. My mother's parents, Moe and Trudy Greenfield, were the owners. Hands firmly on the wheel, my dad then steered the conversation to the late Ernie Kovacs, the brilliant comedian from Trenton who used to play the pinball machines at Greenfield's, banging on the glass top so forcefully when he'd lose that my grandfather regularly threatened to throw him out.

Kovacs led Donald and my dad to other famous people who'd come into Greenfield's. Willie Mays topped that list, having played a year of minor-league ball for the Trenton Giants. Mays led to baseball, baseball led to the Dodgers, and the Dodgers to my dad's detailed descriptions of going to Ebbets Field as a kid, courtesy of a cousin who knew a few of the players. My dad was on a roll, regaling Donald with stories of driving Pee Wee Reese home or taking Roy Campanella to dinner at Mamma Leone's.

From there, he brought the conversation closer to home, describing the couple of shoe boxes he had stored in our attic, each filled with autographed baseballs wrapped in crinkled cellophane. The crinkles made it tougher to decipher the names, but my dad was always able to make them out whenever he'd take them down to show me: Robinson, Snider, Hodges, Reese, Furillo, Erskine—autographs he'd picked up on those trips to Ebbets Field. He stopped just short of issuing the potentially plate-cracking invitation to Donald to come over and look at the old baseballs.

It was time to pivot.

"Have you been flying much?" my dad asked, seamlessly turning the topic to Donald's well-known hobby. This was his patented sleight of hand. Whenever he felt the conversation was veering dangerously close to real intimacy, as the subject of the old autographed baseballs was clearly doing, my father would move quickly to establish a "special relationship" by probing the other guy's passions, locking him in with a series of thoughtful questions. This provided the breathing room he needed. Peppered about the number of hours he'd logged at the stick, the cost of flying, and what it was like to land at Newark Airport in between all those big jets, Donald never saw my father palm the ace. Naturally, Donald graciously took the conversation to the next level, knitting baseball and flying together into a generous overture.

"Bob, why don't you, me, Jimmy, and Willie all go to Cooperstown? We'll pick a Saturday. Fly up in the morning. Have lunch. Hit the Hall of Fame. Fly back. We're home by dinner." Donald snapped his fingers. "Piece-of-cake trip. And it would be a terrific day."

I didn't bother digesting the fantasy itinerary. I'd seen the trick before and knew what was coming. Reaching out with his right hand for another shake, this one to close the conversation, my dad patted the back of Donald's upper right arm with his left hand.

"That sounds great, Donald," my father promised. "I'll get back to you with a good date."

Even at twelve, I knew it was never going to happen. It never did. Bob Axelrod was an enchanting escape artist who compelled people toward him. They reached out when they got there, gathering nothing but warm and charming air.

He was happiest when expectations were clear, unencumbered by any confusion about how to proceed. He was happiest in the courtroom. There the rules of law and advocacy dictated his behavior, providing clear lines to guide everyone's conduct and making it that much easier to knowingly overstep them.

The courtroom liberated an honest confidence in him and a nimbleness that was missing at home. Early in his career, he was arguing a motion, fiery and passionate, when the judge interrupted him.

"Mr. Axelrod, your argument is very compelling on behalf of the defendant. But may I remind you that in this case, you represent the plaintiff."

The courtroom was silent for a few moments, while my father gathered himself, the air turning sour with embarrassment for him.

"Of course, Your Honor," he parried back with a twinkle. "That is the argument I anticipate the defense will make. Now I will explain why that position is entirely without merit."

It was no surprise to anyone watching when he won the motion.

This was the purest part of my father, the maverick trial lawyer who subpoenaed a German shepherd in a dog-bite case and sang the jingle for the Roto-Rooter plumbing franchise while suing a proctologist for perforating his client's rectal wall.

He never wore a three-piece suit to the courtroom. "I can't stand vests," my father would explain, introducing himself to the jury. "You can hide something behind a vest. One thing I can tell you about this trial: I won't be hiding anything from you." He'd slip off his jacket and roll his shirtsleeves halfway up his forearms. "Look, nothing up my sleeve," he'd say before leaving the courtroom to his adversary, who was almost always wearing a vest.

Once a year, on a school holiday, my dad would take me to court with him. I'd sit in the back row, heart thumping in my chest, and watch him carve up a doctor on the stand. He was especially vicious with orthopedists. To hear him tell it, they were the most arrogant and dismissive doctors going. Of course, they were exactly the kind of doctor he'd wanted to become until he couldn't hack premed at Cornell.

Just before lunch on a visit during one spring break, I watched my dad fearlessly badger a notoriously tough judge to dismiss the other lawyer's line of questioning. Finally, as the badgering edged toward hectoring, the judge had heard enough.

"Motion denied," thundered the judge. "And, Mr. Axelrod, may I remind you that I'm not a big fan of wasting the court's time."

I was shaken, listening to the snarling man in the black robes. I had no idea what my father had done wrong, but it didn't seem to be a small matter. The judge was red-faced and raising his voice for the first time that day. He seemed intent on sending a harsh message that no shenanigans would be tolerated in his courtroom. Then he dismissed everyone for lunch.

My father struck me as the only person in the courtroom who was not intimidated as we walked out. "Jimmy," he asked, cheerfully throwing an arm around my shoulder, "you want a hot dog?"

On our way to the lunch counter, we bumped into a man in the hallway who seemed to want to chat with my father. They were chuckling. I could pick up enough to know that it was all about the scolding. It took me a second to catch on, because he was no longer wearing those scary black robes. It was the judge, looking shockingly less sinister in a suit jacket. Even so, given the way he had just spoken to my father, I was still petrified once I figured out who he was.

He looked down at me. "Are you Mr. Axelrod's son?" he asked. I snapped my head straight down at the floor. He was wearing black orthopedic shoes that laced on the side.

"Head up, Jimmy," my father softly commanded. He liked me to shake hands firmly and look other men right in the eye when they spoke to me. I lifted my chin to see the judge's round face and full head of gray hair. He used some sort of hair tonic and a comb with wide spaces between the teeth. His hair looked like smooth, wet pieces of gray spaghetti, swept back uniformly off his face. I wanted badly not to be there.

"Are you going to be a lawyer when you get older?" he asked. I quickly nodded as my eyes broke away again and darted right back to the ground.

"Pick your head up, Jimmy," I heard my dad command again, this time a little less gently.

The judge pointed in the direction of my father. "Well then," he said in an unmistakably kind voice, "be just like him. Your father is a very good lawyer, you know." The judge walked away with a compact, squat stride.

I looked at my father, expecting to see a wide smile. There was nothing. He'd already moved on.

"Come on, Jimmy, we've got to hustle if we're going to get that hot dog," he said blankly, his eyes steeled.

Bob Axelrod moved sure-footedly through his professional life, a fierce and unyielding advocate, untroubled by anyone's opinion of him. But outside the courtroom, where life was more complex and harder to control, he got lost in the shadows. That's where the danger lay for him, in the responsibility and obligation meaningful connections entailed. Those interactions were far messier than the ones conducted under the prescribed rules of the courtroom.

He didn't seem to cultivate a group of close friends the same way the other dads did. It didn't seem to matter to him. The other men in our largely Jewish upper-middle-class central New Jersey neighborhood always loved to see him at parties. His skill with a jury translated seamlessly to a cocktail hour or dinner. When they once commandeered a basement to watch dirty movies, my dad was right there, helping to devise a system of rotating projectors that minimized downtime between the end of one film and the start of another. But he always stopped short of becoming one of the guys. Confidences were reserved for clients.

He wasn't a joiner; he didn't play tennis and wasn't about to take up cycling and become part of the pack who got up early on Sundays for forty-mile rides. He'd loved golf as a kid but had put the clubs away in his mid-twenties, leaving me to wonder what those black shoes with the fringed flaps and metal spikes on the soles were for when I would root around his closet as a five-year-old.

It wasn't that the master of the "special relationship" couldn't connect. He could. Too well, in fact, for his own liking. It was a question of accountability. He didn't see friends as ballast for his listing ship or cushions for life's sharp edges. They were simply another demand to balance when he couldn't handle any more. By the time I was eight, he'd already started to resent the ones he had.

This wasn't something that was particularly tricky to figure out. My dad may have been confused about the place where life had taken him, frustrated with how elusive sustained happiness had turned out to be, angry that he was flailing, even embarrassed that he couldn't do a better job balancing all the competing demands. But one thing he was not: capable of hiding any of it.

A dozen kids lived on the two or three long blocks named for U.S. presidents on the north side of Highland Park, our small town in the middle of New Jersey. We'd all convene for kickball or tag when the weather got warm. Our yard on Lincoln Avenue was nice-sized and heavily shaded by enormous oak trees, so we hosted our fair share of games.

For the neighborhood kids, the shade was a nice feature that prevented the sun from beating down on us directly. For my dad, however, it was a curse that prevented the sun from shining uniformly on his lawn. He routinely spent parts of his weekend sprinkling Scotts seed on the pesky dirt patches he could never get to sprout grass, fuming that his lawn, like his life, wasn't turning out as he expected.

Pulling into our driveway early one evening after work, when the kickball game had drifted to our lawn, he took in the scene—half a dozen kids running around his front yard, trampling the fresh seed he'd spent the weekend spreading. I caught his face behind the wheel of his Saab, his eyes popping in rage. He drove into the garage, which was around the corner of the house and out of my view. I heard my dad before I saw him next, although he was trailing his scream by only a split second as he came charging back around the corner from the garage to the front lawn.

"Jimmy! Get these kids the fuck off my lawn!"

The other kids were startled by the eruption at first, then paralyzed by such proximity to an actual F-bomb detonated by an adult. Never mind that we weren't supposed to say the word; we weren't supposed to even hear it. Everyone froze for an instant before realizing it was now or never. They all made a break for it, sprinting for the safety of their own homes.

I tried to come into the house gingerly, using the back door to stay out of sight, desperate to avoid setting off another explosion. This was a challenge, since I wasn't exactly sure what part of a neighborhood kickball game could have caused the first one. As always, I forgot about our perpetually malfunctioning screen door. The device at the top, the long silver tube that was supposed to slow the door down so it didn't slam shut, never seemed to work. The screen door's crash gave me up as I walked into the kitchen.

"Jimmy, please come in here." His voice was raised, but he was past yelling. I walked through the living room and found him at the blue table, with his head in his hands.

"Look, son," he said, a slight pleading in his voice. "I'm sorry I yelled. I was only mad at myself." Now I was really confused. Just a few minutes earlier, I'd heard him clearly. He wanted the kids the fuck off the lawn. In my twelve-year-old mind, that meant he was mad at the kids. Now he was telling me that he was mad at himself.

He couldn't sue life and make it conform to the set of rules he knew so well. Instead, he thrashed about in total exasperation, mystified by how quickly and deeply he'd been buried in obligation, clueless how to dig out.

He was doing everything he understood was required of him, his ambition and work ethic properly channeled in pursuit of providing for his family. And yet the payoff seemed so hard to capture. Just when he figured he should be reaching for the contentment and satisfaction—if not the happiness—due someone busting his ass in all the right ways, they would reposition slightly out of his grasp.

He tried all the traditional anesthetics. But this was beyond Bombay Gin with a twist. Or a bright-green Porsche two-seater. Or an affair with a young client. It might have been his growing desperation, or possibly the thirty pounds and two extra chins he'd gained since college. Maybe it was both. But as my father hit forty, searching for a way to bleed out the toxins and rage generated by his confusion, he found just what he needed. Bob Axelrod took a run around the block.

The running boom was perfectly timed for him. It couldn't have fit his personality any better. Running didn't require teammates or partners, like softball, tennis, or golf. Running depended solely upon him. Unlike managing money, which required some alchemy he could never quite divine, running had a simple calculus: what you put in, you got out. He needed a transaction like that in his life—immediate and dependable. Running allowed him to sweat his anxieties, disappointments, and fears right out of his system.

It was also quantifiable. Not just how far he'd run, but how fast. Over time, he'd accumulate the markers—the certificates, plaques, and medals—that bore witness on the largest wall in his office to just how many miles he'd managed to cover at precisely what pace and exactly what age.

I knew something had a hold on him as I walked up the block from Steven Factor's house late on a Saturday afternoon in the fall of 1976. The twilight was gathering in burnt oranges and dark greens, casting long shadows. The air was crisp, and the chimneys on Lincoln Avenue were pushing out chestnut-scented smoke from some of the season's first fires, filling the neighborhood with coziness.

I approached the corner of Second and Lincoln, the beginning of my block. On the other side of the intersection, about twenty yards away, a bulky figure slogged toward me in a gray sweatshirt, baggy gray sweatpants, and Jack Purcell tennis shoes, huffing hard for air. He reached the corner before I did, turning right and plodding away, his focus on the pavement ten feet in front of him.

This was my first hint—how completely lost in the act of running this man seemed. As I watched him come toward me, something about the concentration on his face struck me as familiar. Suddenly I was hit by a giant swell of astonishment. I knew where I'd seen that expression: on my dad's face. In the nook. Paying the bills. That was my father—running! I stopped and watched him shuffle up another block on Second Avenue, until he took another right on Grant and disappeared from view. He never took his eyes off the pavement.

By the next spring, the Jack Purcells were gone, replaced with a pair of top-of-the-line blue New Balance 320 running shoes. The gray sweatshirt and baggy sweatpants, which smacked heavily of Rocky Marciano doing roadwork, were exchanged for a nylon Frank Shorter all-weather running suit. My dad was no longer puffing his way once around the block. Instead, he was taking long runs through parks two towns over.

That May, my mother and I stood in the clearing of a heavily wooded park at the finish line for a ten-mile road race. We felt out of place, intruders in a community we knew nothing about, jittery with anticipation and uncertainty.

The first runners emerged from the line of trees, circled the meadow where we were, and crossed the finish line. We waited for my dad, expecting him any moment. Five minutes went by. Twenty, maybe thirty more runners finished. There was no sign of my dad. Five more minutes went by. My mother looked puzzled. Her husband wasn't a back-of-the-pack kind of guy. A dozen more runners finished. They were clearly the stragglers; older stick-thin men, some frail-looking women. When a few more minutes passed with still no sign of my dad, concern replaced confusion on my mom's face.

Finally, we saw him pop out of the woods, a racing number safety-pinned to the front of his Fruit of the Loom T-shirt. By then he'd picked up a pair of Nike Daybreak trainers, which looked like a couple of yellow-and-blue pillows strapped to each foot, then stapled to a stack of waffles. He was dead last. I didn't know what to do, or even what to think about that. I certainly had no idea what to say.

He stopped a few strides after crossing, put his hands on his knees for a couple of seconds, then straightened back up and started to walk again. Still breathing hard, he made a small loop of a dozen halting steps away from us, then circled back, approaching my mom and me. I could see his face for the first time. His expression was unfamiliar, somewhere between blissful and delirious—a goofy smile with his lips parted and the tip of his tongue poking through his teeth. His eyes were sparkling, eyebrows lifted, raising the lines on his forehead.

He didn't say much of anything as he got close. He just hugged my mother, then me, and mumbled, "Wasn't that great?" After a few minutes, he shuffled over to the registration table and claimed his certificate for finishing. He motioned with his head toward the parking lot and started to make his way toward our station wagon, a blue Oldsmobile Custom Cruiser with faux-wood paneling. Then he did something I'd never seen before. He climbed into the passenger seat, content to let my mother drive home.

D riving to the White House on the Monday morning after our North Carolina spring break, I dialed my brother's office number. I was almost certain I wouldn't get Peter, since it was just after dawn in San Francisco. But I could never be sure with him, a hard-driving federal prosecutor with an overdeveloped work ethic.

He didn't pick up. I left a voice mail letting him know I had a few questions about my training. I always deferred to Peter when it came to exercise. He was in great shape, certainly more fit than me. He'd run several marathons and started three mornings a week with a mile and a half swim in San Francisco Bay.

The executor of my will, godfather to my sons, a discreet confidant and straight-shooting counselor, Peter was my go-to guy on just about every important life issue, from questions about my CBS contract to what kind of running shoes I should buy. He was eight years younger, a span that had always minimized any sibling rivalry, if not eliminated it entirely. That mostly worked in my favor because with his killer looks, charming personality, calming karma, Phi Beta

Kappa key, Stanford Law degree, and wave-shredding surfing skills, I could've worked up a fair amount of envy.

My phone rang on the drive home. "Big Doc," I heard Petey bellow sharply, his standard hello. He was the only one in the world who called me that and I had no idea why. It didn't matter. Every time he blasted me with it, I brightened, no matter what my mood.

"How's it going?" he continued, asking about our spring break. I answered with a slightly too-long soliloquy about my frustrating battle to get back into shape.

"I'm a fat fuck, Petey," I spit out in self-loathing, starting to build to an agitated climax. "It's bad. Pathetic, actually." I stopped for a second to gather myself. "Let me tell you what kind of lousy shape I'm in," I continued. "I'm out running and I get passed. By a mother. Pushing a stroller. Like I was standing still." I hit the crescendo hard.

"Understand? I am now so out of shape I am being walked down by mommies and their FUCKING BABIES, PETER."

There was a pause. Ordinarily, I would've expected his high-pitched hyena cackle. Peter loved it when life cast one of us in the role of poor schmuck. But he could also read me better than anyone. I wasn't looking to laugh. His voice took on a sober tone, meant to calm me. "Tell me about your recent runs," he said.

I described everything—the incapacitating leg swelling, the awkward struggle back to the beach house, the Pop-Pop Moe climb up the stairs. "Petey, you know how it works with me. Every time I've let myself go, what's it taken—three, maybe four weeks max?—then I'm right back to where I should be. That's not what's happening. It's like I woke up in someone else's body."

Petey let a few more seconds pass while he considered his next question. "When you do go out for a run, how fast are you going?"

I described my standard operating procedure in the month since I'd started running again. "I go out as hard as I can for as long as I can, then I walk."

Again he was silent for a few seconds. He was piecing together everything he was hearing in his typical, deliberate way. Finally he offered up his take.

"Here's what I'm thinking." He let a few more seconds hang silently before continuing, in full Yoda. "I think you're pushing too hard and your body is rebelling. Next time you go out for a run, take it easier at the beginning. No pushing. It'll feel different, no question. It'll seem all wrong. But try it." I turned down my block as Peter offered up his final piece of advice. "Slow down, Jimmy. You'll go farther."

I rushed off the phone, up the steps, and in the front door. My kids immediately came barreling toward me. I didn't stop for the next three hours of dinner, baths, and homework. By the time I crawled into bed, I'd been unable to steal even a second to chew over my conversation with Peter.

I slid under the covers, closed my ears, and heard Peter's voice: "Slow down, Jimmy. You'll go farther."

Since Houston, I'd been running without any real objective beyond "Can I beat him?" I'd seen my dad's times and become entirely focused on "faster." I hadn't given two seconds of thought to what else running might provide, aside from another way to compare myself with my father.

I went to sleep turning over the ways my brother's advice applied far beyond a five-mile training loop.

One of the perks I had as the CBS White House correspondent was setting up tours of the East Wing for visitors to Washington. I loved watching the awestruck faces of friends and relatives as I walked them through the East, Green, Blue, and Red rooms and into the State Dining Room, throwing out some insider's knowledge about the White House movie theater, bowling alley, and swimming pool along the way.

Each spring, I'd get a stream of calls as the tourist season bloomed with the cherry blossoms in Washington, asking if I could arrange a tour. It was a big win-win. They got through the White House gates. I got to be the guy who could make something special happen behind a prestigious set of curtains.

But the tour I set up on the Thursday after spring break for the family of Paul Douglas left me with another set of feelings entirely: hollow and disgusted with myself.

Paul was the CBS cameraman killed by a car bomb in Baghdad nearly two years earlier. A sparkling Brit, tall, strapping, and broad, with a shaved head and a goatee that framed a gap-toothed smile, he was beloved by anyone who ever spent five minutes with him. I didn't know him well. We'd worked together fewer than half a dozen times over half a dozen years. But like everyone else, I'd fallen under his spell.

We'd first met in Skopje, Macedonia. It was ten minutes after ten on a Monday morning when I'd walked into the lobby of the Aleksandar Palace Hotel, our team's gathering point before heading off to shoot a piece in the camps that had been springing up for refugees fleeing Kosovo. Our rendezvous time had been set for ten sharp.

I hadn't meant to be late, but unlike the crew, which was staying at the Aleksandar, I had posted up instead at a house CBS had rented. The house was a mile from the hotel, and I had taken a wrong turn on my walk over. I didn't give it too much thought. Under the unwritten pecking order governing TV news, no one gave the correspondent any shit for being late.

As I walked into the lobby, I instantly recognized Paul based on the description I'd heard more than once before. After all, how many six-foot-one, two-hundred-and-forty-pound black men were sitting around hotel lobbies in Macedonia, with veins popping from their necks as they pointed to their watch yelling, "You're late, mate. You're fucking late." There was no smile. And certainly no deference.

We headed to the camp in silence, riding in an armored car CBS kept for covering stories in nasty places. I tried to make small talk to ingratiate myself with Paul. He was having none of it, answering me in single-syllable grunts, when he answered me at all.

Half an hour into our walk through the camp, we stumbled across a Catholic priest ministering to the refugees. The priest had been working around the clock for several days, seeing to the basic needs of thousands of bewildered Kosovars who'd been suddenly uprooted from their comfortable lives and were now living six or eight to a tent. We sat down for an interview, weariness dulling the natural brightness in the priest's eyes. I asked him about the personal toll of his work. He put his head down, attempting to ward off a rush of emotion.

"I'm sorry," he told us in heavily accented English. "I am not thinking about this until now you ask." He began to cry softly. It was a tender moment that perfectly captured the pain of the refugee crisis then unfolding in the Balkans. It was also terrific television. After that, I was good to go with Paul. Any lingering irritation about my late arrival to the hotel dissipated in the glow of nailing a story, which was all that really mattered to him.

A pissed-off and sullen Paul Douglas had driven us out to the camp. I headed back with a very different Paul Douglas—exuberant and joyful. Driving through downtown Skopje, Paul stuck his head out the window at every red light, shouting "I am Spartacus" at startled Macedonians.

I was baffled until Paul's soundman, a barrel-chested, redheaded Welshman named Phil Sparks, saw my confusion and explained the whole bit. It was Paul's favorite line from the Kirk Douglas movie, the dramatic high point when all the rebellious slaves captured by the Romans claim to be Spartacus so they don't know whom to punish.

Of course it was his favorite line. He lived for the trust and deep friendship that developed among coworkers on assignment in some of the world's worst places. He took special pride in keeping his CBS colleagues laughing and feeling safe. He'd scream "I am Spartacus" across some darkened dining room in a shelled-out hotel in Sarajevo, delighted to hear a gleeful soundman bellow back "No, I am Spartacus." Of course, that would prompt a producer to yell "No, I am Spartacus," in turn eliciting a correspondent to get in on the action: "No, I am Spartacus."

The building exuberance, buoyant and infectious, would spread to other teams from other networks. Soon the entire dining room would be engulfed in the Spartacus chorus. Paul would sit back and behold it all, unimpeachable evidence to support his long-held theory: camaraderie was the best way to burn the gloom off a shithole.

I would see Paul twice more: in Kuwait just before the start of the Iraq War, and in April 2005, covering the death of Pope John Paul II. Both times he greeted me with a bear hug and a booming "Hello, mate," before reminiscing about the interview with the priest. I never felt more proud. The great Paul Douglas and I had an old story to share.

Thirteen months later, Paul was killed by a car bomb in Iraq. He was forty-eight years old, on a regular rotation in the CBS Baghdad bureau. I got a call with the news and sank into a leather chair in my living room, devastated and disbelieving. He was too smart, too careful, and too experienced to have died that way. The next day, I got an e-mail from a soundman in London, one of Paul's closest friends, who filled in some of the details of the bombing, helping me cut through the shock and get to the grief. At the end of the e-mail was an address for Paul's family.

"Send condolence note to Linda Douglas" went straight to the top of my to-do list. But somehow, shamefully, I never did.

It wasn't as if there was some insurmountable degree of difficulty involved. A drugstore a block away from the White House sold plenty of cards. But a week turned into two, and I never got there to buy one. Two weeks turned into a month. I was getting pummeled by the most demanding job of my life, arriving at the White House briefing room first thing in the morning and often not leaving until after the broadcast that night. The drugstore was still open when I left for the day, but I'd walk right past it, overwhelmed. Or at least that's what I told myself. One month turned into two, two months turned into three.

When my father died, I'd drawn deep comfort from the many cards and warm wishes we'd received. I'd also kept a mental list of colleagues who'd never sent a condolence note, nor even offered a word of sympathy when I saw them in the halls. I remembered who'd contributed to his memorial fund and how much they'd sent. I knew well the power of a gesture to ease the grief, and yet I couldn't find twenty minutes to go to the store, buy a card, write a short note, get the correct postage to England, and send my sympathies to a family mourning someone whom I'd deeply admired.

Judging from my feelings walking down Pennsylvania Avenue two years later to meet Paul's family, I hadn't done a very good job of pushing the guilt away. I was haunted by my self-absorption. Paul's widow, Linda, was here, with their two daughters, Jo and Kelly, and three grandchildren who had traveled to the United States for a ceremony honoring journalists killed while doing their jobs. They'd asked CBS to arrange a tour of the White House. I couldn't have been happier to have some small way to do something for Paul's family.

We met in front on Pennsylvania Avenue, at the northwest gate, which meant a walk of a couple of blocks around to the east side of the White House grounds where the tours started. Linda greeted me with a warm handshake and a kiss on the cheek. "Paul used to come home from stories and describe the Americans," she said, looking into my watering eyes. "He always said you were very nice." I wanted to kill myself.

We chatted about their trip as we strolled. My voice cracked briefly as I told Linda about the first time we'd met in Macedonia. "So he's pointing down at his watch. He's furious because I should've been there ten minutes before. And he looks at me and starts to yell . . ."

I turned away. She was smiling when I'd composed myself and turned back toward her. After two years, she'd grown used to people needing to share their stories about Paul with her. But I knew from responding to people after my dad died that she might appreciate a chance for a simple, quiet walk in the brilliant spring sunshine without having to summon the strength to be gracious. I let the story trail off.

Linda and her family loved the tour through the White House. Her two granddaughters were especially taken with the Gilbert Stuart portrait of George Washington hanging in the East Room. It had been saved by Dolley Madison, who took it with her when she fled the White House during the War of 1812, just ahead of the advancing British troops.

"We studied that in school," one of his granddaughters announced softly, hushing her British accent bashfully.

"Although from a somewhat different perspective," Linda cut in archly, as we all broke up laughing.

In the Blue Room, one of the three parlors linking the East Room and the State Dining Room, Linda and the girls were focused on the early-nineteenth-century furniture as Paul's three-year-old grandson Kai absentmindedly reached up and grabbed my hand. I took it and started to amble on with him, welling up as I realized I was walking Paul Douglas's youngest grandchild through the Blue Room at the White House, casually holding hands. I looked back to Linda to make sure she saw Kai was with me and hadn't wandered off. "Paul was crazy about that one," she mouthed silently to me while pointing at Kai.

Still holding hands, Kai and I meandered through the State Dining Room, into the front hallway, out the North Portico, and toward the front gate. When Kai saw a heavily armed Secret Service sniper by a security booth, he dropped my hand and wandered ahead to stare at his automatic rifle. Walking with me past Kai, who was engrossed by the agent, Linda lowered her voice and began to tell me a story.

"A couple of months ago, I decided to take them all away to the seaside for the weekend. I said, 'Come on, Kai, we're going to Devon.' Do you know what he said back? He said, 'Are we going to see Granddad?'" Linda's eyes filled.

"I had no idea what he was thinking," she continued. "I said, 'No, Kai, what would give you that idea?' He said, 'But you always tell us Granddad is in Devon.'"

Kai's little-boy ears had confused "Granddad is in heaven" with "Granddad is in Devon." She laughed with a surprising lightness. Something about Kai's innocence in the face of unspeakable pain seemed to tickle her.

Her resilience startled me, her ability to balance the humor of Kai's sweet misunderstanding with the crushing weight of her loss. Here was a woman wrestling real grief with discernible grace, a sharp contrast to my own grasping as I confronted issues that were disorienting but hardly devastating.

Outside the White House gates, I hugged them all goodbye and thanked Linda for giving me the chance to spend some time with them. I crossed the portion of Pennsylvania Avenue right in front of the White House that's blocked off to automobile traffic, and went to find a bench in Lafayette Park.

There were several rows of them but all had filled up on this gorgeous early-April morning. At the far eastern edge of the park, I saw an empty bench and made my way over. I was dazed. I could hear Linda's voice: "Granddad is in Devon." Slowly the emotion built in that park across from the White House until it overran me. I started to shake. Then I began to cry.

I was crying for Paul Douglas to be sure, and for Kai, who couldn't see him in Devon, and for Linda, who'd never again share a cup of tea with him in their garden. But the tears came from someplace even deeper, heaving sobs of shame for never having reached out to the people most wounded by his death.

I called Stina, sobbing, and choked out the story. "Honey, two years and I never wrote to them. Two years, Stina. I can't believe I never even sent Linda a card. How's that possible?"

"Jimmy," she answered, "that's so unlike you."

I was crying on that bench precisely because it was no longer so unlike me. I couldn't explain why I'd never written to Paul's family, only that I hadn't, and it clearly had something to do with running too fast in pursuit of . . . I wasn't sure what.

I'd been recording my runs in a journal: 59:58 for running and walking my 5.1-mile loop the Monday we got back, then 58:19 two days later. But my phone call with Peter had put a new spin on my relationship to time. How far now trumped how fast.

On the first Saturday after spring break, I did 6.2 miles in just under an hour and ten minutes. The big deal for me was running three straight miles before I had to walk, the farthest I'd run without stopping since I'd started up four weeks earlier. It was all a little strange. For the first time in thirty years of running, I wasn't worried that I wouldn't go fast enough but that I wouldn't go slow enough.

I averaged three or four runs a week in April, running two days, then resting two days. My body couldn't handle more than two days in a row. My knees would ache, my balky ankle would throb, my calves would tighten, and my shins would swell. Though I still wasn't bouncing back as quickly as I had in the past, I was steadily increasing my distance. Nearly three months after receiving that first e-mail from Dave, I could feel slight traces of satisfaction. I was starting to get somewhere.

Still, no matter how consistently I ran during a nice stretch at home, it wouldn't mean much until campaign coverage resumed. I might have thought I had a new approach, but until it was tested by the demands of the trail, it wouldn't count.

During the last week of April, Hillary Clinton kicked off her homestretch run, a grueling three weeks that saw us bouncing between Indiana, North Carolina, West Virginia, and Kentucky, with a few side trips to other states crammed in whenever possible. It was a string of days that might start with a 7:30 a.m. news conference in Washington, D.C., and end with a midnight check-in at a hotel in Portland, Oregon, after stops in Charlestown, West Virginia, and Sioux Falls, South Dakota, along the way. Never mind running, the goal was surviving.

The next time I checked my journal, I hadn't run in a month. When I finally got home for a couple of days in late May, the same 5.1-mile loop I'd been able to run and walk in just under an hour right after spring break now took me an hour and fifteen minutes. As I looked at my watch and saw the time, my heart sank and my mood soured. The benefits of all the work I'd done since getting Dave's e-mail had been virtually wiped out. It was right there in cold, brutal clarity on my wrist.

I needed the campaign to end. It may have been a chartered jet with a fully stocked bar and plenty of shrimp cocktail, but Hillary

Clinton's campaign plane was flying me backward. I was holding on for dear life as she desperately whipped around the country, her campaign aides hoping Obama would somehow self-destruct. I was trapped until she finally read the writing on the wall the same way the rest of her party did.

I'd loved the chance to cover history, to get a peek behind the curtain of a presidential campaign and have an occasional beer with one of the world's most famous women. Assignments like the Clinton campaign didn't come along very often in a reporter's career. That had always been enough to counterbalance the consequences of taking them. Not anymore.

When I was growing up, our beach house at 7 East Eighty-first Street in Harvey Cedars, New Jersey, took on a distinct vibe during the last two weeks of every summer that was absent the rest of the year. Three lots from the beach, the 1930s cedar-shake bungalow had been raised up eight feet on pilings in 1962 after a vicious nor'easter split Long Beach Island in half and washed the house halfway down the street.

My parents bought it in 1970 for $35,000, their dream come true—just an hour and a half down the Garden State Parkway, their own place at the shore! Their pride and pleasure that first summer blazed as bright and hot as the August sun.

The house had one main floor with a kitchen, an open dining area that flowed into the family room, a front sunroom (where my mom kept the jigsaw puzzles she assembled each night on a long, rectangular dark-wood table pocked with knots), three bedrooms, and a bathroom with a shower only my parents could use. The kids had to take their showers in the dark, mildewed room underneath the raised house.

The shower-segregation policy ensured that we never tracked in sand from the beach. It also required us, once we'd washed off, to lift a freshly laundered towel from the pile my mother always had re-restocked on the unfinished wood shelf over the nearby rusted washer and dryer, wrap it around ourselves, and shuffle quickly up the flight of outside steps that was the only way into the house. Since we were naked under the towel, the run up the steps always felt slightly racy.

The entire second floor of the beach house was an unfinished attic with a queen-size bed and extra-soft mattress that swallowed us when we lay on it. There was also a half-bathroom that my mother covered in contact paper featuring bold pink-and-yellow flowers, hoping to make it a bit more appealing for my older sister, Lisa, who'd claimed the space for her own.

We were small when my folks bought the beach house. Lisa was ten that first summer, I was eight, Teddy was five, and Peter was still a baby. The day after school ended in June, my mother packed us, our summer clothes, a dozen beach towels, and a bunch of groceries into her Oldsmobile Custom Cruiser, with no intention of returning until the day before school started in September.

In those first few years, the house had a breezy, relaxed feel. Lisa, Teddy, and I would hit the beach first thing in the morning ready to stay out all day, coming back to the house only to use the bathroom or eat lunch. My mother would square away the house after breakfast, then follow us to the beach, burying the metal frame of her green cloth beach chair into the hard, wet sand exposed by the low tide going out. With her cheerful infant, Peter, on her lap, she'd watch her three older kids catch waves on their rubber rafts until the siren from the local firehouse signaled noon. Then she'd stand up, brush the sand from her lap and off Peter's diapered bottom, and head back to the house to make sandwiches.

On those summer weekdays my mom had a calm and contented air. No matter what else was going on in her life, nothing could diminish her satisfaction in giving her children more than she'd had as a kid.

Work kept my father up north most of the summer. He drove down to the beach midweek for an overnight, and then again every

Friday for the weekend until the middle of August, when he'd take the last two weeks off, plus the Labor Day weekend.

On that Friday night in August when he was coming down for the last stretch of summer, no matter what else we were doing, everyone would have an ear out for the sound of his car turning into our crushed-pebble driveway. Traffic was so unpredictable that we never knew when he'd arrive. The flow of fathers driving south from New York merging with those driving east from Philadelphia often bottle-necked at the bottom of the one bridge onto the island.

Sometimes he'd show up in the late afternoon, just as we were coming off the beach and headed to that dank shower room under the house. Other times he'd show up while we were eating dinner, chomping on cobs of sweet white Jersey corn my mom had bought that day from Frank the produce man, a schoolteacher who peddled fresh fruits and vegetables in the summer from the back of his truck. If the traffic had been really bad, my father wouldn't get to the house until we were already settled in watching TV on the cream-colored pleather couch with overstuffed pillows shiny from wear and sticky with late-August humidity.

But starting midafternoon on that second Friday in August, if we were in the house, we were on high alert. The sound of any car turning up East Eighty-first Street sent us scrambling to the sunroom, where a strip of half a dozen windows overlooked the driveway. Looking down from the raised house, we might catch a glimpse of him through his windshield as he drove his car underneath the house to park. But the peek was never long enough to give us what we needed most—some clue about his mood.

We'd all wait anxiously, my mom too, listening to him climb the same set of steps we'd used to scamper into the house in our towels. We hoped to hear him whistling, or maybe even singing if he'd settled a big case. "Zip-A-Dee-Doo-Dah" meant especially good things for us. It was a favorite from his childhood. "Zip-a-dee-doo-dah, zip-a-dee-ay. My, oh my, what a wonderful day." The words signaled the arrival of the light and springy version of my father.

But after those first few summers at the beach, we heard it less and less. Whatever kind of marker it had been for him when he bought it, whatever success and satisfaction it represented, the beach house now seemed to elicit no particular joy.

"Dad's here!" Sometimes that meant running to hug him at whatever height we could, knee to midriff. Other times it meant quietly steering clear. We'd know which it was just by the way he came up the stairs.

His vacation had become serious business, his one sustained break that was scheduled into his calendar every year. The sunshine and easy breezes of the rest of the summer were overtaken by the heaviness my father increasingly brought with him as he pulled the screen door open and walked inside, his face blank and impassive. Stillness would overtake 7 East Eighty-first, falling over the house like a dark cloak. It might lighten at points during the next two weeks, depending on how much solitude he was able to enjoy, but from the moment we heard him coming up the stairs on getaway Friday, everyone was on notice: This wasn't a family vacation. This was dad's time off.

He had a routine he adhered to with the discipline of a Trappist monk. In these years, while I was developing the first wisps of darkened hairs above my lip, the father who had swooped in to pick me out of the boat at the World's Fair ten years earlier had split. And with him went the well-defined vision and the determination to execute it. In his place was a man determined to relax during the last two weeks of August, which was becoming an increasingly solitary exercise.

He'd take his rainbow-striped folding chair to the beach each morning and find an isolated spot to sequester himself. After slathering suntan oil on his face, chest, and legs, he'd sit down, slip on his prescription sunglasses with the dark-red lenses, and crack open a Michener novel. He'd cross his extended legs at the ankles and make it crystal clear in one-syllable grunted responses to anyone who might even think about checking in with him that he wasn't there to talk, he was there to broil.

The sun was my father's narcotic. He'd sit for hours, soaking it up until he looked like an overcooked lobster. It seemed to soothe if not purify him, drawing a year's worth of frustration, confusion, and anger from his pores and vaporizing it.

We knew not to breach his space. Whatever pleasure he once had taken in throwing me those baseballs that arched high into the sky was gone; my dad was no longer a guy who wanted to play catch. My mom had secured a visa, and she'd sometimes sit next to him in silence, reading. But for the kids, the only safe entry was provided by the jingle from the ice cream truck. When the stick-thin, long-haired teenager, no doubt stoned out of his mind, stopped his Good Humor truck at the top of the street, walked to the entrance of the beach, and shook a thin metal bar with three bells hanging from it, we knew we could breach the no-man's-land and raced to my father's chair.

Once we'd encircled him, he'd hook a thumb into the waistline of his madras bathing suit, pulling it out just far enough to reveal a little pocket sewn inside. With a mischievous smile, he'd reach two fingers from his other hand into the pouch and extract a few sweat-soaked dollar bills, handing them to Lisa or me.

We'd take off up the beach, out of breath by the time we got to the top of the dunes, but still pushing hard to get to the ice cream truck before the line built. Back we'd come with our treats and give the change to my dad, who'd meet our eyes for a quick smile before returning to his book. In that moment, we'd get a flash of our father when he was younger and still the man with a plan. Buying ice cream for his kids at his summer home must've been on his to-do list when he'd written it up years earlier. But since then it had become crystal clear that whatever he needed, he wasn't looking to us to provide it. And we would trudge back through the sand to our towels twenty yards away, pecking at our ice cream before the late-summer sun melted it down our hands.

Once he started running, the broiling sessions took a backseat to his new infatuation. He'd usually go in the morning, before heading to the beach. Every once in a while he'd wait until after the heat broke in the late afternoon. Long Beach Island was made for running. An eighteen-mile-long sandbar that sat a few miles off the New Jersey mainland, LBI had one main road running north to south with a shoulder on each side for bikers and joggers.

He'd get up before six to be out on the boulevard before the heat started to climb, running five, six, sometimes seven miles down the island before turning around and coming back. If my mom was headed off the island for a big grocery run, he might wait and get dropped off a dozen miles from the house and then run back, which meant going up and over the high hump-backed causeway linking the mainland to LBI.

During the summer before my sophomore year of high school, after I had told Dave I wanted to try out for the cross-country team that fall, I began to run a little myself, up and down Long Beach Boulevard. I was in nowhere near the kind of shape my father was, able to go only four or five miles at the most, but I was starving for time with him. He no longer tossed baseballs. But he ran.

A Hollywood vision danced in my head, the two of us striding side by side down Long Beach Boulevard in the late-afternoon golden light, my father helping his uncertain adolescent son forward with sage guidance and lighthearted chat about girls and the Yankees. But this wasn't Hollywood. It was New Jersey.

When I floated the idea of tagging along on one of his afternoon runs, he shrugged his shoulders in a manner I couldn't entirely translate, but that vaguely suggested "your funeral." He knew he couldn't say no in all good conscience, but he didn't do a thing to encourage the idea, either.

The setting was different—the road, not the beach—and I was a few years past running to him for ice cream money. But the principle was the same: he didn't want anything or anyone cutting into his treasured time alone. At fifteen, I wasn't sophisticated enough to extract his ambivalence from a simple shoulder shrug, which was probably a good thing, since I wouldn't have been able to understand I wasn't supposed to take it personally.

We walked out to the boulevard, turned right toward the Barnegat Lighthouse, and started to run. There was no easing into it with him, and certainly no casual conversation. He went out hard. Within two blocks we were no longer running side by side. I was looking at his back.

His upper body stored all his tension. He tightly scrunched his shoulders, the blades pinched together just below the base of his head. The shoulders forced his chin up at a slightly unnatural angle, bringing much more of his bald spot into my view. His upper arms, from his shoulders to his elbows, stayed glued to his torso. At the bottom of his rib cage, each forearm stiffly jutted up and away from his body at a forty-five-degree angle. He looked like he was in bad need of the Tin Man's oilcan.

While his upper body remained rigid, his stride was a relentless, jaunty bounce from one skinny leg to the other. He was strutting as much as running. I kept my focus on his lower legs, below the knee. I'd always been fascinated by the stretch from his bony ankles up to the compact knots of calf muscle. Both lower legs had been skinned clean by years of wearing too-tight dress socks. It was as permanent as a tattoo, an indelible mark of the long hours building his practice. Each time one of his feet struck the pavement, I'd see the calf defined for one split second in sharp, pulsing relief.

A quarter mile into our run, my father had moved four feet in front of me. The whole reason I'd asked to go running with him had been rendered pointless by a four-foot gap between us, opened so subtly I hadn't even detected it was happening. He stared straight ahead, oblivious to his son trailing behind. Forget the relaxed side-by-side father-son chat. I would've needed a bullhorn to grab his attention.

I wasn't exactly sure what was going on, but as we made our way farther north, in the August air thick with humidity, it started to become clear. As I picked up my pace, he picked up his. As badly as I wanted to close the four-foot gap, my dad needed to maintain it even more.

Frustrated, I backed off a bit, knowing I couldn't sustain the faster pace I'd hoped would draw me even. But as I started to slow down, he eased up too. Not enough to let me catch up, of course. Just enough to maintain the integrity of the four-foot gap. No matter how fast or slow I ran, he adjusted his speed accordingly, determined to keep his distance at all times.

He offered neither encouragement nor explanation. Instead, his head cocked slightly to the right, eyes staring off at some indeterminate point in the distance, he straddled the solid line separating the slow lane from the shoulder. He either didn't notice that his left leg was actually in the slow lane, or didn't care. The cars coming up quickly on him had to swing wide to avoid him.

"Dad, what are you doing? You're in traffic," I shouted from four feet back.

He didn't answer, nor did he move back over the line and into the safety of the shoulder. That would've defeated the purpose. It began to dawn on me: he wasn't unaware of the cars. In fact, he enjoyed making them swerve. However much happiness his obligations bled out of him was returned in some small measure by making those cars veer around him. Each angry honk from an annoyed driver elicited a slightly more chipper stride in acknowledgment, a crucial piece of pushback from a man fighting desperately not to be swallowed whole by the life he'd created.

As the two of us passed the telephone pole that marked the midpoint of the run, I was enveloped by the futility of ever overtaking my father. He was chasing some private vision of happiness, which clearly didn't include me. Worse yet, it might even have excluded me.

We finished at the corner where East Eighty-first intersected the boulevard, in front of the Neptune Market, where a few years earlier we would walk together in the morning to get the papers and see how the Yankees had done. Walking the fifty yards up East Eighty-first Street to our house, trying to catch my breath, I could feel a sharp edge of anger starting to build.

"Dad," I blurted, "why couldn't we just run together?"

As furious as I was, I still wasn't ready to take him on directly. Not at fifteen. I forced a half smile on my face to conceal my emotions, but I could feel a vague tickle in my nose as my eyes moistened. I really didn't want to start crying.

Bob Axelrod was never subtle, least of all when challenged. Half a smile wasn't going to cause him to pull any punches. Not even with his son.

"Not my fault if you can't keep up," he said.

I shook my head, although more in resignation than in surprise. He really didn't get it. The four-foot gap had nothing to do with how fast either of us could run. It had remained constant the whole time. We could've just as easily been side by side.

But even at fifteen, I could sense my father wasn't out to hurt me. Whatever demons he was trying to keep at bay, my hurt was collateral damage in his battle with himself. He was confused, not malicious. He hadn't just lost a clear vision of how to raise his son; he'd lost a clear vision for his own life.

Running was my father's escape, his one dependable break from his many burdens. It was his certain and secure sanctuary. He couldn't tolerate any trespassers, not even his kids. The father who'd taken the training wheels off my bike and knew the exact moment to let go of my seat was still in there, but he was encased in cold layers of overwork, frustration, and unhappiness. And two weeks of sun at the Jersey Shore each August weren't about to thaw him out.

s I ran side by side with Dave across a stretch of park, it felt as if we could've used a machete to hack our way through Washington's late-June air. Dave and his son, Theo, were in town on the last weekend of June to celebrate Stina's forty-third birthday, and the humidity was already in midsummer form. With Dave living in New York, I was able to run with him only a couple of times a year. I savored every opportunity to retrace the steps we'd first taken as fifteen-year-olds.

Looking at my buddy, a touch stockier yet still running with the same effortless, rhythmic grace I'd been watching for thirty years, I was overtaken by a wave of homesickness. As kids, Dave and I would sometimes end our Saturday-morning runs at his house, where Mrs. Moughalian would make us breakfast—a high stack of pancakes fluffy as feather pillows with melted butter dripping down the sides. We couldn't possibly have known then how small the circle of people would be later in life who knew the taste of your mother's pancakes.

The previous night, we'd all gone for dinner to La Ferme, a quiet French restaurant half a mile from our house. Stina, her mom, the kids, Dave, Theo, and I had walked into the village, ambling down a long hill on a narrow sidewalk that sometimes forced us into a single file. Our leisurely stroll had set the mood as we settled around the big, circular table—calm and serene.

I'd looked across the table at Stina, watching her through the soft glow radiating from the squat circular candle on the table. Her peaceful, soothing smile reflected contentment. She was surrounded by her family, and her husband was home. Beaten up, worn down, deeply disoriented—but finally home.

My eyes moved quickly from face to face around the table. Stina, deeply satisfied. Her mom, Trudy, beaming with delight, sitting next to her daughter and across from her grandchildren. Dave, grinning as he watched his son and my boys pass dinner rolls among themselves, the next generation forging friendships. Stina, Trudy, Dave— each could've been the happiest person in the room. I was the only one at our table not in contention, though my prospects were brightening. At least now I had a plan.

Three weeks earlier, Hillary Clinton had finally yielded to the inevitable and bowed out, giving a poignant farewell speech on a brutally hot day at the National Building Museum in Washington. It had been her best event, offering a moving consideration of the deep cracks she'd made in our national glass ceiling. The room, a vast, four-story atrium dominated by eight Corinthian columns, was stuffed with supporters. Many wept, deeply moved by how close Hillary had come and by her own heartfelt consideration of what they'd all accomplished together.

Leaving the museum after the speech, I started to shape a script in my head about what might've happened if only she'd summoned that kind of authentic emotion earlier in the campaign and displayed it more frequently. I was working over a last line—"Perhaps, if she had shown this side of herself sooner, she would've never had to give a concession speech at all"—when I got to the exit.

As I stepped from the dark, cool air of the museum into the bright, sweltering afternoon sunshine, all thoughts of Hillary Clinton vanished. I paused on the steps to let my eyes adjust to the intense light. A simple, powerful thought settled on me: it's over. The half a year of all-consuming chaos that accompanied covering her campaign was finished.

Emerging from what felt like a coma during the next three weeks, I began to survey the mess I'd made of myself during the last push of her campaign. Not only had I not run once during her march through West Virginia, Indiana, North Carolina, and Kentucky, but I'd relapsed into eating like a pig and drinking like a fish. Once again, when I stepped on the scale, I was more than two hundred pounds. A lot more. I was shaken at how quickly all the progress I'd made in March and April had been wiped out by another nasty stretch of campaign coverage in May. But at least it was finally over.

Yes, I was leaving the campaign trail disoriented, with unmistakable question marks hanging over my career, something I'd never dealt with in my dozen years at CBS. I didn't have any answers yet, but putting the campaign havoc behind me would be a crucial first step toward establishing some equilibrium. No longer would I have to claw through some inhuman travel schedule that undermined any shot at sustaining a normal life. No longer would I spend weeks away from Stina and the kids, home just long enough to grab some clean clothes before heading out again. No longer would I live on a frat boy's diet, watching my stomach turn into a gut. I had a lot of repair work to do, but finally I was out of obstacles. That filled me with relief. Of course, I was also out of excuses. That filled me with dread.

By the time Dave visited for Stina's birthday, I'd been back at it for three weeks, hammering out a dozen runs and beginning to recapture some of what I'd lost during the last couple of months on the campaign trail. But heading down a wooded path with him on the Sunday after Stina's birthday, through a chute of overhanging branches and heavy leaf cover, I was reminded that Dave was simply a much better runner. Even though he'd hardly been running regularly, I was the one with the labored breathing, struggling to keep up.

We'd been running for a little more than twenty minutes when we hit a slight upgrade. Weirdly, almost as if some long-dormant instinct was awakened, honed four feet behind my father years ago on Long Beach Island, I started to push the pace up the incline. Suddenly, instead of savoring the too-rare treat of a Sunday-morning run with one of my closest friends, I was racing to get ahead of him. It was all completely unconscious, which would've been a relief had I stopped and apologized once Dave made me aware of what I was doing. Except he did, and I didn't.

Stina had long thought that in another life Dave had been a refined European diplomat known for his impeccable manners and sophisticated salon. He had a knack for expressing his displeasure in a disarmingly nonthreatening way that still got the message across. Halfway into the upgrade, as I started to move a few steps ahead of him, he picked up his pace, drew even with me, and gently tried to help me see for myself that I was running too fast.

"How're you feeling?" he asked earnestly, in a remarkably steady voice. I was breathing so hard I could barely answer. "I don't know, buddy," I gasped, pulling hard for air. "The humidity's killing me. I think I gotta stop soon."

For the last couple of months, Dave had been hearing a steady stream of how my brother had changed my approach to running with his "slow down, you'll go farther" wisdom. And now here I was, ignoring every syllable of Petey's advice, and threatening to corrupt the pleasure of our Sunday-morning run by pressing the pace. Even the diplomat was getting a touch testy.

"Why don't we slow it down just a bit?" It was stated in the form of a question, but that was just to keep me from getting defensive. Dave was still hopeful that he could gently nudge me into seeing what I needed to do.

I tried, leaning back from the shoulders and chest to break my pace, like a jockey pulling at a horse's reins. As long as I focused solely on running slower, I was fine. But the instant my mind began to wander, the reflex took over and I started to speed up again.

Here I was, the guy who should have known better than anyone how lousy it felt to have your running partner leave you behind, and I was trying to dust mine. Making me even more of a moron, I was trying to run into the ground a guy who was in much better shape and could've dropped me like a stone whenever he wanted to. The only lesson that seemed to have stuck from running down Long Beach Boulevard with my dad when I was fifteen was that four feet ahead beat side by side and certainly beat four feet behind. I was just as bad as my dad had ever been.

When I started to pick up the pace once again, Dave abandoned any hope in subtlety. Abruptly, he raised his right arm chest high, like a bar at a tollgate, so that he could touch his forearm against my sternum and regulate my speed. "Hey," he said, this time with an unmistakable edge, "slow down."

That did the trick, snapping me out of my spell. You had to work awfully hard to annoy Dave; I'd just done it effortlessly. In my embarrassment I slowed down and didn't pick it up again. Looking down at my watch, I saw we were at 27:00. In the four months since I'd started running, I'd never made it half an hour straight without walking. All I had to do was hold on for three more minutes and I'd have an important benchmark for my running diary. I was fading fast as I looked down again and saw 28:15, breathing hard, my legs growing heavy. I began to work the numbers in my head, looking to make a deal with myself.

"Forty-five seconds. Just get to 29:00. You can put up with anything for a minute after that."

Dave and I ran in silence. I fell into his rhythm, hoping he could carry me through. I looked down again: 29:03. Less than a minute. As I'd done for thirty years, I fell half a step behind Dave and let him pull me along: 29:45. No matter how bad my legs felt, they certainly had another fifteen seconds in them. I was going to do it. I looked down to see the time on my watch go from 29:59 to 30:00.

I stopped immediately, as if I'd just broken the tape at a finish line, and bent over, hands on my knees, my back heaving up and down. Dave slipped his arm inside mine, prodding me to straighten up and keep walking. I folded my hands together behind my head as I did, elongating my rib cage and allowing as much air as possible into my lungs. Gradually I got my breath back as we walked. I pumped my fist in self-satisfaction a couple of times.

In the old days, running thirty minutes straight would've been entirely unremarkable, and certainly no cause for celebration. But in the old days I wouldn't have split my suit pants or climbed a staircase like my crippled grandfather.

Ten minutes later, Dave asked if I wanted to run a little more. We picked up a slow jog and made it all the way back to the house, another mile and a half. We finished the entire 5.1-mile loop in just under an hour, 58:55. Checking my journal, I saw it was almost exactly the time I'd recorded for running and walking the same loop two months earlier, just before I'd headed back out on the road for Hillary's last shot. Measuring strictly by the numbers, I'd made a full recovery from my latest spell of neglect.

Better yet, when I got on the scale right after our run, the needle settled just on the left side of two hundred. In the three weeks since the Clinton campaign ended, I'd dropped more than seven pounds. With the exception of a little tightness in my right calf, my body was cooperating. My shins weren't swelling, my feet weren't flopping, and there didn't seem to be any new mothers lurking behind me with their strollers. I was sleeping in my own bed, eating like a human being, and running regularly. Every part of my life had slowed down. And as I'd just proven, running half an hour straight for the first time, I was going farther. At least I could, if I wrestled certain instincts to the ground.

The run with Dave was just the motivational spike I needed. I ran four times in the next five days. The following Friday, the Fourth of July, I ran forty minutes straight. I was a long way from marathon shape, but for the first time in a long time I gave over to a sense of hopefulness. I was on a roll.

The next day, I boarded the White House press charter for a twelve-hour flight to Sapporo, Japan, to cover the G8 Summit, the annual meeting of the world's leading industrialized nations. I had red-flagged this trip, nervous about the threat it posed to my growing momentum.

The White House press corps traveled comfortably, to say the least. Forget the stale pretzels and warm cans of soda. Boarding the plane at Andrews Air Force Base, the reporters were met at the top of the steps by a flight attendant holding a tray with champagne. That gave us something to sip as we walked to the front of the cabin and a smorgasbord of fine cheeses, fancy crackers, shrimp, and fresh salmon. God forbid we should take off on an empty stomach.

There was a general giddiness on board as the plane leveled off at thirty-five thousand feet. Usually, I was right in the middle of things, drink in one hand, plate piled high with jumbo shrimp in the other, doing my part to get the traveling cocktail party going. Not this time. I slipped on my headphones, turned on my iPod, and popped an Ambien, hoping to sleep all the way to Japan. Not only did I want to avoid the potential to pig out, but I'd need the rest.

The twelve-hour time difference made for a grueling schedule, working overnight in Japan to meet New York deadlines for the evening news, then staying up most of the following day to cover a full schedule of events at the summit.

Historically, I'd addressed the sleep deprivation with a regimen of constant eating. A full buffet set up in the back of the workspace was standard operating procedure on foreign trips, so reporters under the gun would never have to waste time looking for food. Between meals there was a constant supply of junk food—trays of cakes, cookies, candy, and soda. I'd be living with constant temptation for the entire trip.

My resolve was still with me as our bus rolled out of the Sapporo airport. The summit was being held on Hokkaido, Japan's northernmost island, with the media headquartered at the Rusutsu Resort, a severely under-occupied, mid-level tourist hotel featuring an odd collection of animatronic dogs that appeared malnourished and an Epcot Center–inspired Bavarian restaurant, which lent a creepy hint of Axis nostalgia to the place.

Built at high altitude into the side of a mountain, the Rusutsu offered thin air and almost no flat terrain, both of which made running a challenge. Additionally, security for the G8 meant the premises were encircled in razor wire, cutting down the distance I could run in any one direction. Leaving for a run wasn't the easiest or safest proposition, since coming and going from the hotel involved long lines and metal detectors, and the only road for miles was heavily trafficked and featured neither sidewalks nor shoulders. But I was determined not to give in to the hours, obstacles, or seductions. Finding a way to run was a must.

Heading to the back of the resort, I saw a chairlift that had been silenced for the summer. It had thick metal stanchions supporting the large wheels that kept the cables and chairs moving during ski season, spaced about a hundred yards apart all the way up the side of the main mountain that rose steeply from the base of the lift, where I stood. I counted three stanchions inside the perimeter security fence and quickly realized this was my best bet for a workout.

Drawing up the workout in my mind, I figured since it was less than a quarter mile, I wouldn't stop once I got to the top. I planned instead to slap the top stanchion, then turn around and jog down the mountainside, staying in continuous motion for half a dozen circuits. All told, that would be a bit less than two and a half miles. While that was a little short of how far I'd been running at home, I figured the altitude and the incline would offer fair compensation.

I briefly stretched my legs, bent at the waist to touch my toes, then gave it a go—three hundred yards almost straight up. The first hundred were easy enough, propelled more than anything by the novelty. I started to slow considerably over the next hundred. Rationally, I knew I was outside, running up a steep, grass-covered slope on a mountainside in northern Japan. But at the moment it felt as if somehow I'd slipped onto a treadmill.

Arms and legs pumping, I'd looked up after thirty hard seconds, expecting to see the second stanchion coming into view. No dice. I'd practically been running in place, progressing no more than fifty yards. Head down, I ran for what felt like ten seconds more. When I took another peek, the next stanchion seemed just as far away as it had the first time I'd checked. I kept pumping, then looked up for a third time. Now it actually seemed farther away. I swore I was going backward.

Finally I got to the second stanchion, finding it hard to believe how exhausted two hundred yards had left me. As I headed to the third stanchion, the mountain felt as if it had grown even steeper. I wondered if I'd be able to generate enough power to get there at all.

I fixed my stare ten feet in front of me, continuing to pump my arms and legs through the burn I was feeling in my lungs. I knew I had less than a hundred yards. The fatigue had turned my run into a glorified walk. I glanced up. Twenty yards left. The incline now felt almost completely vertical, downgrading my glorified walk into a near crawl.

I got to the top stanchion and slapped it with my hand, just as I'd planned. The high altitude of Hokkaido was clearly going to require me to tweak my idea of staying in motion during my six trips up and down the side of the mountain. I walked to the bottom, instead of jogging, and was still breathing heavily when I got there. I decided to give myself a couple more minutes at the base to catch my breath before trying again.

My pace for the next trip up the slope was considerably slower. No longer did I have any interest in how quickly I made it to the top stanchion, only that I got there at all. This time when I slapped that third stanchion, I stopped and put my hands on my knees, hoping not to vomit before starting my walk down. Slapping the stanchion on my third trip, I knew I'd never make six. I pushed myself up the mountain twice more and called it a day at five.

While the mountainside had chewed me up, the workout provided at least a small measure of inspiration to go with the exhaustion. I'd negotiated the obstacles, solved the problems, avoided the traps, and got in my run. Finally, it seemed to me, I had a bead on consistency, the essential component of accomplishment that had proven to be so maddeningly elusive.

The next morning, I was back at the base of the chairlift. I made five trips running up the mountain, and threw in one more to make the six I'd originally planned to have done the day before.

I had plenty of time to exercise: thanks to the lame-duck presidency of George W. Bush, Barack Obama and John McCain were the new headliners. With the end of Bush's second term now measured in months, the bar the president had to clear for me to get airtime on an overseas trip had been boosted several levels higher. Certainly nothing at the G8 was going to help him. It was getting to the point where he'd have to mug an old lady to get a minute and a half of coverage, and even then she'd have to be blind to make it a sure thing.

While this meant a slower pace for my work, along with plenty of time to exercise, the downside was further confirmation that my career had hit the skids. As my once certain climb up the ladder stalled, I turned even more urgently to my training and to the idea of running a marathon. It felt so much more dependable. I couldn't control whether or not I got on the news. There were executives, producers, and editors who all played a role in that call, not to mention the news value of whomever or whatever I was covering. But getting to the top of the hill to slap the stanchion—that was entirely up to me. Drawn to the reliable return offered by my investment, I squeezed in four circuits up and down the mountainside before an early departure on our final day. I'd run all three days of my trip to Japan, and thirteen of the last sixteen days.

Boarding the plane home, I asked the flight attendant for a club soda, reclined my seat in satisfaction, and let myself contemplate the idea that perhaps I'd turned the corner. Finally I was safely over the hump. Nothing was going to destroy my progress now. I still had no idea if I'd ever come close to the old man's marathon times, but I was clearly under way in the march toward meeting the larger goal of reclaiming my health, and my sanity.

Not exactly. I got back from Japan and proceeded not to run for the next twelve days straight. Not one run in the next dozen days, a remarkable act of self-sabotage produced by a crippling apathy that settled over me like a toxic cloud belched from the smokestack of a third-world slaughterhouse.

Before I'd left for Japan, I'd started to get signals from CBS hinting that I wouldn't be part of the general election campaign coverage in the fall. With President Bush no longer a guarantee of airtime and the Clinton campaign over, I would have no defined role at CBS News. So I suppose that it was entirely predictable that after arriving home from Japan, I started to spiral down, pulled low by a gnawing anxiety. What kind of correspondent wasn't assigned to cover the biggest story going?

Each morning of those first twelve days, I'd open my eyes at 5:30 when my alarm began to buzz, certain it would be the day I'd seize control, hop out of bed, and head out for a run. And then, I'd close my eyes, roll over, and go back to sleep.

It wasn't a question of wanting to run. I needed to run. But my hard-won momentum was no match for my depression-based lethargy. In the two weeks that followed my trip to Japan, staying up late with a drink and punching the remote was much easier than rising at dawn to slog my way through four miles. Sleeping in and reading the sports section with a toasted bagel slathered in cream cheese won out over lacing up my running shoes. Every time.

The news division's planning wasn't in high gear for the fall yet, but I knew I wasn't going to be assigned to either convention, the traditional events where the network showcased its coverage team for the general election. No trip to the convention meant no role for the fall.

No one called to tell me I wasn't going to be in the mix. It didn't work like that. Instead, someone from the department who handled logistics for big stories called Chloe to tell her there must have been some mistake, because while she'd been assigned a hotel room in St. Paul, where the Republicans were holding their convention starting Labor Day, I hadn't.

There was no mistake. A historic campaign was unfolding, and I wasn't going to have any piece of the action. My contract was up in half a year and I couldn't have been more useless, which among other issues wasn't exactly my best bargaining position. I'd always known how brutal the TV news business could be. I'd collected plenty of stories of talented reporters whose careers suddenly hit brick walls. Up-and-comers who'd morphed into down-and-outers in a flash.

But I'd never treated those stories as cautionary tales, as warnings of what could happen to me. I'd figured careers didn't just fall apart overnight. There must've been a legitimate reason for each horror story I'd heard about a correspondent's having his salary cut or, worse yet, not getting his contract renewed at all. In my mind, I was just too talented and hardworking for anything like that to ever happen to me.

I'd lived by a few simple professional principles: Never say no. Don't complain. Outwork everyone. Do difficult things well. The way I understood it, if I took care of business along these lines I'd make a lot more money when my contract was renewed. This was a blatant violation of the rules. I was stunned. My dad would've been even more surprised to learn the rules no longer held. After all, they were his rules.

Suddenly I had to absorb a significant change in status with no warning. Each morning it hit me in the gut, leaving me heavy and sad, riddled with embarrassment and self-doubt. And if I stayed in bed long enough, those emotions would be overtaken by an even more powerful one: panic. Running would've been a wonderfully healthy way to deal with the trauma, but I was simply too drained.

If I'd been counting on my July breakdown to magically abate when I flipped the calendar to August, I was sadly mistaken. My malaise thickening, I ran just four times the entire month of August. When getting a morning cup of coffee exceeds your goals for a day's achievement, running five miles is simply not going to happen.

After twelve successful years at CBS, I had a new challenge— wrestling with irrelevance. For any political reporter, there was nothing lower than walking the streets of Washington when the conventions were under way somewhere else. The city seemed vacant, as if its energy had been temporarily transferred to Denver and St. Paul. I felt as if I'd been left behind with instructions to water the plants and bring in the mail. It was worse than being invisible. I felt as if I'd been held down and branded with the word LOSER across my forehead.

No one knew what to say to me. On my way back from getting a sandwich the day after Labor Day I bumped into Fred Jones, a cheerful former White House spokesman, in front of the CBS news bureau. He fixed me with a look of utter confusion, asking, "Aren't you

supposed to be somewhere else?" I mumbled that I hadn't been assigned to cover either convention. He quickly broke eye contact, wanting to spare me embarrassment but not knowing exactly how to react.
Finally he said, "Well, why don't we get lunch one day this week,"
before hurrying off, hoping whatever I had wasn't contagious.

Franco, my kindhearted Italian barber, was similarly perplexed
when I showed up for a haircut. He lowered his voice and asked, "Is
everything all right?" But in Washington, even the barber knew the
game. When I told him I wasn't covering either convention, he didn't
miss a beat. "You could use a little rest after the year you've had." I
could have kissed him for his courtesy.

But there was no hiding. Even the guy who sold fruit from a
street-side table two blocks from the bureau was perplexed. A short,
plump black man with sagging cheeks and a booming voice, he looked
confused as I approached in search of a banana. He said, much more
directly than Franco would have ever dreamed of, "What the hell you
doing here?"

Without a good answer, I had to confront the fact that after losing most of July and all of August, I was now in just about the same
pitiful condition as when I'd stood on that platform in Houston in
February six months ago. I had every incentive to keep training—I'd
convinced myself that nothing less than my long-term happiness depended on it—and yet here I was, half a year later, in the same place
I'd been when I started. Maybe even worse.

I needed a jump start. If I didn't figure out how to regain my
momentum soon, I'd have no chance of finishing a marathon. On
the morning of September 1, I woke up and headed back out to my
neighborhood streets, bringing a healthy helping of now or never
along with me. But given my inconsistent record during the past six
months, the smart money was on "never."

The first week of September was uneventful. I ran my bread-and-
butter 3.7-mile loop four of the first seven days, adding some push-
ups and sit-ups when I got home. I went four for seven during the
second week, including three loops of my 5.1-mile circuit. Twice
during the first two weeks of September, I woke up at 5:00 feeling

sluggish and vaguely depressed. Both times I managed to struggle out of bed, throw on shorts, shirt, socks, and shoes, and get my ass out on the street. Each time I felt my head clear and spirits lift—creating a strong incentive that I hoped would lure me out there when I was tempted not to go.

The third week of September was even better: getting out six of seven days, including a 6.2-miler that I ran and walked—as long a loop as I'd tackled since February. The air was now a touch more crisp in the early morning. I had to slip on a nylon shell and sweatpants. The sunlight was sharp and brilliant. I'd run fourteen of the first twenty-one days in September. I wasn't ready to cue the trumpets just yet—not given my history of inconsistency—but I felt strong, understanding more deeply than ever before the proud look on my father's face when he came in sweat-drenched from a morning ten-mile run at the beach, in his maroon Bill Rodgers shorts that seemed a little tight even by the standards of the late 1970s, bellowing "You should only look this good when you're my age."

I had to head off to Florida for a couple of all-day shoots the last week of September. Between the travel and the shooting, I ran only once. I got home on Friday, determined not to slip, and ran a quick four miles. I got out five of seven days during each of the first two weeks of October.

But it was a losing battle. The link between running and my well-being was clearer than ever before in my life. And it still wasn't enough. Whatever momentum I was able to create was still no match for the mounting evidence of my cratering career.

The country was riveted by the building sense of history about to be made. As Obama steadily pulled away from McCain in the national polls, I was watching from the sidelines with no role in the coverage. Twenty years spent preparing to cover a story like this one, and the closest I could get was watching the *CBS Evening News* each night at 6:30, just like the rest of our viewers. In a repeat of the cycle that had crippled me after the Japan trip in July, three weeks before Election Day I surrendered to the darkness and stopped running.

On Sunday morning, November 2, 2008, two days before the

election, I dropped off the kids at Hebrew school, came home, slid a couple of bagels in the toaster, and settled into the couch with the sports sections from *The New York Times* and *The Washington Post*. I stretched out, turned on the TV, and nearly threw up.

Clicking along the cable menu, the listing on ABC stopped me cold: the 2008 New York Marathon. I was now officially one year away. One year away from running a marathon and I couldn't sustain a training regimen for more than a couple of weeks before I yielded to something—travel, apathy, frustration, depression—and stopped. I watched for a couple of minutes as a pack of elite male runners ran effortlessly up First Avenue in Manhattan before a crushing sadness started to settle on me. I turned the TV off.

The next morning, I woke up hoping a run might be just the thing to nip my growing despondency on the day before the election. I'd never find out.

Three-quarters of a mile in, I felt my left calf start to lock up. This wasn't any garden-variety tightness. The muscle completely seized up. I stopped running and started walking. Then I stopped walking and started limping. Nothing helped. Every step triggered a jolt of searing pain.

Each of the next three days, I tried to run. Each time my left calf sent me the same message: forget it. I missed the next thirty-six days in a row. I was back to climbing stairs like my grandfather. I was—in a word—lame.

I picked up my freshly flung mortarboard from the grass and started to make my way off my high school's football field, stopping for handshakes and hugs with classmates along the way. Crossing the running track that ringed the football field, I saw my dad standing next to the long semicircular Quonset hut where the pole-vault and high-jump pits were stored. Decked out in a tan windowpane sports coat, open-collar dress shirt, olive slacks, and loafers, he was waiting for me. He seemed bewildered, with hunched shoulders that signaled an unmistakable anxiety entirely at odds with the joy of a high school graduation ceremony.

He walked toward me, spreading his arms wide as he got closer. We slammed together in a clench. It was a Bob Axelrod special—tight, deep, and full—designed to convey significance. I could feel him cinching me closer, his right arm up over my left shoulder and his left around my ribs. Mirroring his position, I hugged him back, my right arm slung over his left shoulder and my left arm wrapped around his ribs, though I was unable to generate a squeeze as tight as his. The moment came to relax the embrace, that point in any hug when both people sense it's time to let go. I loosened my grip. He was oblivious, continuing to clutch me.

I couldn't remember the last time I'd been wrapped in one of his bear hugs. When I was a little boy he would grab me on the beach and pull me in close, snaking his palm around to the back of my head, then pressing my face to his chest. Cradled in tight, I could smell sea salt, suntan oil, and musky sweat. Even when I was eleven and twelve, he'd still put down his Michener every now and again to come tenderly throw an arm around my back, a way to maintain contact with me and, perhaps more important, with himself. I couldn't nestle in close enough to the scent I craved. It wasn't the smell of vacations, or even of summer. It was deeper: the scent of love and protection.

At first, neither of us said anything during our postgraduation clench. Then my father started to whisper in my ear. "Congratulations, Jimmy. You did it. I'm just so proud of—" His voice broke and he started to shake. A moment later, he reared his head back, then buried his face in my neck. I could feel his tears on my skin, warm and wet, as they started to trickle down to my collar.

I grew vaguely aware of people watching us. At first, I was proud of my father's emotion, apparently overcome by his love for his son. But the longer it went on, the more uncomfortable it started to feel; the moment morphed from moving to awkward. I squeezed him tight once more, then fully loosened my grip. At last he took the cue and broke the hug. We stepped back from each other. I looked at his face. He was in the grip of some deep emotion, the lines on his forehead reflecting anguish and strain. These weren't tears of celebration. They were tears of grief.

The commencement exercise had just made it formal. My childhood was over. My father knew he'd missed so much of it.

Standing next to that Quonset hut at the end of June 1981, I was just about eighteen and a half years old. My father would die almost exactly eighteen and a half years later. We didn't know it then, but locked in that powerful embrace, my father and I were halfway through our relationship, almost to the day, if not the hour.

But whatever profound conclusion my father reached watching my graduation, it didn't prompt some dramatic flick-of-the-switch change. He still seemed deeply distracted, unable to broker any lasting peace for himself. I headed off to the same college he had graduated from twenty-three years earlier and many calls home that ended with his promise: "We gotta get a beer when you're back after finals, I really want to hear about school." Each January, I'd drive myself back to Cornell after winter break feeling as bleak and gray as the Ithaca landscape, having never managed to get that beer.

At the end of my junior year in college, ten months after a four-week family vacation in England, where my parents seemed genuinely compatible, if not happy, my mom called and volunteered to come pick me up. It was odd, as neither one of them had ever been the type of parents to drive me back and forth from college. I wasn't sure what was up, but I could sense she wasn't asking if I wanted her to come, as much as telling me she needed to.

She arrived in the late afternoon, the day after my last exam. We went out for dinner at the Greek restaurant up the block. She loved nothing more than sharing a meal with one of her kids and having a chance to catch up. I loved it too, expecting to fall into our familiar, gossipy conversational agenda: what her friends were up to, what my friends were up to, how Lisa was doing in law school, what Teddy had planned for the summer, how well Peter had done in his last year of middle school. Instead, she was surprisingly sullen.

"Okay, Jimmy, let's get out of here," she said, as I finished shoveling the last of the souvlaki into my mouth. We walked silently back to my apartment building, a nondescript seven-story cinder-block rectangle that, in a stroke of great fortune, had been built over my favorite bar. I motioned to my ratty couch. She looked pained and weary as she sat down, lowering her eyes. "Mom, what's the matter?" I asked gently.

"I have something to tell you, Jimmy." She choked a little, overtaken by her own disbelief. "Your father is leaving."

It took me several moments to absorb exactly what she was saying, which was so far from the realm of possible answers that I had expected. A spirited, black-haired beauty, my mom had never shrunk from battle with Dad, no matter how loud or fierce. But here, sitting in my apartment with her eyes welling, she seemed stunned and embarrassed, if not a little frightened.

"He wants to move out," she continued. She stiffened, trying hard to steady herself. "He's got a new therapist," she continued. Her voice strengthened and took on a hint of ridicule. "After one session, the guy told him he should leave, that we'd never get it all worked out."

I absorbed what she was telling me, focusing on not reacting to it. My mind was racing with enough follow-ups to last us the night, but I sat on all of them. She'd explained enough. I wanted to avoid her humiliation, not examine it. We sat silently for a few moments.

"When's he going to split?" I finally asked, in the gentlest voice I could summon.

"Next week," she said. "I wanted you to know now, so you'd be there for your brothers."

"Wow, Mom," I said softly. "Holy shit."

After a few minutes more of silence, I stood up, motioning for her to get up as well. I wrapped her in a big hug. "We should probably get some sleep. We've got to get going on the early side tomorrow." It was the best I could do: revert to the normal in the face of the absurd.

She kissed me good night without saying a word, cupping my left cheek with her right hand, then patting it gently. Her face started to break, and she folded her arms in front of her as she shrunk back into my hug. "I can't believe it," she said softly. "We're not going to be buried next to each other."

She cried silently for half a minute in my hug, then collected herself and headed off to my room, which I'd given her for the night. I heard her rustle around for a few minutes, and then it was quiet. I stretched out on the couch and stared up toward the ceiling. I couldn't see a thing in the darkness.

In a masterstroke of parental vision, my dad had picked the day Peter would graduate middle school to drop the bomb on the rest of the family. As I watched my youngest brother, at the outset of his adolescence, going through his ceremony blissfully unaware of what was coming, I felt my left eyelid twitch. A series of spasms surged through the far part of the upper lid, each lasting two or three seconds. I rubbed the lid slowly with my left index finger, pushing the skin against the part of my eye socket closest to the ear, hoping to smooth out whatever nerve was misfiring. A few minutes later, it twitched again.

When we got home, my dad called us all into the living room. He didn't turn on any lights, not even a single table lamp. In fact, he drew the shades. In the dull shadows, he announced he was no longer happy being married to my mother. Teddy didn't let him get in another sentence, jumping up immediately, grabbing our sheepdog, Dashki, by the collar, and storming off. I heard our poorly functioning back screen door slam. A few seconds later, Teddy gunned the station wagon in reverse out of the driveway, screeched to a halt in the street, and then floored it down Lincoln Avenue.

My mother and father sat there for a few minutes with their heads hanging. Peter's face was creased with a naïve look of confusion that even my father couldn't miss. "Peter, I love you. This has nothing to do with you," he said.

"But you are leaving, Dad?" Peter asked, trying to understand what he was being told. "You aren't going to live with us anymore?" My father tried to meet Peter's eyes with a meaningful smile reflecting unconditional love. I got the feeling that my father had run through the lines with his shrink. "Peter, I think this will make me a better father. I need to be happy to be the best father I can be."

I'd heard enough. I got up and kissed my mother. "Come on, Peter," I said, "let's go for a ride." I had to get to the beach to start my summer job at a local lobster joint. Once I knew what my dad had planned, I'd told my mom I would take Peter with me after it was over. I looked at my father. "Congratulations, nice work," I said, mustering as much sarcasm as I could, and led Peter out of the darkened living room.

We took the back roads in the forest-green Volkswagen Scirocco I'd bought with money I'd saved from my summer job at the restaurant. Peter was silent for long stretches, staring straight ahead. Half-way there, I popped in a Sam Cooke cassette. We had a routine where we'd bellow the call and response at the end of each verse of "Bring It on Home to Me." I handled the Sam Cooke part, the first "yeah," which Peter would answer just as Lou Rawls had, batting a slightly lower "yeah" back to me, and then we'd repeat the exchange. We usually broke up laughing before we got through all three back-and-forths.

Peter wasn't even listening. Sam Cooke got only midway through the first verse—"About leaving, leaving me behind"—before my little brother lowered the volume.

"I thought they loved each other."

He was entirely unaware that this was our parents' second split. That made sense, since he wasn't even four years old the first time my father left, capping off an affair with a client. I was eleven then.

My father was gone all of a couple of days that first time, slipping back home while we were out running errands. I heard my mom hiss, "What the hell is he doing here?" I popped my head up from the backseat of the station wagon. There it was, his bright-green two-seat Porsche in the driveway.

We walked in to find him sitting sheepishly at our round kitchen table. She repeated the question to him, in a sharper, louder voice. "What the hell are you doing here?" I made a beeline for the stairs, not wanting to be anywhere near the kitchen for the answer. I sweated it out in my room, worried that somehow I might do something to chase him away.

Ten years later, going through it all again, I looked at my mysti-fied younger brother in the passenger seat of my car. He was thir-teen, sucker-punched by the trouble in our parents' marriage. I thought for a moment about telling him what had happened when he'd been a toddler. My left eye started to twitch. I turned up Sam Cooke instead.

I spent a lot of time rubbing my left eye that summer. My dad kept inviting me to see his new apartment, spectacularly unaware of how proud he was when describing it. He didn't have the sense to temper his undisguised glee at making what sounded like a clean get-away. The thought that this was gutting my mother and turning his four children's lives upside down was beyond his emotional capacity.

Stopped at a red light on the ride over to see his place for the first time, I stared hard out the passenger-side window at a Kentucky Fried Chicken, as he tried to casually let me know that life would be changing.

"You know, with your mom and me living separately, there just isn't going to be as much money in the house." He paused a moment, letting this sink in. "Don't worry, I'm going to support everyone," he said with a loathsome hint of obligation in his voice. "But I'm not living there anymore. That's not where my life is. You need to understand, Jimmy—this is the start of a new way of living. For all of us."

I couldn't tell if that meant no more twice-a-year trips to Bloomingdale's for clothes, canning the cleaning lady, Breyers Ice Cream instead of Häagen-Dazs, or selling the house. I looked at him, wanting to summon rage or disgust. At the very least, some spite. But I remained flat and detached. For the first time in my life, I pitied my father.

This time there was no other woman. Instead, my dad offered up a tortured explanation that seemed to have been written especially for the occasion by his new therapist and delivered to him on a set of five-by-seven note cards. "You see, Jimmy, I've known your mother for so long, we met when we were so young, that I was never able to develop as an individual," he said, as if I didn't know they'd started dating in their early teens. He was converting what had always been a source of romantic pride in our family mythology into the root of all trouble.

"We've been too dependent on each other," he continued. "It's stunted my growth. My only chance to really find out who I am, as an individual, not a husband or a father, is to separate. It's my best shot at happiness."

I clung to my nagging suspicion that he had no earthly idea what he was talking about. At least I hoped that was the case. It was a lot easier to contemplate that my father had fallen under the spell of a new therapist than to acknowledge that he saw his role as husband and father as incompatible with his own happiness.

Toward the end of that summer, having had no contact with him for a few days, I called his office. Even in the midst of this turmoil, it wasn't normal to go more than a day or two without his checking in with one of us.

He wasn't there. I asked for Chris, one of his two long-serving, devoted secretaries. She told me she'd yet to speak to him that day, but she knew he had depositions in Providence, Rhode Island. I asked her to please get in touch with him and have him call me.

"Jimmy, I can't," she said.

"Why not?" I countered, with an edge sharpening in my voice.

"He didn't leave me any contact information," she answered.

My anger, which had been building steadily over the summer, since the night in Ithaca when my mother told me he'd be leaving, started to spill over.

"You've got to be kidding me, Chris. You've got no numbers? No way to get him a message? He's completely out of touch?" I paused for a second, my anger building. "You're telling me if something happened to one of us, there's no one at the office who's got any way to let him know?"

I could sense her discomfort as she treaded ever closer to territory she wanted badly to avoid. "I'm sorry, Jimmy. I don't know what to tell you. I don't have any way to contact him."

My father had crossed a line. I walked into the kitchen, where my mom was making lunch, and unloaded.

"Goddamn it. He's got a thirteen-year-old son. What happens if Peter gets hurt surfing? How the fuck are we supposed to get in touch with him?" My left eyelid started to twitch. I rubbed it a few times with the middle finger of my right hand. I'd grown more comfortable over the course of the summer using my right hand to massage the twitch out of my left eye than using my left hand. I was able to generate more pressure with it.

A few hours later, as late afternoon turned to early evening, I heard his car pulling in under the beach house. Then came the familiar sounds of his steps up the stairs, heavy and foreboding. But no longer did he have a wife and four kids waiting anxiously inside, hoping to hear a few bars of "Zip-A-Dee-Doo-Dah."

Apparently he'd called his office for messages and Chris had filled him in on our phone call. "Hi, Jimmy," he said as he walked in. He nodded at me, trying to communicate a serious sense of purpose. "I drove down to talk with you. I know you're upset." He was speaking deliberately, in the lowest register he could maintain, as if he could defuse the situation simply with bass tones.

I wanted desperately to match the calm in his voice, but all that came out was an agitated growl. "Jesus Christ, just where the hell were you today? What if one of us needed you? What if there had been a fucking emergency here?"

Bob Axelrod didn't like being held accountable, certainly not by his son. My father tossed the olive branch he'd brought with him right off the beach-house deck.

"Don't be so dramatic," he countered, staying calm but adding an insulting edge. It was a tone I'd heard before, a technique he brought home from the courtroom. He wanted to regain control over the situation by casting me as an annoying, hysterical pain in the ass.

His attempt to dismiss me lit a fuse. "Dramatic? Dramatic! Don't fucking tell me I'm being dramatic. I don't want to hear that shit."

As I moved toward him he registered what was rapidly unfolding. I got nose to nose with him, unafraid and unconcerned. But as he braced for a confrontation, I detected what looked like the slightest trace of a flinch.

"Whatever shit you're working out for yourself or whatever's going on with you and Mom, you've got four children," I said, my voice hardening. "And if something happens to any one of us, we need to know how to get in touch with you. You can't suddenly decide not to be our father."

He stiffened, then backed down. All the aggressive energy drained from him. He broke eye contact, mumbled "All right, all right," and walked away sad-shouldered, heading upstairs to the private deck off the onetime love nest he and my mother had designed when they'd renovated the beach house a few years earlier.

I was late for work. I changed and headed off to my shift waiting tables. When I got back at midnight, he was gone.

At the end of August, I returned to Cornell for my senior year. When I spoke to Peter a few weeks later, he reported that my father had been dropping by the house a couple of times a week, taking my mom out to dinner. Neither of them had said a word to him about it.

By the end of September, my dad had given up his apartment and moved back into our house. I found out when I called home one Saturday morning and heard my father's surprisingly chipper voice say hello.

"You're back?" I asked.

"I'm back," he answered. Just as with the first time he'd left and returned, the explanation never got any deeper than that. Almost immediately, we were one big happy family again, everyone in on the plot to bury the body quickly and deeply.

I was as complicit as anyone. My dad and I never mentioned the confrontation again. I told myself it was pointless, that it had been more a vent for anger than a search for understanding anyway. The truth was, our face-off had given me a case of vertigo, disturbing my natural order of things. I didn't want to be nose to nose with my father. I wanted to be tucked under his arm.

There was no lingering, awkward hug following my college graduation the next June, but I could tell he was trying. Whatever vision had been restored by his wandering in the wilderness of therapy and separation, he intended to apply it. With me, he was short on time. I was headed off to New Orleans and a job teaching seventh-grade history.

At the end of August, as I backed my Scirocco out from under the beach house, the hatchback stuffed with clothes, books, stereo equipment, and golf clubs, my dad extended his right arm toward me, palm outstretched in the universal command for me to stop. I hit the brakes and rolled down the window. He approached. This was it:

my final instructions, a father's words of wisdom imparted to a son setting out to make his way in the world.

"Remember, Jimmy," he said solemnly, "if you break down, I got you Triple-A PLUS." He'd been fixated on the roadside-protection service he'd bought for me since he'd handed me the card for my wallet two days ago.

"I just want to make sure you understand. It's PLUS. This is different from standard Triple-A. PLUS means they've got to come to you anywhere within a hundred-mile radius. If they give you any shit—make sure you tell them it's Triple A-PLUS."

I still craved the centered certainty my dad had when I was eight, a father with a vision for raising his son and the will and the means to implement it. But as I set off for New Orleans, he was sending me out into the world with the best he had to give. Not just Triple-A. Not when there was another layer of protection available. Triple-A PLUS.

My father was in transition. Just because I no longer lived in his house, he was unwilling and unable to let go of doing better by me. When I decided to give TV news a shot after a couple of years of teaching, he had his chance. Something deeply paternal stirred in him. Somehow I'd wandered into his wheelhouse. Maybe he felt that he now had something more to offer me. A son embarking on a demanding, competitive career that blended talent, patronage, and risk was right up his alley. That was one facet of his life he'd gotten unerringly right.

He knew exactly what to do. Twenty years after teaching me to ride my bike, my dad returned to once again hold the back of my seat while I figured out how to maintain my balance.

As I weaseled my way into my first TV job, he couldn't talk to me enough, wanting to chew over every detail of the broken-down ABC station in Utica, New York. He needed to learn the underpinnings of a business he knew nothing about to better guide me down the path I wanted to travel. He loved the chance to pepper me with questions about who did what at the station, wanting to figure out who had the power to push me up the ladder and how I could get them to invest it in me.

He left standing instructions with both Chris and his other secretary, Roberta, to interrupt whatever he was doing when I called. Nothing made me feel more important than Chris's saying "Hang on a sec, Jimmy. He's taking a dep. I'll get him." I'd start to swell at the thought of him leaving a room full of lawyers, witnesses, and clients in mid-deposition to spend a few minutes gaming out whether it was too soon to try to jump from Utica to Albany.

He worked double shifts trying to make up for what he'd missed during my teens, wanting to make sure he was familiar with every part of my life. He was happy to drive five hours across the New York State Thruway for a long weekend in Utica, with a side trip to the Baseball Hall of Fame an hour and a half away. Fourteen years after I'd heard him talk to that other dad at a neighborhood bar mitzvah about flying to Cooperstown, knowing it would never happen, we'd finally made it.

Like the rest of the small cities in upstate New York—Watertown, Oswego, Oneonta, Binghamton, Elmira—Utica was hard-pressed for celebrities, beyond the players who filled out the rosters of their minor-league baseball and hockey teams. Local news personalities filled the vacuum.

We started one weekend visit at a breakfast joint outside Utica. After ordering, I headed off to the bathroom. I returned to find my father sitting there with his head cocked mirthfully, a perfect match for his elated smile. He looked as if he was fresh from the opium den.

"What's up with him?" I asked my mother.

"Well, Jimmy," she said, making "well" into a three-syllable word. "You see those two over there?" She nodded at a couple of pretty young women who looked to be in their early twenties. My father couldn't contain himself, cutting her off. "As soon as you left the table, that one"—he turned his chin down and lifted his eyebrows in the direction of one of the girls—"came over and asked me, 'Is that Jim Axelrod?'"

For the first time since I was eight, when life began to overwhelm him and his search for distractions corroded his connection with me, I felt as if once again I mattered in some sustained way. Staring at my dad, I was looking into a magical mirror, for I saw myself registering completely in his eyes. I'd found my ambition. He'd found his redemption.

He had something to offer me and the motivation to try. Perhaps he was grateful that a thriving, ambitious son had emerged despite his neglect. Perhaps he wanted to make up for his silence and distance during my adolescence, for the unfortunate case of bad timing when my needing him coincided with his most urgent need to escape. Regardless, he was back, determined to be my loudest cheerleader. I wasn't about to argue. Happy to have cracked the code, I wanted to make up for lost time as well.

Working in Syracuse a few months before my wedding in 1993, desperate to find a higher-paying job at a TV station in a bigger city, I climbed several hundred feet to a platform at the top of a rickety ladder set up over a strip-mall parking lot and bungee jumped live on the news. Stina and my mom were horrified that I took such a risk. There hadn't been a single pad to break any fall.

My father told them all to pipe down. My outsize example of literal ladder climbing appealed to his trial-lawyer instincts never to be too worried about being too obvious when making a case. "Joan, Stina—listen to me," he boasted. "That's what you gotta do to get ahead."

When I landed a new job in Raleigh, North Carolina, a few months later, having caught the station's attention with a new audition tape featuring the bungee jump, he was incapable of handling the news with grace. He reminded them frequently with I-told-you-so delight how it had happened—by my taking risks others wouldn't.

The Raleigh station was a huge step up—talented cameramen, top-shelf equipment, a helicopter on the roof, and a satellite signal that could be picked up around the country.

To watch my stories from North Carolina five hundred miles north in New Jersey, my dad installed a small telephone pole and full-size satellite dish in front of his house. This was well before satellite TV had become commonplace and small satellite dishes the size of garbage-can lids were mounted unobtrusively on the edge of a roof. His treasured front lawn, the one he'd once issued death threats to protect when the neighborhood kids played kickball on it, was now dominated by an eyesore that gave the place the feel of a NASA compound. And he couldn't have been happier, proud to explain his front yard's new look to anyone who asked. "My son's on the news."

On a May morning in 1996, I was shaving in the bathroom of our town house in Raleigh. Stina was across the hall, tucked into our bed, nursing seven-month-old Emma, when the phone rang. I picked it up, holding the receiver far away from my ear and face to avoid coating it with shaving cream, but close enough to hear the person speaking to me. It was my agent, Carol.

"You're in," she said in a sparkling voice perfectly matched to the news she was delivering. "CBS wants you. It's Miami. It's $130,000. You start in September." I screamed, feeling shaving cream squish out from under the phone I'd unconsciously pressed closer to my ear to make sure I was hearing her right. She'd just told me that my professional dream had come true, and I'd nearly quadrupled my income in the process. My yell spooked Emma. I could hear her start to wail. I told Carol I'd have to call her back.

I'd already started dialing my dad when Stina poked her head in the bathroom to find out what was going on. As the phone rang I mouthed to her, "CBS . . . CBS . . . we're going to Miami." We locked eyes in a meaningful stare, neither of us mentioning that I'd called my dad before I'd told my wife.

He picked up. I blurted the same phrase to him that Carol said to me. "I'm in. I'm in. CBS. Miami. I'm going to CBS. Dad, the network!"

"Yes, Jimmy. Holy shit. Yes, Jimmy. Yes. Yes. *Yeh-esssssssss!*" His scream was louder than mine, fuller, more primal, like a Native American war whoop. He took a breath, gathered himself, and got down to the task of figuring out exactly what we were talking about here.

"Six figures, Jimmy?" he asked breathlessly, his voice rising in pitch and intensity. "You getting six figures?" When I answered yes, he started screaming into the phone again. "Yes. Yes. Yes. Yes. Six figures, Jimmy! You're making six figures. Six fucking figures! That's my boy. That's *my fucking boy*!"

Calling him eight months later from Peru, on my first big story, he picked up the phone right after the broadcast. "Dan just called you 'our man in Lima.' Did you hear that, Jimmy? You're 'our man in Lima.' You are doing it, son." Thrilling him intoxicated me. Like any drunk, my vision grew dull and blurry. I wanted more. Much more.

The next year, CBS called, dangling a job in Dallas with greater responsibility, more airtime, and the chance to further establish myself. They wanted a quick answer. Stina didn't want to move. Not only had she fallen in love with Miami; she was also six months pregnant.

During a string of phone calls, my dad and I went through the motions of gaming out the pros and cons of taking the Dallas job, but we both knew there was no question I'd take it. Rule number one for him was "never say no." Rule number one for me was following my dad's rules. If CBS wanted me to move to Dallas with a few weeks' notice and a pregnant wife, then I was going to move to Dallas with a few weeks' notice and a pregnant wife. One day we'd tell the story and laugh, looking back from a position several rungs higher up the ladder.

My dad asked Stina about the move, trying valiantly to hear her out as she described her conflict.

"Bob, I just got settled here. I've got a good doctor. I want to have the baby here. It all seems like too much disrup—"

He couldn't help himself. "You'll be fine," he said, cutting her off curtly. He sounded slightly annoyed that perhaps she wasn't quite clear on the concept of the price one paid for success. He was worried that her reticence would cause me to back off on my pursuit, just when I should be pressing the accelerator down flat. He loved her, but he didn't want anything interrupting my career climb.

"Really, Stina," he said, trying again. This time he added in a layer of warmth, aware of how dismissive he'd just sounded. "You'll be fine."

If he saw the postpartum depression she suffered six months later after Will was born, he never said anything. And if he'd been alive the next time she was pregnant and I was headed off to Iraq to embed with the army for the invasion, he would have said the same thing. "Really, Stina. You'll be fine."

But he wasn't. So I said it for him.

My mother, Peter, and I stopped at the thick polished-wood door and hesitated just a beat before pushing it open. It was a few minutes after 10:30 on the morning of January 23, 2000, a Sunday. The bustle of the hospital seemed subdued, creating the sense that even disease and death adhered to a slower Sunday-morning pace. But a phone call an hour earlier from the nurses' desk had revealed that to be an illusion.

My mother was taking a bath when the phone rang. Petey was sleeping in a guest room with no phone. Occupied with getting Emma and Will settled in front of the TV while letting Stina catch up on her sleep, I didn't get to the phone the first time it rang. Five minutes later it rang again. Fifteen seconds after that Peter and I both heard a scream. *"Baaahhhhhhhhhhhhhhhhhhhhhhhhhhh!!!!"* It was my mother's voice, piercing, even though it came from behind two closed doors.

We called Lisa and Teddy to tell them the news, then threw on some clothes and raced to Robert Wood Johnson, the teaching hospital at Rutgers University. My dad had been admitted there just after New Year's when his legs, swollen grotesquely with lymphedema, had given out and he'd fallen down a flight of stairs.

Forty-five minutes later we were standing outside his room. We steeled ourselves, and Peter pushed open the door. I followed him in. We both paused just inside the doorway to wait for my mother, who'd taken still another moment before stepping through. We collected her in the small entryway, each of us putting an arm around her, and took the last few steps together out of the vestibule and into the room. We moved toward the bed. There was my father, draped by a thin white sheet, pulled high then turned down under his chin. Or rather, there was my father's body.

He'd been dead for ninety minutes by the time we arrived, but we approached the bed gingerly, as if not to disturb him. His eyes were closed and under the sheet I could make out his hands resting on his sternum, folded one on top of the other. Unlike the night before, there were no lines attaching him to any monitors, no needles connecting him to suspended bags dripping medicine. The room was peaceful but sad, like a battlefield after one side had surrendered.

Peter and I both drew close to him. First I kissed my dad's forehead, then my brother did. "He's still warm," Peter said softly. We'd arrived quickly enough to feel the last remnants of his life slipping away.

I dropped a CD into the Bose player my father had set up in his room. The notes of Fats Waller's "Ain't Misbehavin' " began to tickle the somber air. I was well aware that the music—mirthful, flirty, and sly—was a bad fit for the mood, but this was the last time I was ever going to see my father. I wanted to hear his favorite song playing. I kissed his forehead again. He seemed colder than he had just minutes before.

Suddenly it hit me. I'd never talk to him again. He'd never field an anxious call about my career again, or dial me out of the blue at my desk to say "Jimmy, you're doing great" when I felt like a dead-end loser in dire need of a pick-me-up.

He'd never again plop down on the couch for an inning of a ball game I was watching. He'd never again buy far too much Chinese food when all his kids were visiting, or beat me to the register when I took my children for ice cream. He'd never again come into the kitchen after a run and ask for a sip of my orange juice, then drain it and slam the glass back down on the table with a mischievous grin.

He'd never hug me again, or kiss me, or put an arm around me on the beach. He'd never calm me down, or pick me up, or reassure me with a trademark gesture—his palms turned up, his shoulder shrugged, his face bemusedly absorbing life's latest kick in the ass— that everything was going to be all right. There'd be no more Triple-A PLUS, or phone calls after stories, or encouragement to push for the next big assignment—"hey, Jimmy, all they can call you is *pisher*." I was out of chances for him to field a question, dispense his spot-on advice, or explain the past.

Never again would I interact with him, only with his influence.

With Lisa and Teddy soon to arrive, Peter and I left, giving my mom a few minutes alone in the room, and headed over to Crabiel's funeral home in Milltown. It was a half-hour drive from the hospital. On the ride there, I could feel the adrenaline drain and a deep wave of fatigue envelop me. It had been an exhausting couple of days.

When he'd called the house late Wednesday night to make sure my mom had arrived home safe from that night's visit, my father was lucid and present. Early Thursday morning the nurse called to report that he'd taken a turn during the night. He was completely unresponsive. I took a train from New York and met my mother, Lisa, and Teddy at the hospital.

It was clear just from looking at him that he was slipping away. He was on his back, eyes closed, his breathing shallow and labored. His eyelids would flutter open at the sound of our voices, but irregularly and for frustratingly short intervals. Even when his eyes opened, he seemed to be looking at us from some other dimension, separated by a hazy, gauzy film that prevented any meaningful connection. His gums were starting to blacken, a sure sign that his body was beginning to die.

By Friday afternoon, he'd been unconscious for more than twenty-four hours. Peter arrived from San Francisco that night, getting to my father's bedside a little after nine. "Hey, Dad," he said tenderly as he sat down. My father's eyes opened. He couldn't lift his arm, but he managed to cock his wrist and roll the fingers of his left hand in a small wave from pinkie to index finger. It was the last interaction he would have with anyone.

Word had spread that my father was failing. On Saturday, old friends started to drift in and out of his room. In the late morning, his law partner, Richard, arrived with a book he'd been meaning to give him, not knowing it was already too late. Mary and Dick Van Riper, friends of my parents since college, drove down from Connecticut, arriving in the early afternoon. They were shaking their heads as they greeted us, baffled at how quickly forty years had passed, from sleeping on the floors of each other's first apartments to one of them now about to die. Then Rabbi Yakov Hilsenrath swept in, bearded and dignified.

The rabbi led a synagogue in Highland Park. It wasn't the one where we worshipped, but Rabbi Hilsenrath had been a client of my father's. My dad always spoke with reverence about him—"this is a holy man"—and we weren't surprised to learn that my father had reached out to him more than once during the last several weeks.

My father's room emptied out when Rabbi Hilsenrath went in; all of us standing vigil understood that whatever he had to say to my unconscious father was privileged communication. Ten minutes later, the rabbi reappeared, walked over to my mother, and took both of her hands into his in a gesture of sympathy. "Your husband—now there was a counselor. What a man," he said, his pitch-perfect tone full of comfort. I watched him walk out, wondering what they'd talked about in the last weeks of my father's life, and knowing I'd never get an answer to the question.

But it was the arrival of my grandmother Trudy, my mother's mother, that jolted me into understanding what was unfolding. I'd never been through this before, the final hours of someone's life. All four of my grandparents were still alive. I had no familiarity with the rhythm of a person slipping away. When Nana Trudy appeared in the hall outside his room, with an expression I'd never seen on her face, nor anyone else's for that matter, I was smacked by the unavoidable reality—my father would soon be dead.

Nana Trudy had known my father for fifty years, and loved him as her own almost since the day her Joanie started dating him in her early teens. Nana never stopped, even during my mom and dad's toughest times.

Nana Trudy was grief-stricken to be sure, but also purposeful and protective, determined to battle the descending darkness. When she saw her grandchildren, she raised her arms and spread them, beckoning us. As her arms came up, her brown wool coat, which she'd unbuttoned but was still wearing, formed a set of wings. I moved under one of them, breaking into tears. "Nana," I sobbed. "I think this is it." She didn't say anything back. She simply hugged me, gently making small circles on my back with her palm.

In the early afternoon my father's brother, Bruce, arrived with my father's parents, Nana Helen and Pop-Pop Aaron, so they could see their elder son one last time. They were both in wheelchairs— Aaron was ninety-one; Helen was eighty-nine.

Aaron had been born in Russia in 1908. His father, William, had moved the family to the United States three years later. They'd settled in Trenton, where William did odd jobs and started a junk business. Helen was born into more comfortable circumstances, the eldest daughter of an established Jewish businessman whose family had immigrated from Eastern Europe a generation earlier.

Helen and Aaron had done it all the right way—he put himself through pharmacy school and then opened a drugstore in Flemington, New Jersey, with his new bride. They worked long hours building their small business, Aaron often falling asleep in the easy chair where he'd sat down for a second to catch his breath after another exhausting day. They sacrificed to make sure their boys had the finest educations, sending them first to the prestigious Lawrenceville School, then to Cornell and Williams, leading to successful careers in law and medicine. As we wheeled them bedside, I was overcome by the cruelty of it all. Their reward for living lives selflessly planting seeds for the generations that would follow was burying their son.

I could bear only a small peek into the room, watching my grandparents lean forward in their wheelchairs, each taking one of my father's hands into theirs. My grandfather raised his voice, as if he could get through to my dad if he just spoke loudly and slowly enough. "Bobby, it's Mother and Dad. We are right here," I heard Pop-Pop Aaron say. He'd slipped back more than half a century, talking to my dad as if he was an eight-year-old boy.

His voice broke. Nana Helen was there to pick up the patter as my grandfather faltered. "We love you, Bob," I heard her call out in a voice that would not waver. "Bobby, we love you, sweetheart." That was it; I stepped out of the room. I couldn't stand the unfairness any longer.

We stayed at the hospital until just before midnight: my mother; my sister and her husband, Michael; Peter; and me. Stina had taken the kids back to my parents' house earlier that night. Teddy wanted to stick around for a few more hours. My father didn't move. Other than his raspy, labored breathing, the only sounds we heard from him all day came just before we left, when a team of orderlies arrived to change his sheets. They asked us to step out of the room so they could move him to make up the bed. They warned us it might be uncomfortable for him, and they didn't want us to see him in pain. But seeing him couldn't have been any worse than hearing him.

We all wished my unconscious father good night, gave him pecks on the forehead, and headed out to the hall. We were moving heavily to the elevator when we heard my father shriek: a high-pitched feral howl that sounded like an animal caught in a trap. *"Owwwwwww!"* I heard once, then again a second later. *"Ayyyyyhhhhhhhh!"* The screams brought us up short, and not just because he was so clearly suffering. He simply sounded so much like himself, which was jarring after having watched him steadily fade away for the past couple of days. Peter and I locked eyes and shook our heads. At the very end, he was still in there. The elevator door opened and we got in. There was nothing else we could do.

When we got to the funeral home, a young woman led us to a desk in a darkened study. We sat across from her in the studied shadows of her office, making a series of selections: a simple pine casket, two limousines, and three local papers for his obituary. Jewish tradition guided families to bury their loved ones as quickly as possible. It was already too late on Sunday to get a funeral together for Monday, so we set it for Tuesday, January 25—my thirty-seventh birthday.

I had been twenty-eight when he was diagnosed with prostate cancer. He'd fought it hard for the next nine years, employing every possible approach. First, he tried conventional methods. The surgery to remove his cancerous prostate was done by Pat Walsh, the nation's top specialist in the field. Initially, Dr. Walsh thought he got all of it. We were ecstatic when he called to tell my father his lymph nodes were clean. My dad was going to be fine. "Let me tell you something about cancer," I said proudly to Stina when we got the news. "Cancer didn't know who it was dealing with when it picked Bob Axelrod."

A second call a few days later revised the prognosis. More lab tests revealed the cancer had not been fully contained in the prostate, as Dr. Walsh first thought. The hope of erasing the threat with a single surgical procedure was lost. Some of the cancerous cells had escaped into his nodes, which meant they'd eventually spread throughout his body. The second call was a death sentence. Only the execution date was unknown.

My father treated it as a call to battle.

With conventional medicine offering him very little in terms of active, aggressive treatment, he turned to the protocols of Nicholas Gonzalez, a controversial doctor who prescribed a regimen of coffee enemas, hair analysis, nutritional supplements, enzymes, and an all-organic diet. Dr. Gonzalez had patients who swore he was a lifesaver, and some of his results in treating pancreatic cancer appeared promising. He also had his share of critics who called him a charlatan, a purveyor of false hope who'd been disciplined by the New York State medical board. Whatever the case, my father, one of New Jersey's top medical malpractice lawyers, desperately needing something and someone to believe in, threw in with a doctor whom many mainstream cancer specialists dismissed.

I rolled my eyes while my father spent thousands of dollars buying supplements and enzymes from Dr. Gonzalez that his insurance didn't cover. More than a few of their friends shared my skepticism. But my mother certainly did not. Each week she'd sit beside him at their kitchen table, packaging up hundreds of pills into small baggies holding his daily doses. She was a fierce sentry, making sure only organic fruits and vegetables found their way into their juicer for the tonics Dr. Gonzalez prescribed. She pushed back hard against any snickering about my father's twice-daily coffee enemas, designed to detoxify his body. In this, his final battle, my mom was right there with him.

History was a powerful adhesive. Since meeting at thirteen, they'd been together in some form or fashion for nearly fifty years. The man who had left her twice in ten years was also the man with whom she'd built her life. This was no time for the complicated process of reckoning. She set aside whatever bitterness she still harbored. She had to. At least for the time being.

If the coffee enemas raised eyebrows and his trips to the Lakota sweat lodges in South Dakota drew a few snickers, my mom never wavered. She preached to my father what she believed in her heart: they had discovered a way to beat this threat, if only he would trust in it. After years as the main source of conflict in my father's life, my mother became his main source of hope. He clung to her. If it wasn't the kind of love she'd always wished to feel from him, it was certainly the kind of need. And at the end of his life, that might've been even more important to her.

On a Friday night nine days before he died, I dropped by the hospital after work. It was a few minutes after eight when I walked into his room. He was propped up in bed, looking as though he'd shrunk since the last time I'd seen him, just a few days earlier. He was staring out the window to his right, his right hand cupping his cheek and jaw. He seemed to be gazing far off into the distance at nothing in particular. I'd walked in on a moment of deep sorrow.

I felt horrible breaking his train of thought. He turned toward me, and I approached his bed. "Hey, Dad," I whispered, kissing him on the forehead. "Can I get you anything?"

"No, Jimmy, I'm fine," he answered. "You did a great job on the Letterman story. That was a hell of a thing that happened to him." A few hours earlier, David Letterman's production company had announced that the comedian had undergone emergency bypass surgery. The news had broken just before six that night and led to one of those beat-the-clock mad dashes to get a piece on the air. I didn't know for sure that we'd made it in time until Dan Rather started to introduce my piece and the stage manager beckoned for me to take my place on the set to deliver the last couple of lines live. They would've never sat me down next to Dan if the story hadn't been ready.

Seeing me on television, sitting next to Dan, always gave my father a thrill, so I wasn't surprised when he wouldn't let it go. "Dan must've been impressed," he continued. I didn't fight him. I loved the chance to slip back into our old dynamic developed in Utica and Syracuse, then polished in Raleigh, Miami, and Dallas: the savvy mentor gaming things out with an ambitious young man on the make.

"It all went well, Dad," I told him. "It got a little hairy at 6:29. Always makes your ass pucker when you don't know if you're going to make it. But all's well . . ." I paused, hanging it out there, hoping he'd pick it up. "That ends well," he volleyed back. We both smiled. This is where the bungee jump and the front-yard satellite dish had led.

"Come on, Dad, what can I get you?" I asked. He tightened his lips into a sad, wry smile and shook his head, breathing in deeply, then pushing one long exhale through his nose.

"Jimmy, you want to head down the hall and see if you could find me a Coke? And if you happened to find some Peanut Chews, it shouldn't be a total loss."

It was one of my dad's classic phrases. In better days, he'd wielded it with his eyes twinkling. Perhaps we'd be out to dinner at the Holiday Snack Bar, our favorite hamburger joint on Long Beach Island, stuffing ourselves silly with cheeseburgers, small mounds of red-pepper relish and pools of homemade sweet-and-sour sauce spooned onto slices of raw Bermuda onion that were perfectly centered on top of the patty. At the moment we kids realized none of us could possibly take another bite, my dad would gesture to the homemade desserts with a challenge: "Well, who wants cake? I mean the night shouldn't be a total loss." But as I listened to him gamely tack it on to this request for candy, devoid of its customary spark, it was the last thing I wanted to hear.

Goldenberg's Peanut Chews, in their red-and-brown wrapper, had been my dad's favorite since he was a kid. But as far as my mother, the enforcer of the detoxification regimen, was concerned, they were verboten contraband. And Coke? That was like drinking antifreeze. For years, he'd dutifully followed every last requirement of Dr. Gonzalez's approach to beating prostate cancer, drinking so much carrot juice his skin took on a slight orange tinge. He continued to visualize the cancer leaving his body as instructed, even when he started to waste away. He never expressed any doubt. At least not to his kids. This was his last, best hope. If doubt was capable of reducing the efficacy of the Gonzalez regimen by the slightest measure, he wasn't about to risk it. Asking me to get him candy and soda was a concession. He was acknowledging that his fight was over.

I found the vending machines at the end of the hall and was back a few minutes later with a couple of cans of Coke and three packs of Peanut Chews. While I poured the Coke into a small white plastic cup I'd grabbed from the nurses' station, I heard him rip open the Peanut Chews.

He had to sneak the Coke and Peanut Chews to avoid disappointing my mother, who still clung faithfully to the idea that my father could rally. A few nights later, Stina and I were back at the hospital. My mom had been there all day and looked as if she needed a break. I asked if we could take her to get something to eat, and the three of us walked a couple of blocks to a small Lebanese restaurant. I tried to gauge where my mother was on the spectrum of acceptance. "Mom, do you think Dad is failing?" I asked gently.

"Jimmy, we can't have any negative energy," she shot back immediately in a steely voice, angry that I'd even raised the idea. "The way we approach this is very important. First things first—let's get him out of the hospital. We need him home."

While I understood my mother's position, I couldn't let this go unchecked. If nothing else, she needed to start considering the possibility that he might not be coming home. "Mom," I said, as gently as I could. "I think Dad's dying."

Her anger gave way to confusion. I'd just slugged her in the jaw, rocking her back on her heels and leaving her glassy-eyed. She managed only to mumble back at me, "Really?" Her defiance drained away, leaving her with just a few drops of diluted disbelief.

"Yes, Mom, I do. Really."

I spoke in a low-pitched, slow-paced voice, hoping she'd hear my compassion. I looked her in the eyes and reached across the table for her hands. "I do, Mom. I'm not sure. I mean, who knows what's going on. But it feels that way. We need to think about that. Get ready for it, maybe." She looked down at her plate, letting go of my hand to push what was left of her dinner away from her.

On the Tuesday after he died, the day we had set for his funeral, I woke up at five to the phone ringing. Overnight, a horrendous ice storm had come whipping down the East Coast, closing schools, highways, and just about everything else. Frank Facchini, the funeral director, was calling. He wanted to know if we were going to postpone. I woke up Petey to figure it out. We looked outside. It was still dark, but glancing up at the streetlights, we could see trouble.

Each light emitted a cone of bright fluorescence that cut through the dark. Peter and I looked at the streetlight closest to the house. We could see thick sheets of snow moving sideways through the light before disappearing. I looked at Petey and asked what he thought.

It had been less than two days since my dad had died. The grief hadn't fully settled in, pushed aside by all the arrangements for the funeral. But now that we'd run through our initial set of distractions and the anguish was starting to gather, the idea of a packed synagogue seemed enormously comforting. A big funeral would validate my father's life, a measure of the man. Over the past forty-eight hours, it somehow seemed easier to bear his death when we'd get reports from his partner, Richard, of the judges who planned to come and the lawyers who'd called to say they wouldn't miss it. There was a cushion in my father's stature. We decided to delay for a day, which provided the additional bonus of not having to bury my dad on my birthday.

That night, my mother made me a birthday dinner, determined to maintain some normalcy in the face of our collective sorrow, or at least try her best. She invited my friends who'd come in for the funeral, old buddies I'd known since fifth and sixth grades. Every few minutes Stina would squeeze my hand, then get up from the table and go into the TV room, returning with one of the kids for me to cuddle. The warmth in the dining room was unmistakable, though it was easy to look past the comforting faces to see the snow still coming down hard outside.

A portrait of my father taken by Teddy a few summers ago worked its way around the table. He'd artfully captured my dad in the middle of his struggle—before it was clear that cancer would win. The tight head shot showed my father with a full beard, his reading glasses halfway down his nose. He looked wise and pacific. His expression suggested that he'd accumulated a deep well of knowledge in his life. It had been painfully acquired, far too much of it far too late, but it was now calming and centering him. The same sadness I'd felt in the hospital room with his body returned for a deeper consideration. For the rest of my life I could look at the wise man in the photo. But whatever last bits of wisdom he had to impart had gone with him. All I'd had with my dad was now all I'd ever have.

The next morning, we walked into the sanctuary of our synagogue, Anshe Emeth. His plain pine coffin was already sitting at the foot of the altar. Every row was filled, just as we'd hoped when we delayed the funeral. I thought I saw a familiar face in the back row, but it couldn't have been who I thought it was. He would have been out of place, belonging, as he did, to another realm of my life. But when I climbed the stairs to the pulpit and took my spot behind the lectern to eulogize my father, sure enough, there sitting unassumingly in the back row was Dan Rather.

Over the years, Dan had always made a special effort to be at the life-cycle events of those who worked with him, weddings and funerals in particular. This was his way. He had a well-developed understanding of the power of his position, that his presence had the ability to enhance a celebration or cushion a tragedy. When he sent a couple of fruit baskets with kind notes of sympathy, word quickly got around the house that they'd come from Dan. No one would've appreciated the gesture more, or been any prouder, than my father.

If his aim was to comfort, he was right on the money. As the funeral ended and our family was walking back up the center aisle of the synagogue to the limousines that would take us to the cemetery, I took Nana Helen's hand to see how she was doing.

"Nana, you need anything?" I asked this eighty-nine-year-old woman who was about to bury her son. She turned, a few feet from the casket, and whispered to me, "Dan's here." Perhaps because it was precisely the observation my dad himself would've made at that moment, I smiled, however slightly.

We made our way outside, through the slush on icy sidewalks, to the limo. We got in and waited for the other cars to line up behind us. My mother sat there awash in grief and disbelief. Peter had his head down. Sitting next to my mom, looking out the window, I saw Dan approach. "Hey, Mom," I said softly, trying to mask any sense of excitement, "I think Dan's coming over here."

I started to push open the door so she could get out and greet him. At the same moment, my mom started to put the window down so she could reach through to shake his hand. She stuck her hand through the window, just as the door started to swing open. Dan didn't know whether to grab her hand or step back to let the door clear. He started to stick his hand through the lowered window, then thought better of it when he noticed she'd pulled hers away and was now starting to step out of the car. Seeing his partially extended arm, however, caused my mom to freeze in the backseat and once again stick her outstretched arm through the window, nearly losing her balance as she did.

Just outside the synagogue after my father's funeral, the casket loaded in the hearse and ready for burial, my mother and Dan Rather were caught in a slapstick routine that would've made Mack Sennett proud.

Finally, she cut off the awkward back-and-forth by getting out of the car. They both chuckled at the clumsiness before he clasped her hands in his and communicated his sympathies. He gave me a big hug and headed off to his own car for the ride to New York.

We all piled back into the limo. As the procession started to the cemetery, a slow drive made even slower by the snow and ice the plows had been unable to keep up with, we began to chat about the service, looking to banish the dread for at least a few minutes before meeting back up with it graveside.

As we paused at a red light, waiting to turn right onto Commercial Avenue in New Brunswick and the last stretch of the trip to the cemetery, my sister said, "How about Dan Rather at Dad's funeral. He would have loved that." I nodded in agreement, the same slight smile I'd given Nana Helen.

Peter cut us off sternly. "I don't really care who was there." His father was dead. He wanted only to mourn. He didn't need, or want, any distractions from the solemnity. Certainly nothing as trivial as which big shot had shown up.

In the back of the limo I registered a brief sense of shame. Something about Petey's tone jarred me. His voice was full of grief, deep and authentic. His sense of loss was unclouded by other considerations, and he was self-aware to the point of refusing distractions. The compass guiding my younger brother afforded him far greater direction than my own.

E verything seemed to be in perfect working order as I walked the five blocks from our house in Montclair to the bus stop in Watchung Plaza, where I caught the DeCamp 66R to the city. The sky was deep blue and cloudless, filled with brilliant sunshine, one of those high-pressure, low-humidity September days when the late-summer air takes on a crisp freshness. "One-for-all weather," I called it, the kind of day I'd choose for all 365 if I had to pick just one. Heading for the bus, I was half an hour later than usual, having lingered with Stina over an extra cup of coffee to count our blessings on the morning of our eighth wedding anniversary.

Our daughter, Emma, a month and a half from turning six, was off to a smooth start in kindergarten, still consumed by Disney princesses, having recently moved on to Pocahontas after two years spent wearing out two different Snow White dresses Stina had sewn for her. At three and a half, Will was a cheery, eager soul about to start his second year of preschool. Emma had been shy and diffident at that age, so we'd been thrilled to see Will purposefully stride into the basement of the church where his preschool met. He had an easy charm that drew his teachers to him and never left him short of playmates.

After pinballing from North Carolina, to Miami, to Dallas, to New Jersey during the past three years, we were all starting to feel settled in Montclair. I could feel roots taking hold, steadying each of us.

I walked toward the rear of the bus, sliding into an empty row, third from the back on the driver's side. I didn't have my computer, having left it at the office as I often did, and my phone wasn't fully charged, but I figured I'd be in soon enough to get myself squared away with batteries and power cords. If news broke and the desk wanted to send me somewhere right after I got to the office, I'd be ready to go in no time. Besides, what could happen in the next forty-five minutes before I got to my desk?

Usually I read the paper on the bus, but the pairing of my anniversary and the perfect weather left me contemplative. I stared out the window, taking stock. My reverie settled on Stina. Maybe it was true—you didn't find out who you'd married until you had kids with them. But the past twenty months had provided a crucial corollary: what you didn't discover about your mate through raising children together, you learned when a parent died.

My mind was wrapped around Nana Helen's new chair, a white leather La-Z-Boy recliner Stina had recently picked out after my grandmother complained that her old one was uncomfortable. Nana had a son, two daughters-in-law, and six grandchildren, but it was Stina who made sure she got what she needed. I was far away, lost in thought about Stina's trip to the showroom to pick out the chair and arrange for its expedited delivery, exactly the kind of thing my father would've taken care of when he was alive—when the bus jolted to a dead stop. We were a mile and a half from the Lincoln Tunnel.

There was nothing out of the ordinary about that. At least not at first. The traffic always built to a maddening crawl in the last few miles before the entrance to the tunnel, where two major highways, each choked with cars, merged. It wasn't uncommon for the bus to stop dead for a few minutes, before starting to creep toward Manhattan again. But after a few more minutes passed, and we hadn't moved an inch, it started to feel as if we were going to be stuck there awhile. Some passengers began to look around the bus at one another, sharing expressions of impatience. Others craned their necks, trying to get some sort of clue as to why we were at a standstill and how late we might be for work.

I felt my pager vibrate on my belt. The message was from Marty Gill, an old-school newsman who worked on the CBS News national desk dispatching crews and correspondents to story locations. "Plane hit World Trade Center. Call desk." September 11 was no longer just my wedding anniversary.

I looked to the southeast, across the aisle, past the opposite row of seats, and out the window toward the Twin Towers, but I couldn't see a thing. What the high walls bordering the highway didn't block from my view, the buildings of Weehawken did. I tried calling Marty but couldn't get through. The DeCamp bus company had an iron-clad rule against using cell phones on the bus, one zealously enforced by passengers tired of listening to self-important seatmates talk loudly about their clients, deadlines, and deals. But as the bus started to buzz with more information filtering in about a plane hitting the World Trade Center, passengers broke the no-phone rule in a unity of curiosity and concern.

Marty paged me again. "Maybe Cessna. Go to WTC if poss." It wasn't. We hadn't budged in fifteen minutes. Our bus driver made an announcement over the loudspeaker.

"Ladies and gentlemen, I just got word from dispatch. The Lincoln Tunnel is closed." He went on, sounding slightly confused. "They're telling us to turn around and head back to Montclair. We're going to drop you off where we picked you up."

Another page from Marty: "Commercial flight. Disaster."

I started to panic. I wasn't concerned about my safety. Nothing that trivial. I was worried about my career.

By now, both planes had hit the towers and I was in a communications blackout. I couldn't get a call in to the news desk, but from the chatter on the bus I'd picked up enough to understand the magnitude of what was happening. A national catastrophe was developing several miles from where I was sitting locked down in traffic. The biggest story of my life, and I couldn't get there.

The bus finally limped to an exit ramp, turned around, and headed back to Montclair. Off the bus, I reversed my stroll from just ninety minutes earlier, when I'd been taking stock of all that was right in the world. My wife, who'd been dreamily recounting our many blessings when I left, was now glued to the TV in the kitchen watching the second tower come down. We debated the idea of retrieving Emma from kindergarten before deciding that would be a bit dramatic.

"She's fine. I'm sure she's fine. Leave her at school," I shouted as I ran up the stairs to our bedroom. I changed out of my suit and dress shoes into khakis and sneakers, stuffed a few days' worth of clothes into a gym bag, grabbed some batteries and my phone charger from our study, and kept moving through the kitchen toward the back door. I paused only to give my bewildered-looking wife a quick kiss goodbye. "I'll call you when I know what's up," I yelled back over my shoulder as I beelined to my Honda Accord in the driveway. "Happy anniversary," I added with an incredulous smile as I closed the door. I started to back out, then stopped. I had absolutely no idea where I was going.

I wanted to get to CBS headquarters in midtown Manhattan, but I clearly wasn't going to be able to take my normal route into the city. The national desk might've been some help with suggestions, but I still couldn't get through on my phone. I headed over to the Garden State Parkway and started driving north. Since all the bridges and tunnels into Manhattan were closed, I figured I'd go up to Westchester County, cross the Hudson well north of the city, then loop back down into the Bronx.

I turned on the radio, which was spitting out details of the once-in-a-generation story I was having no part of reporting. My anxiety starting to spike, and still unable to get through to the desk, I began calling various CBS bureaus around the country hoping they might be able to get through to New York.

In Dallas, a correspondent named Maureen Maher picked up the phone. "Mo" to her friends, she covered the Midwest, though she'd lived in New York for a while and knew the city well. She'd had trouble getting through to the desk as well, but could tell from what she'd been watching on TV that coming in through the Bronx was indeed my best bet. She also knew me well enough to give me the full rundown on the CBS coverage—which CBS reporters were downtown and who was getting on the air.

I barked at her in the high-pitched agitation of a man whose years of career planning were disintegrating in the matter of a single morning as he drove like a crazy man on the Cross Westchester Expressway looking for an open road south to the Bronx. "Can you try the Broadcast Center again, Mo. Please, Mo? Once more. You gotta find out where I should go. I gotta know where to go. *Tell me where to go, Mo!*"

She said she'd try, promising to call me back in a minute. She did. "Jim, listen—it's chaos in there. Total chaos. All I can tell you is to get downtown if you can and look for our trucks."

"Okay, got it. Thank you, Mo. Thank you so much." I ended the call, put my phone down, punched the steering wheel, and screamed. This was definitely it—the big one—and I was driving in the opposite direction, away from the story. Never mind the historic tragedy, the nation under attack, the hundreds, maybe thousands dead, the rumors of other targets, my sole focus was on getting to work.

Traffic was slow. The shutdown of the main bridges and tunnels into the city clogged every major highway in the metropolitan area with drivers looking for alternate routes. It took me a couple of hours to get over the Tappan Zee Bridge and get on the Hutchinson River Parkway, which started to take me south through Westchester County. I crawled along the Hutch for a couple more hours, until I got to the Bruckner Expressway. I talked my way through a couple of checkpoints on the Bruckner with my New York City press pass and made my way over to the Grand Concourse in the Bronx. After another half hour, I found a parking spot on the street, a couple of blocks from a small bridge that was open to foot traffic over the Harlem River.

I threw my bag over my shoulder and walked into Manhattan, hailing the first gypsy cab I saw and heading to the CBS Broadcast

Center at West Fifty-seventh Street and Tenth Avenue. I walked into a newsroom that had worked through the initial pandemonium that accompanies a huge breaking story and was now operating with urgency and efficiency. I looked at my watch. It was a few minutes after four o'clock. The unsettling but inescapable fact was that in covering the biggest story in a generation, CBS wasn't missing a beat without me.

Several teams were already in place at Ground Zero. It wasn't as if I could just assign myself downtown. No matter what kind of story I found, I'd still need a cameraman to shoot it, and they'd already all been paired up with reporters. I went to see Bill Felling, the national editor, to find out what I could do. He gruffly told me I'd be working on a story about all the cancellations—professional golf tournaments, the Emmy Awards, a Madonna concert. CBS News was going to be on the air round the clock covering every aspect of the biggest story in recent memory. There were a gazillion different angles that needed to be checked out, many going directly to the root of our country's security. But in the first come, first served world of breaking news, I was last to the table. My slice of this once-in-a-lifetime story was going to be school closings.

Determined to get a bigger, more relevant piece of the action the next day, I got a cameraman assigned to me and headed downtown first thing in the morning to shoot a piece about the hundreds of firefighters from other cities spilling into New York. I was back at the Broadcast Center by early afternoon to get the story on the air as quickly as possible. I'd met some compelling characters, got a couple of good sound bites, and wrote a nice, tight script—but I knew it was all small change compared to the central story line developing at Ground Zero.

I felt hollow and humiliated, and I needed to take a leak. I walked into the men's room across from Studio 47, where Dan Rather broadcast the *CBS Evening News*. The bathroom was entirely unimpressive. The small, yellowed squares of institutional wall tile lent an air of a junior high school circa 1957, which was probably the last time it had been remodeled. There were three urinals to the right of the door and two stalls beyond them. On the opposite wall were three sinks and a couple of paper-towel dispensers.

I was lost in self-pity as I pushed open the door, knowing this story was going to make some careers, solidify others, and apparently do neither for mine. There was someone at the urinal farthest on the right. I could see only his back as I walked in and passed by him, but that was enough to immediately snap me out of my self-absorbed calculations.

CBS was on the air without commercials. Dan Rather had run across the hall for a quick bathroom break while a correspondent in the field was encouraged to yammer on for a little longer than usual.

"Oh hello, Jim," he said, as I slid in front of the urinal next to him. "How's it going out there?" I knew he didn't want to have a long conversation.

"Honestly, Dan. Not so well," I replied. I needed to be quick and surgical. "I missed it," I said with a hint of a sad smile. "I couldn't get downtown." I wanted to strike the right tone, something he might relate to from his own days climbing the ladder: an ambitious reporter aware of the grand-scale death and destruction in lower Manhattan but not distracted by it. I wanted him to know I was still focused on the story.

He looked straight ahead at the yellowed tiles in front of him. But he nodded enough to indicate he understood. I figured I'd better wrap it up. "You know better than I do—stories like this don't come along very often. I can't seem to get any part of it."

"You never know what's coming next," he said. "Keep working hard." He walked briskly out of the men's room and back to the anchor desk for another long stretch in the chair, leaving a cryptic, hopeful air to compete with the strong smell of urinal soap.

I hadn't spoken with Stina since I'd burst back into our kitchen the previous day, leaving her a couple of voice-mail messages to let her know I planned to stay in the city for the next few days. When we were finally able to talk that night, she listened to me on the edge of despondency. She was home in our TV room watching reports from

Ground Zero, where thousands were feared dead, and I was on the phone describing a glimmer of optimism derived from pissing next to Dan Rather.

Walking the streets in Jersey City two days later, following leads that FBI agents were investigating reports of terror cells rooted there, my phone rang. It was Marcy McGinnis, the CBS executive in charge of coverage for our daily broadcasts. "Hey," she said, cutting right to the chase, "can you go to London?"

Pacing down a block of dollar stores and bodegas, I could feel a faint rekindling of hope. My mind was racing, trying to figure out if Marcy was actually asking the money question.

"Would that be my final destination?" I responded. I didn't want to go to the London bureau and fill in for the regular London-based correspondents who would then follow the story to Afghanistan, Pakistan, and the Middle East.

"I'm not sure yet," she said. She was being cautious, not wanting to make any commitments but also gauging which correspondents were willing to go somewhere dangerous and demanding. "I am going to need people to go to Afghanistan. They'd leave from London. Would you be up for go—"

"Absolutely, Marcy," I said, jumping right in. "Absolutely. That's me. I'm in." I made a fist with my free left hand and pumped it several times. I was back in the game.

Afghanistan. The mysterious, primitive place where the mastermind behind the worst attack on American soil was thought to be hiding. Americans knew next to nothing about Afghanistan, but that was about to change. Being one of the first journalists to report from there could make up for missing the story at Ground Zero the day of the attack. I silently thanked Dan Rather, and his bladder. I couldn't be sure he had anything to do with this, but it certainly seemed like something that had come from our conversation in the men's room.

Marcy told me to get ready as quickly as possible; she wanted me to go to London the next day and work from there for a couple of weeks while applying for my entrance visa into Afghanistan. I was ecstatic, though still not completely trusting that everything would end up working out so well. But one short phone call with a CBS executive had lifted me instantly out of a three-day depression.

My mind was joyfully racing as I sat down on a curb in Jersey City and started to compile my to-do list for my imminent departure to London. At the top was calling Peter. Even after eight years of marriage and two kids, Stina and I still hadn't drawn up a will. I wanted to make sure my brother the lawyer was clear about my basic wishes in case something happened to me in Afghanistan. I suppose it shouldn't have been exhilarating to be worried about my basic wishes in case something happened to me in Afghanistan, but it bestowed some seriousness of purpose that I found thrilling.

It was insane logic: that I was performing at the highest level of my profession and getting my ticket punched for the next level up was confirmed because the coveted assignment I was now in line to get carried the risk of dying. In my euphoria of getting ready to go, I was wholly unaware that I was sewing a deep and painful rift into the fabric of my marriage.

Leaving over the weekend meant I'd miss Rosh Hashanah, which would start after sundown on Monday, September 17, and Yom Kippur, nine days later. I didn't think about any of this before I dialed home to tell Stina about my conversation with Marcy.

"When do they want you to go?" Stina asked.

"Saturday, maybe Sunday," I answered.

"Did you tell her you couldn't leave until Tuesday night?" she pressed, sounding exasperated that I hadn't automatically done so.

"Honey," I said, "I've got to get over there."

It was clear. I hadn't told Marcy I needed to call Stina and discuss the idea with her. I'd already decided and committed. I wasn't asking Stina whether she thought I should go. I was telling her when I was leaving. I dressed it up in the familiar clothing of how I couldn't say no to this opportunity, but accessorized it with a specific pitch that she'd been listening to for four straight days now, that I'd practically blown up my career by not being in lower Manhattan when the towers came down.

"Stina, please understand."

It was silent on the other end of the line. She knew I'd already said yes. She was astounded, listening to her husband and hearing someone she didn't recognize.

After a few more seconds of silence, I heard her voice. It had an edge, strong and disapproving. "Jimmy, what about the holidays?"

Growing up atheist in North Dakota, where nearly everyone else was Lutheran, she'd been painfully aware of her outsider status. When we talked about a family, she told me that wasn't going to happen to her kids. Raising them with a religious tradition wasn't optional, it was essential. She'd converted to Judaism to get her whole family on the same religious page and chose the Hebrew name Behira. It meant "clear," which perfectly described her state of mind when she decided to become Jewish.

She'd always had an affinity for Judaism. She'd had Jewish roommates and dated Jewish men during college. She wanted to build a Jewish home where she'd raise Jewish kids celebrating Jewish holidays. And now her Jewish husband was casting all that aside without a shred of conflict to run off to Afghanistan in some misguided hope that he could correct the self-perceived damage he'd done to his career by not being able to run from the falling Twin Towers.

It had been twenty months since that first day back at work after my father died. When I'd opened my office door and flipped on the light, I'd been drawn immediately to my phone. I'd stared at it, overcome by a dreadful sense of loneliness.

I'd expected something like cleaning out his closet to level me, perhaps when I came across some piece of clothing that was "him." The thick off-white wool Irish fisherman's sweater with the brown leather patches. I'd thought that would've been the thing to do it. Or maybe taking down the medals and ribbons he'd proudly displayed on his "me" wall when we packed up his office. It even might've been something as simple as a pack of Goldenberg's Peanut Chews at a newsstand. But no, it was my office phone.

It looked like a prop from *Mad Men*, a relic at least a quarter century old. Made of dull black plastic, the phone had half a dozen small squares of clear plastic lined up across the bottom under the number pad. Each was assigned to a different line. The square farthest on the left was the Hold button.

Staring at my phone that first day back, I was consumed by a deep isolation. I didn't feel abandoned as much as unaccompanied. In the last ten years of my father's life, I'd come to lean hard on him, relying on his counsel, reveling in his attention, applying the Bob Axelrod rules and thriving.

During my time in Miami and Dallas, my first two stops in the CBS system, he'd always been good about calling after one of my stories ran on the *Evening News*. If he didn't catch me at the bureau before I left to tell me how much he'd enjoyed it, I'd get a call at home that night. But when I moved to the New York headquarters, his enthusiasm intensified to an entirely different level. My dad became a bit of a fanatic.

Within seconds of my signing off at the end of a piece—"Jim Axelrod, CBS News, New York"—the phone would ring. There was no other way to explain such a rapid response other than that he must've started dialing before the story had even ended. Or if I tagged out my story live on the set with Dan, he'd have that black phone ringing as I was walking back into my office. "Jimmy, that was terrific. Dan must've loved it."

Our relationship had grown deepest and our bond tightest when I was no longer living in his house. Our new dynamic was established almost entirely over the phone. On that first day back, I had stared at my phone, with its cold, dull black finish, entirely unsure how to proceed in its silence.

Twenty months later, the best I'd come up with was to conform as closely as I could to what worked when he was alive. In fact, I'd doubled down on it. Searching not just for the right path but for the proper way to proceed along it, I'd felt most sure-footed following his tracks, if not stepping directly into his footprints.

Afghanistan? No-brainer. "Jimmy, get your ass back in the game," I could hear him say.

Missing Rosh Hashanah and Yom Kippur? "Are you kidding me? You'll celebrate them next year. Twice as devoutly." I could see him, with his head cocked and eyebrows raised, the lines on his forehead sharply defined. "You're not going to let that stand in your way, are you? There's a fine line between being a good Jew and a schmuck. Get to London as quickly as you can before someone else gets in line in front of you."

Stina? "I know what she's thinking, and I love what she's thinking," he'd say, reaching to squeeze my arm tenderly. "Look, you've got a supportive wife. You're lucky. A supportive wife who doesn't understand why you've got to go right now." I could see his eyes twinkle while he paused for the payoff. "She will later, Jimmy, when she's looking at Emma's tuition bill."

I could still hear him pretty clearly, even without the phone. It all still sounded good to me.

Off I went, the day before Rosh Hashanah, confirming what Stina feared about my priorities.

I didn't go to Afghanistan out of some long-held interest in the Panjshir Valley, or some burning commitment to inform the public about this far-off country that overnight had become the best-known place no one knew anything about. Please.

I went to live in harsh conditions. "I know, I know. You want to pick dirt out of your teeth," the London bureau chief said to me when I started pressing him after a few days to send me to Afghanistan. His voice had an oh-no-not-another-one weariness, the residue of years of managing eager, ambitious TV correspondents.

I went for the adventure, to get shot at by the Taliban in places named Singedurrah and Golbahar. Walking with a CBS crew through a village a quarter mile from a Taliban outpost, a mortar came whizzing over our heads. We dove for a hole. The mortar hit forty yards behind us. The cameraman, a Dutchman named Wim de Vos, who'd spent years dodging violence in Soweto covering the end of apartheid, came up smiling.

"Nice shirt, James," he said. I'd worn a long-sleeve, button-down dark-blue cotton shirt. The kind I'd sworn I'd seen on veteran combat correspondents in nasty places. Wim thought it smacked of a rookie mistake, giving the Taliban lookouts a good target through their binoculars. "Next time, why don't you just paint an actual bull's-eye on your back?" I was getting kidded by a legendary CBS cameraman, and taught an important lesson at the same time. I loved it.

Our guide through the village, a mujahideen commander named Khademuddin, did Wim one better. Climbing out of the hole, shaking his head at our close call, he started whistling a tune. It was familiar, though it took me a second to place because it was more than a decade old. In his accented English, learned at school in Pakistan, Khademuddin stopped whistling, turned to look right at me, broke into a big grin, and gave me his best Bobby McFerrin impression: "Don't worry, be happy." It was positively absurd. My war stories were getting better by the minute.

I went to Afghanistan to establish my reputation as someone who would go anywhere, do anything, and never say no. I went to prove to anyone watching that I was fully committed to CBS News in a way that all the biggest players had been. I went to prove—to CBS management and myself—there was nothing I wouldn't do to succeed.

I went to Afghanistan so I could say I'd gone to Afghanistan.

On our journey out of Afghanistan at the beginning of November, I called home. It was a Sunday, the day Stina had chosen for Emma's sixth birthday party. I was posted up at a government guesthouse, hoping to catch a lift on an Afghan army helicopter over a mountain range to the neighboring country of Tajikistan. The road was already covered in so much snow that driving would have been impossible. We didn't know if it was going to be one day or ten until the chopper arrived.

I assembled a bunch of cameramen, soundmen, and producers

from other networks and countries to form a "Happy Birthday" chorus. When we called to serenade Emma, I could tell Stina wasn't happy. The satellite-phone connection was spotty. Emma couldn't really hear. I'd called smack in the middle of her party and she was distracted.

It certainly didn't help that on Saturday the sewer main had backed up in the basement. Stina had spent the morning stuffing Playmobil mummies and sheets of sphinx stickers into goody bags, then rushing off to the bakery to pick up the Great Pyramid birthday cake she custom-ordered in keeping with her daughter's desire for an Egyptian-themed party, and the afternoon shoveling crap out of our basement. She didn't think the International Birthday Choir was cute or charming or anything but disruptive.

"If you really wanted her to enjoy your singing 'Happy Birthday,' why didn't you just wait until we weren't in the middle of her birthday party?" Stina asked angrily. I may have been fine with the grand gestures, professional and personal, but Stina hated them. "They make great stories, Jimmy. But I find them hollow," she told me when I got home seven weeks later, "and a little bit sad." She hoped my trip to Afghanistan meant my ticket had been sufficiently punched, and we could put all the tension and conflict it produced behind us.

Which is why a year later, when U.S. tensions with Iraq escalated and CBS started to plan its coverage for a possible war and I raised my hand again, Stina began to feel desperate. She needed Afghanistan to have been a one-off, not a pattern. It wasn't that my choices seemed strange and foreign to her. Rather, they were starting to look too familiar.

Her husband was now the guy who came home from a week of training by former British commandos all hopped up on his new survival skills. I was eager to share with her how the role-playing I'd done there—kidnapped, then blindfolded at gunpoint—left me with much better odds if I was taken hostage for real.

"The key to everything, honey, is not to go to your knees," I told her, with a forced calm designed to channel the understated man-of-the-world bravado of the commandos. "You don't ever go to your knees, honey. Even if they order you to. Don't do it. It's a death sentence. Once you're on your knees, they're going to pop you." I pantomimed putting a pistol to my temple and pulling the trigger. "Instead, what you want to try to do is engage the people holding you hostage in conversations that create some kind of common ground. You've got to let them know you've got a family—'I've got children, please don't do this'—then ask them if they've got kids."

Her face looked strained as I continued my fictional dialogue with my fictional captors. " 'Come on,' you say to them. 'Please. Think about it. Imagine your kids suddenly without their father.' " I couldn't tell whether it was a forced smile on her face or restrained disgust. Maybe it was just morning sickness.

Stina was pregnant again. Her due date was the end of May. No problem, I told her during our holiday break in late December. The way we were hearing it at CBS, the fighting itself wouldn't take long. The military expected to have it wrapped up in a matter of months. The thinking was to begin the fighting in February or March in order for the war to be over before the brutal heat of the Iraqi summer. According to this time line, I'd be gone for a month, two at the most, and definitely be home for the birth of the baby.

She didn't want me to go. But she understood why I was doing it, that a full-scale military invasion of another country was not a story any ambitious reporter would miss. Besides, at the time Iraq didn't seem as dangerous to her as Afghanistan had been. In Iraq, I'd be embedded with U.S. troops. I'd travel with the military, which would provide a certain kind of protection I didn't have in Afghanistan.

She also had some advance warning, months of escalation where I was able to inform her about every step that took us closer, unlike with Afghanistan, where I gave her two days to get used to my going away for two months.

She understood why I was doing it, perhaps. But increasingly, Stina was having a harder time understanding why *she* was doing it. She knew my dad's rules as well as I did, having lived with the consequences of them for years. But for the first time in our marriage, she was starting to ask herself a critically important question: What good was the satisfaction I got from running off to war zones if it made her miserable?

The night the war started, a few hours before the first bombs fell, we made a last check of our equipment. There were three of us, the CBS News team embedded with the U.S. Army's Third Infantry Division for the invasion of Iraq. The tip of the spear, we liked to say, proud of our assignment covering front-line combat.

When our photographer, Mario DeCarvalho, popped open the case housing our night-vision lens, he was horrified. The adapter required to attach the lens to the camera was gone. Since it was an expensive piece of equipment, we figured it might have simply been ripped off. But we didn't have time to worry about why it had disappeared. We had to figure out what to do. The start of the war was imminent. We couldn't just call CBS News and get a replacement shipped to us. I started to panic at the thought of all our training and preparation, the days and weeks acclimating to conditions in the desert, being wasted. If we couldn't take pictures at night, when so much of the heaviest shelling and bombing took place, we'd be useless to CBS. We were looking at professional disaster.

But Mario was tough and resourceful and didn't give up very easily. Before working in TV news, Mario had served with the Portuguese Special Forces, living in the jungles of Angola and fighting the Cubans in the mid-1970s. Our satellite engineer, Geof Thorpe-Willett, wasn't about to give up easily, either. He'd spent twelve years in the British army before his TV career, then covered wars and conflicts in Bosnia, Kosovo, Somalia, Rwanda, Yemen, and Gaza. Mario and Geof went right to work. Half an hour later they'd come up with an idea to jerry-rig one of the three pairs of night-vision goggles CBS supplied to us to the front of a camera lens. It was off-the-charts clever in theory, but attaching and stabilizing a pair of night-vision goggles onto a camera lens with no specialized tools for the job would be a bit of a challenge, to say the least.

In addition to his big, industry-standard TV camera, Mario had brought a small video camera with him. It was an everyday Sony that anyone could pick up at any electronics store. "My bar mitzvah camera," he called it in his Portuguese-accented English, a phrase that always made me chuckle. Mario popped the camera's eyepiece out. He inserted the night-vision goggles in front of the lens, so the camera was now seeing through the goggles, giving it the capacity to take pictures at night. In a stroke of exceedingly good luck, everything fit together perfectly. The only issue was to figure out how to stabilize the contraption to be able to function on a battlefield. Three and a half hours later, using the cardboard insert from one of the military's Meals Ready to Eat, gaffer's tape, and tie wraps normally used to secure cables, they'd done it. We were back in business.

Well, we were back in business as long as one of us gave up his night-vision goggles to use on the bar mitzvah camera. There wasn't any question who would be volunteering. Mario clearly needed his goggles. He was the photographer. Our team's success depended on his ability to see. Geof needed his as well. He was the engineer, a job that required him to climb onto the top of the Humvee at a moment's notice to get to the satellite dish. He was also the first one out of the Humvee to pop the hood whenever there was engine trouble, unclogging the air filter, for instance, which often became choked with desert sand. He certainly wasn't about to try that in the dark without goggles. Geof and Mario also split the driving and navigating.

That left me. The price of getting our nighttime pictures, of doing our job successfully, would be my spending hours in the back of the Humvee, riding blind through a war zone, able to see only what tracer bullets and explosions in the distance might illuminate every so often. I was terrified at high noon, when I could see everything. Not being able to see only made it worse. Far worse. No longer was my sense of the threat we faced governed by what I could see outside our Humvee. Now my fear was limited only by my imagination. Sitting petrified in the backseat, all I could do was yell every now and again in the wake of an explosion, "Hey, would someone tell me what the fuck is going on up there?"

Driving without seeing through a war zone was a top-shelf metaphor for blind ambition. But I was just getting warmed up in the symbolism department.

Four days later, the unit we were traveling with passed by a group of captured Iraqi soldiers. We signaled our escort to pull over. We hadn't seen anything like this yet and wanted to get some pictures.

We got out of our Humvee and walked fifty yards to a makeshift holding pen, where a dozen captured Iraqi soldiers were on their knees in three lines of four, arms secured behind their backs, guarded by U.S. soldiers. Mario was getting some great video when he suddenly snapped his head back from the viewfinder. Looking at me, he barked "batteries." I took off running to the Humvee to get some fresh ones. I didn't know how much time the old batteries had left, but I didn't want to be the reason the camera shut down and we missed out on pictures like these.

I hustled back, handed him the batteries, and then doubled over panting with my hands on my knees. My eye was drawn to my left hand. Something didn't look quite right. "Oh shit," I thought, registering what it was that struck me strangely. "Where's my wedding ring?"

At some point during my sprint to the Humvee and back it had slipped off. Maybe my ring finger had been slickened by the sweat generated by the triple-digit heat. Or perhaps it was all the weight I'd been shedding living in an extended state of fear, which stoked a metabolic overdrive that did wonders for my waistline. My hands were noticeably thinner than when Stina and I had married. It really didn't matter how it slipped off; the bottom line was, I'd lost my wedding ring.

I started to frantically retrace my steps. The ring was nowhere to be found, swallowed by the powdery sand. I couldn't believe it was gone. As my disbelief spiked, my anxiety skyrocketed with it. A deep sense of dread started swirling in my gut. Stina and I had gone to a funky jeweler my parents knew in Cold Spring, New York, and asked her to make our wedding rings. We had a thought that we wanted to express with our rings. The jeweler nailed it, designing bands divided in half by a line encircling the ring's equator—two halves joining as one. Both halves were now buried in the Iraqi desert.

We were traveling across the desert with the Third Infantry Division. The 3rd ID, as it was known, was broken into three brigades. Each network had a correspondent embedded with one of the three. We were with the first. Ted Koppel, however, had the run of the division, moving from brigade to brigade as he and his *Nightline* team saw fit. Long one of my heroes, Koppel had hooked up with the First Brigade for a few days. I'd been thrilled to meet him. He was everything I could've wanted in a hero—generous and gracious, spinning romantic stories about the good old days as we sat in the desert after dinner.

One night, after I mentioned Stina's being pregnant, he reminisced about the challenges of having young kids while he was covering Vietnam. I couldn't believe I was comparing notes about the personal costs of pursuing professional goals with Ted Koppel. To me, it was no different from playing catch with Mickey Mantle.

Now Koppel came upon me digging frantically around the desert sand. "What seems to be the problem?" he asked. I held up my left hand and pointed to the white band of skin where my ring had been protecting it from the sun.

"It's gone," I said, my voice quavering. "I lost my wedding ring." I was trying to play it cool—all part of life as a combat correspondent—but failing miserably.

Just then a captain yelled, "Two minutes." Our convoy was getting ready to push ahead. Koppel did the math before I did, and realized I'd be leaving my ring in the Iraqi desert.

"Don't tell her," he said immediately, knowing exactly what I was thinking. His tone was stern but tipped with kindness. "Whatever you do, don't tell her. Trust me on this, she'll see it as some kind of omen."

I looked him right in the eyes, mustering as hard-nosed an expression as I could. "Got it. Thank you, Ted. Not a word," I said, trying to shrug off the whole mess with an air of nonchalance.

Ted headed off to his Range Rover. I slinked back to our Humvee. Alone for a moment while Geof and Mario squeezed every last second of our remaining time shooting video of the prisoners, I climbed into the back, pulled out the satellite phone, slunk down in the seat, and called home. It was seven hours earlier there. I realized Stina would just be getting up, although I was so panicked I didn't care if I woke her. I needed to hear her voice.

She picked up. I jumped right in, ignoring everything I'd just promised Ted Koppel. "Honey, I lost my wedding ring!" I started to cry. "It's gone, Stina," I said, choking. "I can't believe it. I'm so sorry."

"Jim?" she asked. I hadn't even said hello.

"Stina, I'm such an idiot," I barked back in my agitation. "I lost my wedding ring. It must've slipped off."

"Wait, wait, wait. Jim. What's going on? Are you all right?"

I took a breath. "Stina, I lost my wedding ring. I was running in the desert. It must've slipped off. I've been looking for it for the last fifteen minutes, and I can't find it, and we're about to get moving again. I don't know what to do. We've got to get back in the caravan. I can't believe this. Stina, this is really fucking awful."

There was silence at the other end of the line. Two minutes ago she'd been sleeping. Then the phone rang, and her agitated husband was on the other end spewing something about losing his wedding ring.

Finally, she spoke to me. "Jimmy, you're okay, right? You're safe? You're not hurt, right?"

"Yes, honey, I'm safe. I am. I'm safe. Ted Koppel told me not to call. That you'd think it was an omen. I promised him I wouldn't, then as soon as he was out of sight, I ran to the phone to call you." I was hoping to make her laugh and gin up a little sympathy at the same time.

"It's fine. Don't worry about it," she said calmly. She didn't chuckle the way I'd hoped she would. She sounded distant. I hoped it was the phone connection, though I knew better.

Once she knew I was safe, Stina had shifted gears. Her concern was moving on the emotional continuum to a place much closer to frustration, if not outright anger. The lost ring was not an omen of my impending death but a well-constructed metaphor for what was becoming of our relationship.

"Jimmy," she said, before we hung up, "all I care about is you getting a new wedding band before the baby comes. I want you to have a wedding band in the delivery room. Promise me that."

"Of course, sweetheart. Of course," I said.

When I got home, I'd realize it wasn't just my wedding ring that was gone; I was threatening to leave my entire marriage buried in the sands of the Iraqi desert.

The pain was sharp and burning, as if someone had slipped an acid-dipped razor blade horizontally into my left leg, precisely where my lower calf met my upper Achilles tendon. It was Wednesday morning, November 12, and I was walking home, unable to finish the 3.7-mile circuit through downtown Bethesda, Maryland, that had become my go-to loop. Never mind finishing—I'd barely started, packing it in before the one-mile mark when the pain in my lower left leg became too intense to continue.

Discomfort was nothing new, an unavoidable part of reclaiming a forty-five-year-old body from sustained neglect. My regular runs had become exercises in managing an endless series of annoying aches and pains, pushing through that day's strained muscle or balky joint until I was properly warmed up and the pain would then subside to a point where I'd hardly notice it.

But this was different, reminding me instantly of that debilitating episode of calf swelling that had left me floppy-footed on the side of the road on the Outer Banks during spring break eight months earlier. Except the pain I was feeling on this morning was much worse. Spring break had been humiliating. This was crippling.

The pain forced me into a sort of limping shuffle that looked like a cross between Captain Hook and a *Super Fly*–era pimp. Every time I took a step, rolling from my heel to the ball of my left foot and pushing off the toes, the stretch of all the muscles involved sent a searing pain shooting through my calf. The peg-legged pimp roll minimized that stretching; I moved my left knee, ankle, and toes as a single jointless appendage, rhythmically dipping my shoulders right to left to create the momentum needed to keep going.

Cars passed me steadily as I limped up the sidewalk that ran along Brookville Road, a busy two-lane street. I felt slightly foolish in my fancy all-weather nylon shell, white with blue stripes, and new Nike running tights. It was a lot of money to spend on hobbling.

I was also frustrated. I'd been doing all right, having run thirty-one of the past sixty-one days following my post–Clinton campaign crash. Every other day wasn't exactly the frequency I'd been shooting for, but it was a demonstrable step up from my summer breakdown. If it wasn't enough to inspire confidence, I was certainly making progress. While I'd started to realize how highly unlikely it was that I'd beat my father's marathon times—understanding in a new way what extraordinary shape he'd been in at my age—I'd been building a solid base in my quest to become fit enough to at least finish. I'd lost twenty pounds since I'd split my pants in Cleveland in February. I felt as if I'd turned some sort of important corner. Well, physically anyway.

There hadn't been any sort of concurrent mental rally. And early November only made it worse. The election of Barack Obama had provided reporters with the chance to cover history. Or, in my case, the chance to watch others cover it.

Correspondents had been dispatched around the country on Election Day, with several of my colleagues called to New York to sit on the set with Katie Couric and Bob Schieffer, commenting and analyzing results as they came in. Others chased down the many profound angles stemming from the country electing its first African American president. Meanwhile, I was posted at the White House trying to figure out what my best play was for lunch and dinner because on a day when Obama, Biden, McCain, and Palin were the head-liners, I was tethered at the hip to George W. Bush. Covering Spiro Agnew would have been a better assignment. At least he could've come back from the dead. President Bush was in a state even worse than death, at least by the standards of journalism and politics. He was irrelevant.

An executive told me that as the White House correspondent I needed to stay put and report on President Bush's reaction to the results, which made a certain amount of sense on the surface. But in the TV news business, Election Day is the Super Bowl; each team puts its best players on the field, even if you have to find a different position for them to play. I'd been relegated to the bench, a punch-to-the-gut kind of assignment that put my diminished status on clear display, the former A-lister who'd become as marginalized as President Bush.

I'd ended up getting on once, for about a minute and a half, provid-ing some details about a phone call President Bush made to President-elect Obama as soon as the race was called. During my live shot, several hundred students from George Washington University rushed to the White House fence, cheering Obama and jeering Bush. The quick-moving crowd made for some reasonably dramatic pictures, which I was able to roll over my report about the Bush-Obama phone call. But the rest of my fifteen-hour day was spent following turnout and election results from around the country on my computer at my White House desk. After playing central roles covering the last two presidential elections for CBS News, I was wholly extraneous. Sitting a hundred yards from the Oval Office, I'd never been farther from the action.

My mind was racing as I left the White House that night. It shouldn't have been a surprise. I'd had months to wrap my arms around my inability to gain traction with the new set of bosses. But just in case I'd forgotten, Election Day had provided an unmistak-able reminder. I spent my drive home up Connecticut Avenue through the placid affluence of Northwest Washington considering the tra-jectory of my career. Four years earlier it had been firing in a satisfying arc toward the clouds. Now it was headed back to Earth, moving twice as quickly. The only unknown was when, exactly, it would hit. As I pulled up in front of my house that night, I thought I heard the thud.

So as I limped home from my aborted morning run eight days after the election, I didn't know what part of me was now in worse shape—mind or body. The stairs to my bathroom suddenly seemed insurmountable. Once again, I was transported back to the beach house where we'd spent spring break in March, and I could barely get up the flight of steps to my bedroom. Once again, the common motion of placing the ball of my foot on the stair in front of me to push up to the next step, stretching the calf and Achilles, created crippling pain. Once again, I was climbing the stairs in the inimitable style of Pop-Pop Moe. I was quite literally continuing to retrace my steps. But I wasn't even fit enough to run in circles, only to limp in them.

I managed to shower, dress, and limp back downstairs. On the wall at the foot of the staircase was that framed black-and-white photograph of my father crossing the finish line of his first New York Marathon in 1980, arms up, fists balled, head thrown back in triumph. There it was, the meaning of the moment neatly captured in my father's inspirational grin beaming through his full beard, the feeling everyone who stepped to the starting line hoped to have 26.2 miles later, the goal that sustained runners through weeks and months of training. Looking at the picture, it hit me hard. What the hell had I been thinking, that I could beat this guy?

Nine months after I'd hatched the idea of running the marathon and committed myself to reclaiming my body, I couldn't run one mile, never mind 26.2. If the idea of running the marathon seemed laughable, the idea of running it faster than my dad was delusional. There was no question: He'd been faster, stronger, and fitter. He had more commitment, dedication, and drive.

It didn't take a mastery of Freud to explain the competition I'd set up with my dad. By so many measures, my dynamic, charismatic father had been enormously successful. He'd built a top-shelf legal practice, enjoyed a sterling reputation as a courtroom wizard, and made a lot of money along the way. He owned two beautiful houses, put four kids through college and a wife through grad school. He wore Armani, drove a Jaguar, and picked up every check he could reach. He'd set a hell of a pace. The marathon offered the simplest, most literal way to surpass it.

And yet, as I lingered at the bottom of the stairs, staring at this picture that captured him at his happiest, I was struck by a competing thought. For years he'd also been plagued by confusion, seemingly incapable of generating any sustained joy for himself anywhere other than the courtroom or a running trail. He was often alienated from his wife and distant with his kids, and he kept friends at arm's length lest they come too close.

I'd adopted his rule book to make my way in the world. His success provided not just a worthy target for my ambition, but a high-value bonus as well. The closer I crept to it, the more of his attention I grabbed. But I'd spent precious little time considering the wider picture. I'd never asked if he and I were looking for the same things in life, and whether his approach would work for me. The question wasn't why was I trying to beat this guy. It was why I was trying to *be* this guy. Looking at my father in peak shape with me barely able to climb a staircase, I realized we were, more than anything, different.

Perhaps it was too late; maybe I'd neglected my forty-five-year-old body for so long it wouldn't meet the challenge. Maybe I simply lacked the physical capacity to run a marathon. That's what my strained left leg seemed to be suggesting. But as I limped to the car, I felt lighter in some crucial way, free from the challenge of beating my dad. I was no longer running his race. That left me with the challenge of simply running my own.

Simpler didn't mean easier. After all, I still couldn't climb stairs. No longer could I ignore the obvious. I needed to go see a doctor.

Although my father, Peter, and Dave had all seen specialists over the years for various running injuries, I'd maintained a sort of immature pride that I hadn't, as if it spoke to my sturdiness and their frailty. Driving down Connecticut Avenue, my left calf once again swollen so tight it felt as if it was going to pop through the skin, I knew it was time for an image update. Sturdiness had left the building and taken vanity with it. I needed to get my broken-down pair of legs to an orthopedist.

Dr. Marc Connell met three basic criteria. First, he took my insurance. Second, he got good reviews from a couple of his former patients, whom I knew. Third, he had the earliest opening. I was starting to feel as if I didn't have any time to waste, and Dr. Connell's receptionist told me he could see me the next day.

Walking into the examining room holding a clipboard with some papers I'd filled out describing my problem, Dr. Connell struck me as a man of good cheer and great intensity. He looked as if he was in his early fifties, with a kind face and hair the color of faded caramel. He introduced himself and got right down to business, remaining silent for the first three minutes while he focused on my legs from under a forcefully furrowed brow. He kneaded the calf muscles and massaged the Achilles tendons of both legs, muttering all the while in what sounded like Latin.

Just as I was starting to grow slightly agitated—I wasn't looking for restrained and clinical, I wanted emotive and passionate—Dr. Connell started to share his impressions, becoming intensely engaged with the health of my legs. He was now highly energized, his speech thick with anatomical references meaningless to anyone without at least a year of med school.

"It seems to me your gastrocnemius and soleus just aren't cooperating with the rest of your leg." He fixed me with the meaningful, compassionate stare of a doctor swept away by the moment of diagnosis, which I met with the quiet of a mystified patient awaiting the English-language version. All that had registered was "gastro," which confused me even more. Whatever else was going on, this had nothing to do with my stomach.

Dr. Connell was in full medical blurt, his eyes locked on mine.

Something about my gastrocnemius and soleus had fully captured his attention. I now had all the passion I could ask for in a doctor, as a torrent of words poured forth, from which I was able to pick out "inflammation" and "tendency" and "injury."

He explained to me that the gastrocnemius and soleus were the anatomical names for the two large muscles making up the calf and that both were highly susceptible to swelling when overused. Ramping up my running during the past couple of months had left both muscles inflamed. In a way, I had heard correctly. Essentially, I had an upset stomach of the leg. "I see this all the time," he told me.

My run-of-the-mill injury didn't require anything fancy. He prescribed Daypro, a super anti-inflammatory, and half a dozen visits to the physical therapist. He told me to stop running for at least a couple of weeks and come back to see him once my leg had "calmed down." Dr. Connell started to stand up from his stool to leave the room. I caught him mid-squat with one last question I needed to ask, even if I wasn't entirely sure I wanted to hear his answer.

"Doctor, I am training to run next year's New York Marathon," I said haltingly while he continued to straighten up.

As soon as what I'd said registered, he sat back down on his swivel stool with a slightly bemused smile. He exhaled audibly, almost sighing, but said nothing and waited for me to continue.

Sitting on the crinkled white paper rolled over the top of his examination table, I was reminded of visits to Dr. Factor, my pediatrician growing up, with whom I'd always felt safe. This aura of security engendered by Dr. Connell's bedside manner left me close to letting loose with a full explanation of why I was going to run the marathon. I was teetering on the brink of verbally vomiting the details of my strained marriage, sagging career prospects, and tortured relationship with my father's race times. Thankfully, I managed to rein myself in at the last second, though I still felt a compulsion to impress him. Finally, I broke the silence by completing my thought.

"It's part of a reclamation project for my life."

His expression didn't change. I was looking at the same bemused smile.

"What do you think my chances are?" I continued.

I didn't want to be too dramatic. Essentially, he had just diagnosed me with an overused calf. This wasn't going to require amputation. But I did want to know, with this awful razor-like pain not fading at all, if I was devoting myself to something I wouldn't be able to pull off.

He didn't hesitate. "I'd say your chances are sixty/forty that you can."

He saw my face fall immediately. His compassion and decency took over and Dr. Connell quickly reset the odds.

"Make that seventy/thirty." He was trying to sound matter-of-fact, but his voice was laced with charity. "Yeah, actually I think it's more like seventy/thirty," he said, trying to sweeten the deal with a little bit of can-do enthusiasm. It was kind but extremely ineffective. His first, unguarded response had said it all.

Totally shaken, I went to fill my prescription for Daypro. While I waited, I called Peter to get his read on physical therapy. "Do you really think I need to go to some therapist?" I asked.

"I'm not sure what your issue is," my brother said, pushing back in response to the cynicism he heard in my voice. "Why the hesitation?"

Lacking any good answers, I threw out some lame ones.

"I don't know. It's a pain in the ass to get to? I don't need anything else chewing up my time? I'm not soft?"

"Oh, really." He launched in. "Just so we're on the same page, you realize it's 2008, correct? I've been to three different therapists the last five years. Groin. Thigh. Torn calf. Look, if want to do this you should go see a physical therapist. It's kind of simple: get some PT and maybe your problem gets solved. Maybe, maybe not. But I'll tell you one thing for sure. If you don't get PT, you're never going to run the marathon. I think it's pretty clear your body's telling you that."

His appeal was pitch-perfect. I could stay reflexively committed to the way I'd always done it and not meet the goal, or I could do business a little differently and give myself a much better shot.

"Jimmy," he concluded, "get some help from people who know what they're doing."

Before I thought through what I was saying, I offered up one last justification. "Dad didn't get any help."

Peter laughed as he punctured my long-held but misguided recollection of my father's go-it-alone approach.

"Don't you remember Dad's coach? That guy he got from the Rutgers track team? Maybe you were gone by then, but don't you remember when he was trying to qualify for Boston and he hired that guy to be his personal coach? You don't remember that?"

I didn't. But he'd made his point.

After ten minutes of calling around, I found a physical therapy practice that took my insurance. I called their office and went back and forth with the receptionist for a few minutes more, trying to match their openings with my schedule. Finally we settled on a therapist named Monica who could see me the following Tuesday.

Monica was warm and cheerful. She projected a purposefulness from the second I shook hands with her that reminded me of Miss Shapiro, my sixth-grade gym teacher. Miss Shapiro had been one of my all-time favorites, her tight, mid-1970s perm paired perfectly with a mid-1970s self-help message that—yes—we could meet all our goals if we just kept trying.

I'd brought shorts and a T-shirt with me, as the receptionist had instructed. After I changed out of my suit, Monica led me to a large room full of examining tables, oversize exercise balls, and treadmills. Other therapists were working on their patients. She motioned me to a padded rectangular table covered in maroon vinyl, and told me to hop up and sit on the edge. This highly trained professional therapist was about to shed any resemblance to the kindly phys-ed teacher who'd cheerfully urged my sixth-grade class up the knotted rope hung from the gym ceiling.

Before she laid a hand on me, Monica wanted to understand as much as she could about the problem she was about to try to solve. She grilled me for fifteen minutes, thoroughly compiling a history. She started with half a dozen questions about the specific pain I was having, then moved on to how often I ran, how far I ran, and what time of day I ran. She wanted to know what kinds of shoes I wore, what kinds of socks I wore, and what kinds of sweats I wore. She wanted to know about other sports I played and other injuries I'd suffered. She was curious about the food I ate, the liquids I drank, and the stretches I did before I ran. She listened intently, scribbling down my answers on an intake form.

As she wrapped up, I looked at her, wanting to get her on my side. "Monica, I need help. I really want to run the New York Marathon. More than want to, I need to. Please." I paused and looked right into her pupils. "The doctor who sent me here says it's only sixty/forty that I can do it. I'll try anything."

She kept her face clear of any expression as she wrote down my answers, careful not to betray any reaction, except for when she asked me to describe my pre-run stretching routine.

"I don't have one. I don't stretch before I run," I said in a tone I'd meant to sound earnest but that must have come across as cocky. "I just lace 'em up and go."

She looked up from the form. I saw what I first thought was a slight flicker of confusion cross her face. I realized later I'd misinterpreted the expression. I was a little out of practice with pure scorn. But with the luxury of a little more time to place it, I realized what she was thinking was much more along the lines of "That's real smart, jackass."

Monica was sitting in a chair in front of me, her head about level with the top of the examination table. This made it easy for her to reach out in front of her and feel the fronts and backs of my lower legs, comparing the left and right for swelling and massaging both to see if they were tender in the same places. After ten minutes of examining my legs, she excused herself for a second and came back pushing a cart roughly the size of those that flight attendants use to serve drinks. A small metal box sat squarely on the top of the cart, with a slightly frayed black cord coming out of the side. At the end of the cord was a device that looked like a miniature handheld showerhead, the kind you might find in a fine European hotel.

Monica picked up a small, round plastic canister from the cart. It had a screw-on top with a long, thin plastic nozzle, the kind you'd see on a diner counter holding ketchup or mustard, except it was white instead of red or yellow, and seemed to be filled with a clear jelly. Monica squeezed the bottle until a stream of the stuff oozed into her hand. She started to spread it on both calves and ankles, telling me, "I think we're going to try a little ultrasound, just to see if we can bring the swelling down." That was fine with me. Ultrasound converted sound waves into heat. The idea was to relax the muscles and tendons that were as tight as steel cables. Better yet, ultrasound didn't hurt a bit, which made it easy to back up my claim that I'd gladly try anything.

Of course, Monica wasn't as up front in advertising what came after the ultrasound. As soon as she finished, she put down the European showerhead and dug into my calf with her powerful hands to start deep-tissue massage. *"Ayyyyyyyyyyyy,"* I yelled. I was a little surprised. Miss Shapiro would've never hurt a fly.

I gripped the rounded sides of the table and began blowing short bursts of air out of my mouth as she held my left ankle with her left hand and slid her right hand all the way down the front of my leg. Her hand was cupped in a semicircle on my knee, her thumb and middle finger on either side pressing hard into the calf muscle as she moved down the shinbone, kneading the muscle as she went. The pain—sharp and steady—intensified as she moved down my leg. Given the choice, I would've preferred acid-dipped sewing needles inserted directly into my eyes.

"How's that feel?" she asked. I think she could tell how it felt just by my scream and the beads of sweat breaking out on my forehead, but she wanted to hear it from me. "I'm okay," I managed to force out. She knew I was lying.

She continued for another couple of minutes. I kept exhaling in short bursts but didn't scream again. In relatively short order, I'd mentally converted this well-intentioned health-care professional into my own personal concentration-camp guard. She wasn't going to break me.

"Okay," she finally said, releasing my leg from the semicircular vise formed by her right hand. "No running for the time being." She used the same expression as Dr. Connell: "Your legs need to calm down." She explained that she wouldn't know how to best treat me until my calves loosened up, which would happen only with time off from any kind of pounding.

"How long?" I asked.

"I don't want you even thinking about running for three weeks. We'll take it from there. In the meantime I'd like to see you for another session next week."

I was officially out of commission. Therapist's orders. Before I could worry about running my own race, I was going to need to reach the point when I could run, period.

In the nine months since I'd started running, the only things that had changed were the reasons why I stopped. The first time had been due to the breakneck schedule of the Clinton campaign. The second time was the depression caused by my imploding career. And now there was yet a third reason for a total collapse—injury.

My second trip to see Monica a week later unfolded much like the first, ultrasound followed by ultra-painful massage. Which is why I dreaded my third trip a few weeks after that. Apparently she'd contained the symptoms. Now she wanted to isolate the cause.

She put me on the treadmill to start the third visit, telling me I was going to jog for five minutes. A close examination of my stride, she explained, would help her figure out how to break the cycle of lower-leg pain that kept preventing me from any sustained training. She wanted to convert Dr. Connell's sixty/forty into Monica's eighty/twenty.

This was the first running of any kind I'd done in more than a month. The treadmill's timer didn't even hit a minute before my breathing became labored, but I was happy to push through, since it seemed that Monica had an idea she wanted to flesh out. She stood silently next to the treadmill, arms folded, laser-focused on the way my feet were hitting the ground.

I'd always been a heavy heel-striker, pounding hard onto the heel as I landed. Watching me on the treadmill, my stride heavy and lumbering, pile-driving my heel into the ground, Monica saw big trouble. My heels and toes did not hit the ground along the same vertical line. Instead, when I ran, my toes pointed straight out from the heels at forty-five-degree angles. If my heels struck the ground at six o'clock, my left toes hit the ground at ten o'clock and my right toes hit at two o'clock.

"I think I've got it," Monica said after a few minutes. She wasn't nearly as gentle as Dr. Connell had been delivering his diagnosis. "Okay, here's the deal. You told me you want to run the marathon. If you want to have any chance, you're going to have to make some changes in how you run." She bluntly cut to the chase. "Your stride is working against you."

According to Monica, the way I ran did not distribute the burden of my weight equitably. "You've got too few muscles doing too much work and absorbing too much of the pounding. I need you to start running with a stride that'll spread it out. Your big muscles need to get more involved and start doing more work."

Monica motioned for me to get off the treadmill, then stood beside me and put her left hand on my chest and pressed the small of my back toward my spine with her right hand. "I want you to run more upright," she told me. "You gotta stand taller and tighten up your glutes." I didn't say anything. "You know, your butt," she added, assuming that I didn't know my gluteus maximus from my elbow.

The posture she hoped to see me develop would bring my butt into a straighter alignment with my head, neck, and spine. That would get my thighs and hamstrings more involved in my stride, the big muscles Monica thought were being seriously underused. She also wanted me to turn my toes in so that if my heels hit the ground at six o'clock, my toes came down in a straighter line closer to twelve.

"You're working your calves too hard," she explained. "You're putting too much pressure on them." Monica's theory was that overburdening the calves deprived them of oxygen. My body responded by rushing oxygenated blood to the calf muscles in order to replenish the supply. "You want to know why they swell?" she asked. "It's all the blood racing to your calves. So get some other muscles involved."

Then she took it up one more level and started to lose me. "Your calves are encased in fascia," she said. "They're kind of like webs of tissue that make up these sort of compartments for each muscle group." I nodded affirmatively though instantly I knew that "fascia" was taking its place next to "gastrocnemius" and "soleus" on the list of words designed to make me drowsy. "When the muscles swell with the blood, they get too big for the fascia."

She must've sensed I was zoning out, because she stopped and broke it down to the kindergartner's comprehension level I required. "Two things happen. One—everything starts to hurt. Two—your nerves stop working."

I wasn't entirely sure, but I was fairly certain that Monica had just provided an explanation for my floppy feet on the side of the road months ago in North Carolina. I had a stride that wasn't working for me. Success, according to her, would require me to make fundamental changes in the way I'd run all my life.

My five minutes on the treadmill were over, but Monica wasn't finished. She hadn't said anything when I told her I didn't stretch, but now she was about to address it. She pointed me to a chair next to the examination table while she went to a desk on the far side of the room, shuffled through some folders, and returned with a few sheets of paper for me, each with anatomical diagrams on them.

"All right. Here's your homework," she said in a no-nonsense voice that wasn't asking whether I was interested in learning some stretches but demanding to know when I would start doing them.

When it came to eliminating my painful calf swelling, my new stride apparently wouldn't get it done all by itself. The thighs and hamstrings needed to be warmed up and ready to fire from the very first step I took, in order to share the load with those overburdened calves.

"In another few days, you're gonna start up again. All I'm looking for is ten minutes before each run," she said with a slight tone of insistence as she took me through half a dozen different stretches designed to warm up all the major leg muscles. "Give me each stretch, a set with each leg, hold every stretch for twenty to thirty seconds." I was looking for a hint of a smile, a sign of hope and bonding. I got nothing. She was all business.

Soon I was pushing hard against living room walls, balancing myself on staircases, throwing my legs up on banisters, and attempting rough approximations of a hurdler on my kitchen floor. Monica had retooled my approach to training for the marathon. It wasn't solely a matter of gutting it out, of gamely enduring the miles, the hills, the tweaks and strains. The race would be more than just a test of effort and desire. Getting fit required some forethought and preparation. Yes, I needed to run hard. But maybe more than that, I needed to run smart.

A few days after I lost my wedding ring in the desert, our Humvee rolled to the base of a bridge. Mario brought it to a full stop. A private approached, short and stocky with a red buzz cut. He rested his palms on the doorframe, arms fully extended. It was time for some final instructions before we crossed. He was all business.

"You're gonna get shot at. No worries. They can't hit you."

My stomach tightened as the adrenaline started to surge. I was scared and thrilled and getting exactly what I'd asked for.

From our position near the front of a caravan of Humvees, tanks, and troop transport vehicles, I could see a line that stretched out to the horizon behind us. We'd be among the first couple of dozen vehicles to cross.

I leaned toward the private to hear him over the chaos outside.

He had simple instructions. Hit the gas, don't stop, and bank on the Iraqis' antiquated artillery to keep us safe.

"They can't hit a moving target, sir," the private explained to Mario. "When we give you the signal, it's pedal to the metal, sir. Just keep moving. Go, go, go. No way they hit you if you keep moving. Good luck. See you on the other side of the river."

Fourteen days after pushing into southern Iraq from northern Kuwait, we were about to cross the Euphrates. We idled for a couple more minutes before the private waved Mario through, giving us a thumbs-up as we rumbled by. As instructed, Mario floored it up the bridge's gradual incline. An uncharacteristic silence filled our Humvee—a mix of intense concentration, uncertainty, and the tension of driving under fire marbled with thick veins of exhilaration and euphoria. We were about to become the first journalists to cross the Euphrates with U.S. troops working their way north, winning an important leg in the unspoken side competition among all the embedded reporters to be first to Baghdad.

"Move over, boys," all three of us were thinking, "here comes the A-team."

Not exactly.

As we reached the crest of the bridge—the rubbery, midrange whistle of artillery shells growing louder—our Humvee died. Lights out. Flatlined. Dead in its tracks.

"Shit," grunted Mario, frantically pumping the gas and turning the ignition, trying to get the engine to catch. Not a sound, except for a sickening *click-click-click* as he turned the key.

"Alternator. Fucking alternator."

The Iraqis may not have been able to hit a moving target, but a sitting duck was an entirely different matter. After a minute or two, we could hear the AK-47 bullets starting to whiz by closer overhead. From the sound of things, the soldiers firing mortar shells were zeroing in as well.

Mario and Geof both hopped out of the Humvee and popped the hood to try to get the engine running. Each had an ability, honed during their years of military service, to block out the swirling chaos and focus on the task at hand. Mario calmly worked on the engine, oblivious to the Iraqi artillery. Knowing Mario was doing all anyone could, and not wanting to get in his way, Geof pulled out his camera and started to stroll around the bridge, calmly snapping pictures of the battle on the riverbank below.

I started to join them, swept out of the Humvee by camaraderie. I stood for a few moments on the bridge, long enough to be enveloped by the strong currents of danger and loud explosions. Overcome by terror, I jumped back into the Humvee, a sense of shame washing over me. I didn't have the balls they did.

I anchored myself in the backseat, staring out at the bedlam. In the midafternoon sun, four Apache helicopters slid in and out of thick patches of swaying palm trees, one or another popping up every fifteen seconds to fire at Iraqi positions on the far side of the river. Plumes of thick black smoke hovered over the targets they hit.

Our Humvee, motionless on the bridge, looked like an old lame cow on a cattle drive, the kind the cowboys shoot because everyone knows it's never going to survive the creek crossing and will just slow up the rest of the herd. I curled into a fetal ball in the backseat, covering my mouth with a thin silk scarf in a vain attempt to ward off the smell of the tank fuel, acrid and sharp. Listening to the bullets draw closer, I repositioned my body so my helmet pointed in the direction of Iraqi fire, as if there was something I could do that would boost my chances of survival.

Six thousand miles away, Stina was gently rousing Emma and Will, all three entirely unaware of the danger unfolding on the bridge. As usual, Stina had gone in to wake Emma first. She always needed a few more minutes than her brother to shake the sleep from her eyes. Stina, seven months pregnant and due at the end of May, moved slowly.

I thought of Emma, my sweet, bookish seven-year-old who'd been sobbing when I left her on the front steps of our cozy home six weeks earlier. "Daddy," she choked out. "Daddy. Daddy. Daaaaaaaaaaaddy," she sobbed as I moved down the front steps. "Daddy," she called from behind me, gathering herself for one last wail. "Why can't you be a librarian??!!" That morning I'd turned back and waved with a sympathetic but self-satisfied smile. A librarian wouldn't have a black Town

Car idling in front of his beautiful center-hall colonial in a fashionable New York City suburb. Emma would understand one day.

Stina's eyes had been bewildered and sad. Sliding into the back of the limo for my ride to JFK Airport, I'd pushed her disappointment from my mind. I knew she wouldn't understand one day.

I'd been okay with that. By my calculus then, what was good for my career was good for my family. It wasn't terribly tricky. Going to Iraq was certainly going to be good for my career. Within a few weeks I'd had my picture in *People* and the CBS publicity department had called with an invitation for Stina to go on *Oprah*. Sure I missed everyone, but as I headed off on this grand adventure, I swore I had everything in place that I needed to be happy.

Now, in a very different backseat, curled up and frightened, Stina's warm sea-green eyes haunted me. For the first time since I'd left home, I had the horrifying thought that should've guided each part of the decision to cover the invasion but hadn't: What if I never saw them again?

I shut my eyes tight and pushed my face into the seat. My brain fiercely pulsed a single thought: How the fuck did I get here? How the *fuck* did I get here? *How the fuck did I get here?*

Bernie Goldberg, a savvy former CBS correspondent, once told me how he'd turned down a request from Dan Rather to go to El Salvador and cover the civil war there. To him, it wasn't about covering a war. Earlier in his career, Bernie had volunteered to go to Vietnam. He just couldn't justify the personal risk he'd be taking going to El Salvador.

"Dan, nobody gives a crap about the war and nobody even understands which side we're on," he'd explained to Rather. "If I'm walking down some road there and get shot in the head, next thing you know I'll be standing on a cloud looking right at God. He'll say, 'Let me make sure I understand this: You got killed covering the war in El Salvador?' Next thing you know, Dan, a trapdoor opens in the cloud and I drop right through it and go straight to hell. So I'm not going."

I'd heard the story, laughed, and totally missed the warning. Not about covering war. About knowing what risks you're willing to take. And why you will take them. The warning to know what price you are prepared to pay and whether your wife agrees it's a cost worth bearing. About knowing why you are doing what you are doing. And, maybe most important, when you should say, "No thanks, I think I'll pass."

Here I was, seven years after that discussion, covering a war from the front lines, and getting dangerously close to Bernie's cloud. More than once. And if I had died on that bridge in Iraq, and God asked me what I was doing there in the first place, I wouldn't have had anything close to a defensible answer. Because I'd never really thought it through beyond a general belief that a big part of getting ahead was never saying no.

There were plenty of valid, indeed noble reasons to go: from discharging the obligation of a free press to keep people informed, especially during war, to taking on an extraordinarily tough professional challenge, to wanting a taste of one of life's grand adventures. Plenty of reporters went for one of those reasons, or many others, seeing risk as part of their job. The gut-punch of Bernie's story wasn't the decision to go or not: it was knowing the reasons for the decision. And if I'd left Stina and the kids without a husband and father for no better reason than that my inherited rule book of ambition stipulated I never said no, I would've deserved my quick trip to Bernie's flames and sulfur.

Suddenly we felt a jolt. We looked behind us. It was an ABC camera crew, one working with Ted Koppel. They were driving an RV customized for war coverage. Seeing us stalled, they maneuvered behind us, locked onto our bumper, and began to push us across the bridge. Mario and Geof started laughing in the front seat, a pretty good signal that we were going to make it. I sat up in back and could feel a charge running through my arms and legs as the adrenaline started pumping, a warm static.

The crew from ABC pushed us all the way down the bridge, onto land, and into a sheltered area where Mario and Geof could safely turn their attention to fixing the Humvee. I sat in the backseat shaking and agitated.

The next night, our convoy pressed on to the airport. A few Humvees in front of us, a brilliant print reporter named Michael Kelly, there for all the right reasons, and the sergeant who was driving him came under attack. Trying to evade the rocket-propelled grenades, they swerved into a canal. The Humvee landed in the canal upside down. Both Michael and his driver drowned.

Mario, Geof, and I pushed on, dodged a few more bullets, and became the first crew to broadcast live TV reports from the runways of the U.S. Army–secured Saddam Hussein International Airport. The cheers and congratulations rang loudly from CBS headquarters in New York, but the euphoria was gone. We'd done our job. But all three of us were around the emotional bend. As Saddam's statue was toppled and other teams picked up the story in Baghdad, we needed to get out.

For weeks Mario, who knew combat as both soldier and observer, had been clear about his plans. "I do wars," he'd say. "I don't do occupations." That sounded good to me. On April 9, I caught a U.S. Air Force transport plane to Kuwait and didn't stop hopping planes until I arrived at JFK Airport the next day. On April 10, what would have been my father's sixty-seventh birthday, I was home.

Stina met me, seven and a half months pregnant, with a face full of tears, a tight hug, and a complicated smile composed of relief, joy, confusion, and a simmering I-can't-believe-you-did-this-to-us anger. I had a backpack, a computer case, and a framed picture of Saddam that a few officers with the Third Infantry had pried off the walls of one of his palaces and presented to me as a farewell present. What neither of us could see was the other baggage I was carrying, which would have been enough to break the backs of a team of skycaps, if only it had been in some physical form.

Over the next few months, we would get to examine what I'd dragged back from Iraq in this other set of bags: my short fuse with Stina, the distance from my kids, my inability to return calls or e-mails from friends. I'd been damaged on that bridge. No matter how many times I told the story with self-deprecating humor ("I was in the backseat yelling 'Mommy' and looking for a clean diaper") or nailed the punch line about ABC pushing us over the bridge with the precision timing of a borscht belt comedian ("We were first over the bridge, with the competition right on our tails"), I couldn't shake the trauma.

The first weekend after I got home, Stina took us all to a peaceful resort in the mountains of upstate New York. She planned long hikes, massages, lots of naps, and a warm, cushioned reentry. What she hadn't counted on was my paralyzing anxiety attack when I went to play golf. All alone in a cart, on the far corner of the resort's property, an unsettling agitation swept over me. I was too far away from our room, suddenly unsure how to get back.

I flashed back to a poorly marked T in the road on the way to Baghdad. In the darkness and dust kicked up by the desert wind, we'd lost contact with the convoy. We got to the T and had to decide which way to turn. There was a small orange cone turned on its side, with a ChemLight flare inside. The nose of the cone was pointing left. Geof was sure what that meant. Left it was. "Whoever turns right is going to get fucked, mate," he said.

Not everyone made the same choice in the days that followed. Jessica Lynch was part of a convoy from the army's 507th Maintenance Company that turned right. They headed toward Nasiriyah and straight into an ambush. Eleven troops were killed. We'd heard about it a few days later, while still pushing toward Baghdad. I was nauseous. Mario and Geof had made the right call. But what if they hadn't? I couldn't shake the idea that one wrong turn could have spelled the end, and that I'd been a passive player at such a crucial moment with life-or-death consequences riding on their decision.

I floored the golf cart back to the hotel, finding some comfort in the breeze that swept across my face as I sped down the fairway. I wanted to get back to Stina as quickly as possible. I needed to be wrapped in her gentle warmth, which would soothe and reassure me. Only once I was, I snapped sharply at her. "Why did you want me to play golf? Why did you want to come here? Why did you make me come here?"

She was alarmed, but wrote off the outbursts as among the inevitable bumps bound to be part of returning home after covering a war. A month later, she began to realize that resuming our lives was more complicated than simply picking up where we'd left off. Worse, she began to understand that the close call on the bridge hadn't left me with some crystal clarity about my priorities, my restlessness and yearning somehow sated by such proximity to disaster.

A few weeks after my golf course freak-out, CBS was planning to fly its team of correspondents who covered the invasion of Iraq to Las Vegas, where the managers of all the CBS affiliates were holding their annual meeting. The idea was to shake some hands, tell some war stories, and take a victory lap for all our hard work. I couldn't wait to go—play golf, drink Scotch, and bask in my newer, higher profile as a combat correspondent. Somehow the fact that my wife was about to give birth didn't seem to factor into my travel plans.

Telling Stina that I was headed to Las Vegas for a couple of days just as her due date approached, as if it was my sophomore-year spring break, was too much for her. She was now officially petrified, wondering what the hell had happened to her husband. One thing she knew for sure about the man she'd married was that she'd never have to worry about where he'd be when she delivered a child. Her Jimmy would be bedside, wiping her forehead, holding her hands, and helping with her Lamaze breathing. Except now I was telling her I was going to Las Vegas, but not to worry, there was no way she would go into labor during the three days I was gone.

"If you do," I added, "I won't have any trouble getting back in time. The planes fly to New York all day."

Every time she raised the subject, we ended up screaming at each other. A deep and troubling trench was widening between us. On one side, there I was—the aggrieved husband whose unyielding wife wanted to deny him his due after all he'd been through. On the other was Stina, stunned by this self-absorbed stranger who'd come home from Iraq, climbing into her bed and sleeping where her husband once had.

Thankfully, Stina's water broke twelve days early, the day before my flight to Las Vegas. Bobby was born the next day. If she was look-ing for me to be ashamed, embarrassed, or even slightly chastened, she was disappointed. In her room, with Bobby sleeping between feed-ings, I told her she was lucky. "Just think, Stina," I said with what I hoped was a rakish smile. "You never had to find out how right I was, about getting back from Vegas if I had to. There's no way I would've ended up missing it." I was shooting for charm, and misfiring badly.

If the distraction of a new baby temporarily created a façade that the worst was behind us, that I'd settled back in, it was at best a bandage far too small for a wound far too deep.

In August, I drove up to Hershey, Pennsylvania, for a guys' week-end celebrating the fortieth birthday of my buddy Mikey, one of my best friends since fifth grade. Friday night, six of us, Mikey's broth-ers and his closest pals, kicked off the weekend with a Springsteen concert in Philadelphia. Saturday morning, Stina called.

She was at Long Beach Island, having taken the kids to my mom's place for the weekend. She'd been loading them into the car to take them to their favorite diner for breakfast, the one built inside an old railroad dining car. She was carrying our infant, Bobby, in his car seat when she slipped and fell, banging into a big clay flowerpot next to the front door. She smacked her left side forcefully, squarely in the ribs. Stina was in tears, in pain, and in need.

"Jimmy, I think I broke my rib," she sobbed into the phone. And then she was silent, waiting. Naturally she expected me to jump in and tell her that I was on my way.

"Is Bobby all right?" I responded coldly. I was pissed off, annoyed by the thought of a premature end to my weekend. Reflexively, I shifted into the same rationalization I'd constructed for Las Vegas—the golf, the beer, and the concert, combined for some much-needed therapy. Listening to Stina on the phone, I desperately and lamely began spin-ning a line of horseshit equating my wife's broken rib with my fragile spirit.

"Stina, are you okay?" I finally asked. "Is my mother helping you? Do you want me to see if I can find someone down there who knows a doctor, someone to come over and take a look at you?"

"Jimmy," she said, mystified and furious, "I can make it home. I don't think driving is an issue." She was silent, waiting for me to snap out of it and tell her I was getting in the car and would meet her in Montclair. But four months after I'd come home, we'd reached a standstill. I wasn't going to volunteer to come. She wasn't going to ask me to. It wasn't a matter of pride for her. She was simply scared of the answer she might get. And heartbroken about the one she expected.

When I got home from Hershey and saw Stina in pain, something gave way inside me. I couldn't look at it any other way. Stina had broken her rib and I hadn't come running. What sort of husband did that? I was mortified. I'd been back for four months and was finally realizing there was no other way to spin it: I had issues. But knowing that was far different from dealing with it.

I didn't like the concept of seeing a shrink. I never had. Over the years, I'd been resistant to the idea the same way I'd refused to get physical therapy. I was sturdier than that. My father's second departure from home hadn't exactly been a ringing endorsement for the benefits of engaging a mental health professional. So it was my extremely good fortune that one of the best bought his bagels at the same place I did.

Dr. Allen Keller, a physician who works with torture victims around the world, was on the Sunday-morning line at Sunrise Bagels in Montclair when I walked in a few weeks after my trip to Hershey. I'd first met Allen in that refugee camp in Macedonia on the day Paul Douglas and I interviewed the priest. Chatting among the desperation of fleeing Kosovars living ten to a tent in an overcrowded stretch of pastureland, we discovered that we lived just a few blocks from each other in New Jersey. We'd seen each other on the bus to New York half a dozen times since then.

Allen asked me how I was. He knew I'd been in Iraq, but his question was nothing more than a casual conversation-starter. I answered, "Oh, I'm fine," following the script of a couple of acquaintances bumping into each other getting coffee. But he was a trained professional. He held my eyes for a couple of seconds to get a better fix on something he thought he recognized. He repeated, "How are you doing?"

I looked back, figuring this was my best chance. "Well . . ." I said, motioning to the door. "Let's, uh . . . let's go outside for a second." On the sidewalk in Watchung Plaza, thirty yards from where I'd caught the bus to New York on 9/11 two years earlier, I told Allen I was having trouble slipping back into my life.

Thirteen days later, I was sitting across from Dr. Anthony Bossis, a warm, teddy-bearish man with a mop of shoulder-length wavy brown hair and a full beard who radiated comfort and safety. He was also a top-shelf trauma psychologist. Dr. Bossis reminded me instantly of my favorite cousin, and I fell into an easy rhythm answering his series of intake questions. I recounted what had happened on the bridge, repeating several times how much "it was like something right out of *Apocalypse Now*." I described how distant I felt from Stina and the kids, detailing my shame about Hershey. We got to the end of our first hour and I asked him, "So is there something here, or am I being overly dramatic?"

Dr. Bossis answered with a kind smile and a tone that suspended the standard clinician's detachment just enough to punch through to me. "Are you kidding?" he asked. He could sense I needed to be reassured that my fallout was legitimate. "You've been through real trauma, Jim. You've seen more than enough to be sitting here. No, you are not being dramatic." He added one more phrase, to address his instinctive sense of what I was getting at with my question. "And you're not being soft."

Over the next several weeks, I would become familiar with "acute stress response," Dr. Bossis's formal diagnosis. I had some classic signs of post-traumatic stress disorder, but nothing full-blown. Essentially, all the death and injury I'd seen, coupled with my own near miss, had left me highly stressed out.

It all made sense to him. I needed to keep the feelings of fear and danger produced by my experience in Iraq at arm's length. They were destabilizing. To prevent the disturbing feelings from somehow slipping through, I unconsciously blocked all feeling. That explained my detachment from Stina and the kids, my emotional blunting, the flat affect.

Then there was my shame at having risked the security of my family. I couldn't bear to think of my children, their lives permanently and painfully altered, had I been killed in pursuit of pulling myself up another rung on the ladder. Add in the survivor's guilt, that I'd come home while Michael Kelly and others had not, and I was a mess. I'd shut everything down because processing such luck-of-the-draw guilt was torturous and, ultimately, futile. My mind preferred not to even try.

Dr. Bossis zeroed in on the bridge, feeling that I needed a safe, empathic environment where I could tell that story over and over. The idea was to drain it of its power through the retellings, the same way a piece of gum is sapped of its flavor when chewed long enough. We worked at it for a couple of months, desensitizing the story of the bridge. Gradually, I started to feel better.

Whatever I was doing therapeutically with Dr. Bossis, my head and my soul were also healing on their own. The way he explained it to me, trauma changed the neuroplasticity of my brain. The longer my brain went without further exposure to new trauma, the more it would naturally return to its original composition. Time, according to this kind man taking care of me, would indeed heal wounds. That was physiology as much as philosophy.

Toward the end of November, I told Dr. Bossis that I thought I was good enough to stop seeing him. He didn't agree, thinking I wasn't quite done yet. He wanted me to work with him a bit longer. He was right. I should have. But I didn't want to think of myself as someone with lingering issues. Taking a couple of hours out of my workday every week or two to see Dr. Bossis underscored that I wasn't yet "normal."

So I stopped seeing him. Despite cutting off my therapy prematurely, slowly I began to regenerate the many close connections that I had let fray. Slowly I began to feel normal. That was good, because I started to live as I had before I'd gone to Iraq. But it was also bad, because I started to live as I had before I'd gone to Iraq.

I couldn't stop staring. I didn't want to, and there were certainly better subjects for my attention, but I had no choice. I couldn't take my eyes off it. After all, Treasury Secretary Hank Paulson's grotesquely disfigured pinkie was pointing out my future.

Paulson had come to the White House pressroom to brief reporters about the financial meltdown. It was September 15, 2008. Lehman Brothers had just gone belly-up, Merrill Lynch had been sold to avoid a similar fate, the government was bailing out AIG, and the stock market had lost five hundred points the day before. Suddenly it seemed the country was careening headlong into 1929. President Bush wanted Paulson to come to the White House, take a few questions, and see if he could calm the jitters rippling across the country. As the CBS News chief White House correspondent, I took my responsibility seriously. In a time of national crisis, the media needed to press for answers. Paulson's pinkie was threatening to get in the way.

Paulson had been Treasury secretary for a couple of years, but I'd never had the chance to watch him up close. Now I was getting it. There were seven seats in the front row of the White House briefing room. I was assigned to the third one in from the left, just next to

Helen Thomas, who sat smack in the middle. I was five feet from the podium.

At Dartmouth, Hank Paulson had been an all–Ivy League offensive tackle. Now in his early sixties, he still projected a lineman's broad heft and muscular dependability. Tall and fit, he filled the room physically, though his bald, egg-shaped head added a slight but unmistakable touch of geekiness. His strong sense of command wasn't uncommon for cabinet secretaries, though its source was. It didn't emanate from charisma but rather from the intelligence he projected and his résumé.

His years of running Goldman Sachs, the alpha male in one of the most aggressive and ambitious wolf packs on Wall Street, imbued him with a certain dynamism. While he left no doubt that he was the smartest man in the room, he also carried the air of a man who didn't need to reinforce that idea every time he met someone. In fact, he didn't seem terribly concerned with what anyone thought of him, a rarity in Washington. You got the feeling that with $700 million in the bank, if this whole Treasury secretary gig didn't work out, it wasn't exactly going to break him.

As he made his opening remarks to reporters, I tried to take in his physicality, wanting to get as full a sense of him as I could. He seemed to be aware of the magnitude of the moment, and that a lot of ears in Washington and on Wall Street were anxiously trained on him. He certainly wasn't awed either by his position in the center of an imploding financial system or by his mission to calm the roiling waters. Still, his constant fiddling with a button on his suit jacket revealed a few stray nerves.

"Good afternoon, everyone. And I hope you all had an enjoyable weekend." The room broke into soft but sincere laughter, as everyone knew Paulson hadn't slept more than a couple of hours during the past several days, working on various deals to keep Wall Street from crashing. Paulson laughed as well. His chuckle lasted a couple of beats longer than anyone else's, bleeding some of his jitters. As he made his opening remarks, which were intended to underscore the resilience of the financial markets, he brought his hands together in front of him every couple of sentences, the tips of his fingers meeting just below his sternum, lightly touching for a moment and then separating again.

I recognized the technique from my own live shots on the White House lawn. Paulson had unconsciously developed a repeating physical motion to use for security, a reliable way to manage the tension that came with high-stakes public speaking in a high-pressure setting. The rhythm of bringing his hands together every sentence or two helped him stay centered while he spoke, insurance against blanking out while delivering the most significant statements of his public life.

Watching his hands, my eyes were drawn to his left pinkie. It was distractingly grotesque, bent away from his other fingers at a forty-five-degree angle and bowed with a large U-shaped indentation between the first and second knuckle. I'd read somewhere that he had an old football injury. This must have been it, a mangled pinkie that he'd caught and twisted in some opponent's face mask while playing for Dartmouth.

After his opening statement he went right to Jennifer Loven of the Associated Press for the first question. That was usually the way it worked. From the president on down, anyone taking questions in the briefing room traditionally gave the first opportunity to the Associated Press. After that, except when it was the president speaking, who commanded a bit more respect, it was a braying free-for-all, half a dozen reporters trying to outshout one another to ask the next question.

This always made for a pointless game of journalistic chicken. One or two of the bellowing reporters would fall off early, their voices either too soft or their senses of decorum too well developed. The rest of us would continue yelling our questions at top volume, hoping to grab the attention of the official behind the podium and suspending any of the social cues and biofeedback that would ordinarily prompt us to pipe down because we were making horses' asses of ourselves.

The official would pause for a moment, properly horrified, until one of the howlers outshouted the others, essentially by having the least-developed embarrassment threshold. The official at the podium would then answer this reporter's question until the others sensed the answer was winding down and began to howl once more. Then the reporter with the second-least-developed embarrassment threshold would ask his or her question. The whole system was faultily constructed, as it depended on shame, which was about as rare a commodity in the White House briefing room as straight answers.

It was meaningless theater. There was no actual reason for all the yelling. At least no journalistic reason. Most of the important facts are covered in the briefing. So would the relevant context and perspective. After all, that's why the White House was trotting out Paulson—to establish the administration's line on the tanking economy.

No, the braying was clearly a question of the reporters sorting out their own power structure, especially the TV guys. Even with the most important briefings, just a portion of the ensuing Q&A session would be carried by the cable networks. Every one of us was jockeying to get called on before the producers in the New York control rooms cut away from the briefing so that everyone watching—White House aides, other journalists around town, and, most important, our bosses—would see us on-screen asking a tough question and know who had juice in the briefing room.

I'd always thought I was a fairly decent shouter, with the requisite imperviousness to embarrassment developed while outshouting my colleagues in city council meetings in Syracuse and at the North Carolina General Assembly in Raleigh before joining CBS. But among the limitations I'd discovered at the White House was my second-tier shouter status. The White House was the shouters' grand stage. ABC's Sam Donaldson had made millions shouting at Ronald Reagan. CBS's Bill Plante was still outshouting his colleagues into his seventies, maintaining his prestige in the process. They wouldn't have gotten there without being great reporters, but being great shouters had vaulted them higher still.

Yet on this September morning, with the financial world collapsing, the Treasury secretary taking questions, and a large audience watching, Edward R. Murrow himself could have been in the briefing room and he still would've ended up waiting behind me. I was determined to get the first question after the Associated Press.

I had a built-in advantage. In the front row, almost directly in front of the podium, my proximity to Paulson was worth more than ten megaphones. I didn't need to out-bellow anyone. I simply had to catch his attention as he wrapped up his answer to Jennifer's question.

"Mr. Secretary," I said, cutting in quickly and locking eyes with him. Paulson nodded at me. It was a slight, almost imperceptible tilt of his head downward, no more than half an inch, but it was more than enough. Once you had an official's attention there was no reason for the others to keep yelling. Paulson's minimalist nod at me was an unmistakable invitation to ask the next question. The other reporters conceded my advantage, and their voices quickly trailed off.

"Could you just put aside for a second the specifics of AIG or Merrill or Lehman Brothers," I asked, trying to project authority with a deep voice and deliberate pace, "and can you tell us just how this happened and how did we get here? I mean beyond the housing correction, take us back and explain to the American people, how did we get there?"

Whenever I asked a question of a big shot, a number of different factors went into choosing what to ask and how to ask it. But constructing a question for Paulson had been a relatively simple process. I'd figured a complicated question about the intricate nature of isolating toxic assets or determining moral hazard wasn't going to do anyone any good. At least not any viewer outside of Washington or Wall Street. Over the preceding weekend, talking with friends, relatives, and neighbors, everyone I'd spoken to was enormously confused on a much more fundamental level. My question was a distillation of all those I'd been hearing during the past forty-eight hours. I wanted to be a proxy for the baffled and try to get someone in power to explain in simple, accessible language just what the hell was going on.

Paulson was the kind of guy who acted quickly and decisively, whether in a boardroom or taking questions from reporters. "Okay," he answered without missing a beat, "first of all, we have excesses, and excesses that have built up for a long period of time, number one. Number two, we have an archaic financial regulatory structure that came in place a long time ago, after the Depression; it really needs to be rebuilt. But again, what we're focused on right now, I think, is the future, and the future is stability, orderliness in our financial markets, and working through this period."

He wasn't exactly answering in the language of Joe Six-pack, but I was only vaguely aware of what Paulson was saying as he was saying it. Mentally, I'd already moved on, formulating a follow-up question to extend my time in control of the room. Knowing that I could read a transcript later, I wasn't listening to comprehend as much as to hear a phrase or nugget I could press him on as soon as he took a breath, before another reporter could grab the wheel. He paused. I jumped.

"And specifically a future with what kind of regulation?" That bought me another couple of minutes of his explaining the balance between regulation and market discipline. I could see other reporters scribbling notes while he was answering my questions. I'd done my job, making news on what was now the biggest story in the world.

My work was far from finished. Paulson would be taking another dozen questions. The headline might still be to come. But as soon as my turn was over, my mind started to aggressively wander away from what he was saying. Paulson's voice took on the muffled, foggy, indistinct enunciation of Charlie Brown's teacher.

I watched as he repeatedly brought his hands together in front of him while he answered questions, my attention returning to the curve of his misshapen finger. The global economy was in a disastrous free fall. I had the Treasury secretary an arm's length away explaining the calamity in full detail. And my focus was on whether he had disfigured his left pinkie against Harvard, Yale, or Princeton.

But it wasn't just the fascination with the grotesque that had captured me. It was the story that led from that pinkie to Paulson, the backstory of the man himself. I started drifting to his career path, wondering what kinds of qualities were transferable from the trenches of an Ivy League football field, where he'd sustained that injury, to the highest levels of the financial world. The pinkie had set me wondering. Where does a master of the universe come from? How is one created? I wanted to know what that pinkie could tell me about what made him tick.

Only that wasn't my job. At least not while covering the president.

Walking to my car that night, I couldn't shake the ghost of Paulson's pinkie. I'd done my assigned job well. I took control of the room and asked a question that elicited a news-making answer from the administration's point man on a developing crisis. Seeing quotes from his answers to my questions in the first stories to appear online after the briefing left me sure I'd asked a question that added to people's understanding of the threat we all were now facing. I wasn't a bad political reporter, just a disinterested one. The backstory of the government's rescue of AIG wasn't what had grabbed my attention. Hank Paulson's pinkie was.

My mind flashed back seven months to that painful meeting in February, when Sean McManus had made it crystal clear that I wasn't what he had in mind for the next CBS Washington wise man. At the time, I'd been crushed by the rejection, unsure how to deal with not being on the A-list, and angry that I had to.

Now, as I slipped out the northwest entrance of the White House, the heavy metal gate clanging shut behind me, I thought to myself that perhaps Sean grasped something I hadn't.

I'd come to Washington for a lot of different reasons.

I'd come to Washington because I wanted a crack at one of the biggest beats in journalism. Dan Rather, Lesley Stahl, Tom Brokaw, Brian Williams, Ed Bradley, Sam Donaldson—they'd all spent time covering the White House. Maybe in the Internet age it wasn't what it once was, but because of sheer proximity to the president of the United States, the North Lawn was still one of the grand stages in TV news.

I'd come to Washington because I wanted to walk through those gates every day and head to my front-row seat in the most famous briefing room in the world. I wanted my chance to fire questions at the most powerful man in the world.

I'd come to Washington because a White House assignment was a time-honored rung on the ladder that any ambitious network television correspondent was trying to climb. I wanted to realize the return on my investments of bungee jumping without a net in Syracuse, diving away from incoming mortar rounds in Afghanistan, and pissing myself in fear on a bridge in Iraq.

I'd come to Washington because it was the natural destination for anyone chasing the red light of a television camera, the one signaling that "you're on." For a red-light junkie jonesing for a validation high, there wasn't a better place to score a fix than the White House, where the steady churn of world-shaping headlines ensured daily appearances on the evening news, the pharmaceutical-grade stuff.

I'd come to Washington to be smack in the middle of it. Checking my BlackBerry from my front-row seat while I waited for Paulson to appear, my back to the bank of cameras in the rear of the room, I had read with delight the e-mail from my buddies around the country watching CNN or CNBC. The cable networks had a shot of the briefing room for their anchors to reference as they set the scene. My BlackBerry buzzed. "I'd recognize that bald spot anywhere," wrote Mitch Weitzner, a CNBC executive I'd worked with for many years at CBS. "If you get this," e-mailed Kevin Rendino, a fund manager watching from Wall Street, "raise your hand." I wasn't just at the center of the universe. I was the link to it for my family and friends.

I'd also come to Washington to finally get a step ahead of my father, instead of remaining four feet behind. Nearly nine years after his death, I was still trying to capture his attention. He'd worked at the Middlesex County Courthouse, where he'd once subpoenaed that German shepherd in a dog-bite case. I worked on the North Lawn of the White House, where Jimmy Carter, Menachem Begin, and Anwar el-Sadat signed the Camp David Accords. He had a bailiff in the corner of a half-empty courtroom guarding a county judge. I had a couple of U.S. Marines posted at the entrance to the West Wing, guarding the president. For years, his desk had been in an office on the second floor of a converted house in downtrodden Perth Amboy, New Jersey. My desk was fifty yards from the Oval Office.

I'd come to Washington to fly on Air Force One and feel the heady self-satisfaction when I flew into the part of the world my grandfathers had fled as toddlers, their parents looking for a better, safer life. Two generations later their grandson had returned to Russia—where Pop-Pop Aaron was born—aboard the plane of the president of the United States and had drinks and dinner with some of the president's senior aides in Riga, Latvia, five miles from the apartment where Pop-Pop Moe lived before emigrating.

I'd come to Washington to sit next to Karl Rove at the Kennedy Center and take my wife to the White House Christmas party and my kids to a screening at the White House movie theater. I'd come to have my name announced by the baritone marine before strolling with Stina on my arm, right by the cameras taking pictures of the A-listers heading into the East Room for a glittering social event.

I'd come to Washington to take my place as a boldfaced name. I'd come looking for a prestige boost, expecting my posting at the White House to get me acknowledged and registered. In a city that worships proximity to power, where guests at cocktail parties look right over your shoulder as they say "Good evening," wondering if there isn't a more important person to corner and a better use of their time, the title of CBS White House correspondent seemed like a pretty good way to hold their attention.

I'd come to Washington to become extraordinary.

What a moron.

Hank Paulson's pinkie had made it as clear as could be. I'd been drawn to Washington, and the White House, for many reasons. But the actual work wasn't one of them.

Peel away all the trappings of being the White House correspondent, and it's a job reporting on public policy. Of course it's critically important work, the most important daily journalism posting there is. Of course it's a demanding job, and extremely difficult to do well.

Of course it takes an aggressive, sharp reporter to succeed. Of course it can lead to even bigger jobs and more money. But ultimately it wasn't for me. A big mistake was not grasping the fundamental nature of the job before I took it. But there was an even bigger mistake—not understanding something fundamental about me.

Posting up on the North Lawn of the White House in my trench coat was never anything less than thrilling. I was aware each and every time I came through the gates to go to work that I was enormously privileged to have the job. Still, after several hundred live shots, I'd started to notice the just-the-facts reporting was rather dry for my taste.

During my whole career, the stories I loved most, the richest and most satisfying pieces, the ones that left me filled with pride and brimming with sorrow, were stories drawing some essential human connection between the viewer and the subject. The kid with cerebral palsy outside Denver whose most effective therapy was riding a wild mustang broken and trained for the job by maximum-security prison inmates, or the team of volunteer doctors delivering babies amid the hopelessness of a refugee camp in Macedonia, or the army unit in Iraq that lost two master sergeants in twenty-four hours during the invasion of Baghdad—those were the stories I'd want my kids to show after I was dead and someone asked, "So, what did your dad do for a living?"

I'd been paid well to travel, halfway across the world at times, and tell exactly those kinds of stories. And yet, without the slightest trace of a second thought, I'd abandoned the job that let me do that, turning away from what I loved most and did best to chase some bullet points for my résumé—and take a shot at fame and fortune. Guided by how a job looked rather than how it felt, I'd sold a house we loved, left a town where we were settled, and dragged Stina and the kids somewhere none of them wanted to go. All to undertake the kind of work that had never captivated me.

It was a bad fit. In fact, I couldn't have designed a worse fit. But that made perfect sense because I'd taken the wrong measurements when I pursued the job. And in life, nothing good ever comes from a bad fit.

I didn't like being there. And my bosses didn't want me there. Unfortunately, they'd figured it out long before I had. Or maybe fortunately—otherwise I might never have identified the self-delusion, never mind confronted it.

From the day I got to the White House, I never had any real sense that they thought I was doing much more than a mediocre job. Oh, my family and friends all thought I was the second coming of Dan Rather, but the people who counted when it came to evaluating my performance were a bit less enthusiastic. Maybe my bosses wanted someone more telegenic, or with a bigger personality. Maybe they wanted someone wiser to the ways of Washington rather than someone who'd just dropped in a few months earlier. Perhaps they wanted to use the position to groom someone they thought more likely to develop into a star.

At various times I was told I waved my hands around too much, or I wasn't edgy enough, or confrontational enough, or thorough enough, or that I didn't do live TV well enough. It really didn't matter what the specific objection was, the bottom line was that my bosses just didn't care very much for my occupying one of the network's marquee positions, standing in front of the White House. My posting at the White House, my supposed springboard to the next level of success, had become instead a very public plank to walk.

Whatever anger I'd had after the Clinton campaign ended and I was left without any role covering Obama's race against McCain, whatever rejection I felt from being marginalized after going to Afghanistan and Iraq, whatever embarrassment I felt when a friend from one of my old stations in Syracuse or Raleigh would call to ask "Are you okay?" in the same tone they'd use to greet a widow at a wake—washing out at the White House was the crucial development of my life, a life I wasn't all that happy living.

I could no longer ignore the destructive pattern I'd been repeating for the past half-dozen years. On a bridge over the Euphrates, my unexamined ambition had almost gotten me killed. Then the same blind striving put me back on a familiar path, again threatening serious trouble as I worked away from home for weeks at a time, eating too much, drinking too much, and waking up far too many mornings hundreds if not thousands of miles from where I wanted and needed to be. But I was lucky. Before I did any irreparable harm, I failed.

The dress she wore for the service, a gray plaid number from Anthropologie, was perfect. She and Stina had paired it with an ultracool short-sleeve black sweater. The two-inch black heels were a sophisticated reminder that this was indeed the day my daughter would become a woman, at least in the eyes of our congregation. The silver Tiffany peace-sign necklace was so quintessentially Emma that two different families we'd invited to her bat mitzvah had sent one as a gift. But my favorite touch was the set of blue rubber bands she'd asked the orthodontist to put on her braces. They'd match the dress she was going to wear to her party that night.

Looking at my little Bean, I had the requisite Tevya moment: Is this the little girl I carried? The two-year-old who insisted on wearing her Snow White costume every day until the next Halloween was getting ready to lead our congregation in prayer. Tevya had asked the question as his Hodel was getting married. Emma was only having her bat mitzvah. But when it came to sentimentality and my kids, I'd always figured, "Why wait?"

Rodney, her stylist at the trendy salon in Adams Morgan, had straightened her shoulder-length dirty-blond hair, parting it in the middle. As we'd expected, Emma's cautious nature had taken over when it came to makeup. She'd gone light on the base, shadow, and mascara that Stina had bought for her at Lord and Taylor earlier in the week.

The three of us sat on the bimah, to the left of the ark in matching modern, high-backed dark-wood chairs with gray seat cushions. I sat closest to the ark. To my immediate left was Stina. Emma sat to the left of her.

As we waited for the rabbi to give Emma the signal to begin, I slowly lifted my left arm and rested it on the chair's flat, wide wooden armrest. Stina reached out with her right arm, turned the palm of her hand up, slid it under my left hand, and knit our fingers together.

A hundred and fifty of our closest friends and family filled the rows in front of us. Their warm smiles reflected our joy back to us, richer and fuller from the ricochet. I slowly scanned the faces: my best friends from fifth grade; my college roommate; my cousin Doug, the one who'd reminded me so much of Dr. Bossis. I saw Chloe, who'd been with me on the platform at the Obama rally in Houston ten months earlier, when I opened up my dad's marathon times on my BlackBerry. There was Oz, Peter's two-month-old son, in the arms of my sister-in-law, Leah. Peter had moved up a few rows to sit with Bobby, just in case he got a little skittish sitting apart from his mom and dad for the two-hour service. My eyes darted from face to face. A few rows in back of Peter and Bobby, I saw my great-aunts Ruth and Elaine, ninety-four and eighty-nine. Right in front of them were Dave and his son, Theo. To their right was my mom. She looked beautiful and suffused with the joyous moment, despite the element of soldiering on alone that family life-cycle events now carried.

I pushed back into the cushion of my chair and crossed my right leg over my left. Inhaling deeply, I took in these close connections, overwhelmed by seeing all of my most reliable sources of warmth in one place at one time. In the third row, directly in front of me, I locked eyes with Mo Goins, an infantry colonel I'd met in Iraq. Six foot three, two hundred and thirty pounds, he was "tough as a woodpecker's lips," to quote one of his favorite descriptions for his best soldiers. Mo had kept a watchful eye on me from behind his wrap-around sunglasses from the moment I embedded with his brigade. He'd flipped me a roll of toilet paper on my first day in camp as I headed into the latrine he knew had none, pulled me to safety when a fast-moving, blinding sandstorm enveloped us so quickly I suddenly couldn't find the command tent twenty yards in front of me, and constantly checked in to see if I was all right during those moments when I most decidedly wasn't. After we'd both returned home in the summer of 2003, he sensed my flailing and drove five and a half hours from northern Virginia to New Jersey to walk the beach with me, reassuring me it would just take some time.

Sitting in Temple Sinai on this Saturday morning in December, five and a half years later, I looked at Mo and flashed back to a conversation we'd had in the desert ten days into the invasion. The First Brigade was posted up in a desert camp, giving the supply lines behind us a chance to be established before we pushed farther into Iraq. Mo was the operations officer for the brigade, an enormously high-pressured position that meant he couldn't walk ten yards through camp without someone stopping him to ask for something. On that day, a Sunday morning, we'd struck up another of our casual conversations—college basketball, family, and North Carolina, where I'd worked and he'd grown up.

I'd asked him how he decided on a career in the military. He started telling me about his role models: Uncle Alan, who'd been a chopper pilot in Vietnam, and Uncle T, who'd done a tour in Korea and two in Vietnam. They were the men whose rule books Mo had followed. On this tenth day of the war, Mo was a few minutes into an animated telling of the story about Uncle Alan returning home from Vietnam, when he suddenly went silent.

I wasn't sure what we'd stumbled into and certainly didn't know how to play it. Just when the silence was lengthening from awkward to uncomfortable, Mo slapped one of his meat-hook arms around my back and slowly started to jog us away from camp and into the desert. He didn't stop until we were at least fifty yards from all the tents and the bustle of camp. We stood quietly next to each other for a few minutes. It was clear he was gathering himself, needing to bleed some of the unrelenting, excruciating pressure that built up while fighting a war. It was just as clear he wanted to be far from any of the other soldiers, should he buckle.

He didn't. For the next forty-five minutes, we stood in the Iraqi desert describing the men in our lives and how they shaped us. A small tear or two might have fallen briefly from behind the wraparounds, but I could feel his strength return as we talked. Uncle Alan, Uncle T, and Bob Axelrod were all getting a good workout, until suddenly Mo clapped his powerful hands together and barked, "All right, church is over," and we made our way back to camp.

Now, thousands of miles from the Iraqi desert, as Emma's bat mitzvah was about to start, a celebration of life, Mo and I nodded to each other, and to a friendship forged in such close proximity to death.

A powerful quiet filled the sanctuary, the energy created when many people sit silent in anticipation of something extraordinary. My nose started to wrinkle, and my eyes began to fill. My tears spilled onto my slightly downturned face. I made no move to wipe them; the moment gathered even more strength as each tear trickled to the crest of my cheekbone, hanging for a second before dropping off my face and onto my talit.

My mind was racing with meaningful memories. I thought of my own bar mitzvah thirty-three years ago. I could see my father standing face-to-face with me. He had a Torah resting on his shoulder. I had a smooth blue velvet yarmulke with fancy white stitching perched precariously atop the heap of dense black curls that covered my head.

My dad was thirty-nine the day I became a bar mitzvah, six years younger than I was now. He was lost and wandering, a little more than a year after leaving home the first time, eight years before he'd leave the second time. And yet it was impossible to mistake his love for me on that day in January 1976, as well as his regret for what he'd already missed.

It was the custom at Anshe Emeth, my synagogue growing up,

for a parent to speak to their child just before passing the scroll to them. I'd have thought this to be right up my dad's alley: a chance to pass on a few words of guidance, publicly articulate some paternal pride, and put his indelible fingerprints on the day. But when he started to speak, he was rendered mute by the heavy emotion. He started to sputter and shake, unable to summon any words, only tears. It was a preview of what I would see five years later, on the football field after my high school graduation. It turned out that my father, the gifted trial lawyer who kept courtrooms enthralled, hanging on his every word, spoke loudest when he couldn't talk.

I suddenly snapped back to the scene unfolding in front of me, my eldest child preparing to read from the Torah. I was crying as well. But unlike my dad's tears, mine were not for what I'd lost but for what I'd found.

"*Baruch atah adonai.*" Emma's voice, strong and confident, filled the synagogue with perfect lilting Hebrew. I could see surprise cross the faces of so many who'd gathered with us. She'd always been a careful sort, shy and guarded about revealing herself to anyone until she was sure they were trustworthy. It was understandable to mistake her caution for insecurity—how would anyone know differently? If you didn't live in the same house with her, you would've never heard her belt out a chorus of "Good Morning Baltimore," from the musical *Hairspray*, in full Ethel Merman at seven o'clock in the morning.

She loved having any stage, especially when she also had a script. Now she had both. Emma's Torah portion told the story of two brothers, Jacob and Esau. They had a tortured relationship and were meeting for the first time in years. In her speech, interpreting the story, Emma delved into the way Jacob handled the reunion, humbling himself and taking the blame. She wrapped together the prophet Hosea, Thomas Jefferson, and her brother William with the concepts of deception, obligation, and supplication.

"There are times when we must bend like reeds in the wind rather than snap like cedars always trying to stand tall," she boomed. A wry smile crossed my face. There were only fifty-four Torah portions she could have drawn. Of course she got the one that doubled as a private lecture to her old man. "There are times when we must bend like reeds." She already understood at thirteen what I'd just spent the most painful year of my life learning at forty-five.

The huge glass windows on either side of the sanctuary allowed us to bathe for a moment in the occasional ray of morning sunlight that pierced the dull gray sky on this mild winter day. I leaned over to Stina. "Freeze this," I whispered.

So much elasticity had been leeched from our marriage in the past half-dozen years by my self-absorbed pursuit of importance instead of happiness. My lurching down a path, setting my course by someone else's map, had sent us careening. And yet here we were in this perfect stillness, sitting together on the bimah, our fingers interwoven. I had only the clarifying pain of the past year to thank for this moment that I didn't want to end.

The disappointments of that year had forced upon me an honest self-examination I would've never undertaken on my own. I hadn't exactly failed at the White House. I just hadn't succeeded the way I'd anticipated when I'd moved everyone to Washington. Either way, the sting had subsided enough for me to finally see what I'd gained, though it would've been hard to miss in the sanctuary that morning.

I'd come so close to repeating some of my father's mistakes, pushing hard after some poorly calibrated, ill-defined vision of success, without clearly seeing how it would produce happiness. I'd let myself lose sight of the things that most immediately grounded me, made me truly happy. That's how I'd ended up on that bridge, stalled out, under fire, and curled into the fetal position by fear.

As Afghanistan bled into Iraq and then into Washington, Stina and I had dug in to our positions, neither of us giving ground until the pain of failure exploded in my foxhole, a direct hit. The way I had been living my life—on the road for weeks and months, allowing my ambition to set a course to the exclusion of all else—had been disorienting and destabilizing. It undermined any chance at sustained contentment and left me both fat and hollow.

Fortunately for me, I'd come up short before doing any permanent damage. At least it didn't feel permanent as I held hands with my wife and we watched our daughter.

The profound well-being from Emma's bat mitzvah was still with me the next Saturday as I got ready to run for the first time in five and a half weeks. Not that I could feel it. I was in too much pain, down on my ass on the hardwood floor in our entryway, left leg extended in front of me, right leg bent at the knee and folded behind me in a hurdler's stretch.

I was diligently attempting to follow the fifteen-minute pre-run stretching regimen Monica had prescribed—three different calf stretches, then a series of others designed to work over my hamstrings, groin, butt, and thighs. This was the first time since high school I'd been in some of these positions, which explained the searing shots of agony as I sat on the floor with my legs splayed, bending and twisting the barely measurable distances my long-neglected body could tolerate as I stretched one muscle after another. Clearly, my body hadn't appreciated being ignored.

My stretching regimen did more than loosen my muscles. While I was trying to hit the Reset button on my training once again, there was a difference this time. Flat on the floor, twisting myself into a pretzel, producing a kind of pain the Marquis de Sade would envy, I had some clarity. Not complete and total, perhaps. But if I wasn't entirely sure why I was running, I'd winnowed down the list of possibilities.

I was running to lose a few pounds. I was running because I liked the rush of endorphins. I was running because I loved bleeding tension from my system and spilling it onto the neighborhood streets. I was running to regain a sense of control over what I could accomplish when my professional life had stripped that from me. I was running because it made my world spin slower, leaving me grounded and, I suspected, that much closer to happiness.

I knew that wasn't all of it. I was running because whatever lesson I'd started to learn way back in Houston was still waiting for me, just on the other side of the marathon finish line. And one thing I knew for sure: I was no longer racing my dad. Even more important, I was no longer racing his ghost.

Still, at that particular moment, legs spread straight out in opposite directions, bent over just enough to feel gravity pull my gut toward the floor, stifling a scream from the burn of taut muscles pulled tight from my kneecap to my crotch, I didn't exactly feel as if I'd figured out the secret of life.

Thirty-eight days. It had been thirty-eight days since my last run. In the quiet of the predawn darkness of December 20, 2008, I carefully followed Monica's instructions for reentry: After stretching, I walked for ten minutes at a relaxed pace designed to warm up my leg muscles. Then I alternated running and walking, starting with a five-minute jog that left me gasping. I then walked for five minutes, jogged again for five, and walked once more for five. I wrapped up my first exercise in more than a month by jogging three more minutes and calling it a day.

I was wasted, my tank drained dry. A post-run reverie washed over me as the endorphins started their dependable surge through my system, my body's way of guaranteeing I'd be back for more. But the reality was disturbing. The New York Marathon was ten and a half months away and I couldn't run a second more than five minutes.

Following Monica's instructions, I took the next day off to let my muscles recover from the shock of being used again. The day after that, I popped out of bed at 5:30, full of resolve, to stretch and hit the road. In the wet December cold, I jogged for eleven minutes, walked for five and a half, jogged for two and a half, and then finished up with an eleven-minute walk. My legs felt fine—no tightness, soreness, or pain of any sort in my left leg, and just the slightest twinge in my right calf, which I attacked when I got home with five minutes of stretching that made it disappear almost entirely.

The next day was even better. I ran sixteen minutes before my lungs gave out and I had to stop and walk. My legs felt great, entirely pain free. This was my third run in the past four days with my new stride: glutes under my spine, heels and toes hitting six and twelve on the clock. Given my performance over the past year, I wasn't going to draw any grand conclusions about my ability to sustain my training. But Monica had already reconnected me to the deep sense of contentment that running always had the potential to generate.

Walking in the predawn, early-winter darkness, my frozen breath dispersing in front of me in small, visible puffs, I felt a soothing afterglow, a sort of energized fatigue. I was spent from the run, but invigorated as well. If I didn't always like running, I always loved having run.

A warm front moved through on Christmas Day, bringing with it the kind of mild weather that let me shed a couple of layers of shirts and leave my hat and gloves at home. For the first time in nearly two months, I knocked out my 3.7-miler through downtown Bethesda, running twenty minutes straight before walking the rest of the way.

During the last six days of the year, I ran four times, the last on December 30, when I ran for more than twenty-seven minutes straight. On the one hand, as an indication of my chances of completing a marathon, it was nothing to brag about. On the other hand, just ten days earlier I couldn't make it more than five minutes. For now, I'd take my positive signs wherever I could find them.

New Year's is the holiday of choice for optimists, the hope of making major changes yet to be crushed by the repetition of corrosive patterns. I'd never been much of a New Year's Eve guy, but this one felt different. I couldn't wait for the ball to drop, the official end to a painful year.

Stina and I went low-key, filling our family-room coffee table with pizza boxes and watching a movie with the kids, who all fell asleep on the couch trying to stay up until midnight. The next morning, I woke up filled with determination. The marathon, scheduled for November 1, 2009, was ten months away. It really was now or never.

My first run of the year lasted twenty-nine minutes before walking, continuing my positive trend of running longer each time out. I felt lighter. The bathroom scale backed me up. But much more important, I could feel the New Year's spirit sticking with me, the fresh-start sensibility. Running down Wisconsin Avenue in Bethesda, taking a New Year's Day inventory, I was struck first by what was missing. There was no drama.

I'd spent many months trying to get my arms around the various strands of my life—work, family, health, sanity—as each spiraled away from me in every possible direction. Now I was confronting something appealingly binary.

I was going to either get out of bed in the morning or roll over and go back to sleep. I was going to put on my shoes and go running, or I was going to eat bagels and read the sports section. I was going to stretch, or I was going to continue to hobble down the street with swollen calves and climb steps like my grandfather. I was going to change my patterns, or I wasn't. In ten months I would have an indisputably simple way to judge how I'd done. I would finish the New York Marathon, or I wouldn't. It wasn't a process that would be dictated, shaped, or judged by the subjective whims of others. I would be the only one who controlled the outcome.

Six days into the New Year, I ran the entire Bethesda loop for the first time since Halloween, without walking a single step. Chugging up the last hill, two blocks before the end of the run, I was overtaken with a sense of possibility. In the two and a half weeks since I'd started to run, I'd gone from jogging five minutes to being able to run nearly forty. Two days later, it was forty-seven. I'd run six of the first eight days of 2009. Perhaps I'd finally buried the demons that had repeatedly sidetracked me and captured one of the most elusive components of making a change—momentum.

I knew I was onto something before dawn on January 13. My alarm went off at 4:30 and fifteen minutes later I was out on the streets making sure I got a run in before catching an early plane to Tampa. It took me a little more than fifty-two minutes, but I ran the whole thing—five miles. I spent the entire rest of the day shooting a story in Florida and glowing with well-being.

Rolling out of the hotel bed before sunup to keep my momentum the next day confirmed for me that I was in control of this process. I would decide whether I was going to get out on the street on any given day, regardless of whatever obstacles I needed to negotiate. The only thing I could control was not yielding to them. That's where my happiness was—tethered to whether I got my ass out of bed and onto the street for a run each morning. I ran two of the next three days on the city's iconic Bayshore Drive, to bring my total to thirteen runs in the first eighteen days of the year.

I came home from Tampa ecstatic over my perseverance. "Honey, it's all about dragging myself out of bed," I explained to Stina. "Nike was onto something. Their marketers are evil geniuses—'Just Do It.' The whole reason it's so effective is because it's so true."

She smiled cautiously. I'd said exactly the same thing to her three separate times over the past eleven months. She gave me a hopeful hug but didn't say a word, knowing I had one last test coming that carried the potential to derail me.

January 20 was Inauguration Day. The end of George Bush's presidency. The conclusion of my stint as the chief White House correspondent for CBS News. January 20. The official first day of the rest of my life.

Inauguration Day, like Election Day, didn't exactly turn out as I thought it would when I took the job. The swearing in of our nation's first African American president was the kind of event journalists dream of covering just once in their careers, the chance to literally write the first draft of history. And yet on this day, when the entire focus of the world was on Barack Obama, I was the guy assigned to chart the comings and goings of George W. Bush.

I arrived at Andrews Air Force Base just before dawn, where Mr. Bush would board an Air Force jet early that afternoon for his flight back to Texas. I cleared security, found a couch near a TV inside the terminal, and sat back with much of the rest of the world to watch the coverage for the next five hours. There was no way they'd be coming to me until after Barack Obama took the oath, at noon.

Once he was no longer president, Mr. Bush would climb aboard a helicopter on Capitol Hill, be taken to Andrews, duck into a hangar for a farewell rally, then climb aboard the same plane he'd flown in from country to country as the most powerful man in the world for one more flight—this one back to life as a private citizen in Texas. That was it. I'd have one or two chances to get a couple of words in on the telecast during the few minutes Bush was at Andrews, tops.

Three years at the White House, half a year away from home on the campaign trail, and I'd get two or three minutes out of eight hours of CBS News coverage. It was going to be a punch-to-the-gut kind of day.

Andrews was dark and frigid when I got there, my own little slice of Antarctica. The icy winds whipping between the buildings near the flight line were nearly incapacitating. My overcoat, heavily lined and usually warm, felt like little more than a Windbreaker. I thought there was a reasonable threat of death from exposure if I had to stand outside for more than twenty minutes in the Siberian winds blowing across the runways at Andrews. The laws of TV journalism forbade me from pulling on any kind of cap. Preventing hat-head trumped preventing frostbite.

I didn't see any other TV reporters. I wondered whether they might've set up their shots along another part of the tarmac. Or perhaps the other networks decided to have their anchors talk over a live picture in the studio of Bush departing Andrews, figuring the event would not be much more than a footnote on the day. Why waste a correspondent?

I watched the helicopter carrying Bush take off from the Capitol on TV. Twelve minutes later, the nation's newest former president was on the ground in front of me. I heard a calm, dispassionate voice from the control room in New York: "Jim, we're going to go to Dan first." As if I wasn't feeling small enough, I wasn't even going to be the first voice from CBS News to report my tiny portion of the Inauguration Day story. First, Katie would hear from Dan Bartlett, a former senior aide to President Bush whom CBS had hired as a consultant. Finally, when Dan had to get off the air to get on the plane with his old boss for the flight back to Texas, they came to me.

I'd been speaking for about a minute, describing the send-off speech Mr. Bush had made at the goodbye rally, when a director got in my ear to tell me to wrap it up. They didn't want to spend any more time than they had to on the tired old president. Not when there was a dynamic, new, history-making president getting ready to start his inaugural parade. As a producer in New York good-nighted me, the TV term for being told to shut down your satellite truck and go home, I felt as irrelevant as the guy I was covering.

My day was over. So was my time at the White House. I packed up as quickly as I could, jumped in my car, and headed for the exit gate. I wasn't entirely sure who left Andrews's airspace more quickly—George W. Bush or me.

I pulled up to our house just as coverage of the parade was starting. Inauguration Day was a school holiday in Washington, and Stina had the kids in front of the TV to make sure they drank in as much of the history as possible. She knew I'd be walking in the door alienated and low. She'd built a fire, hoping to create some coziness to greet the brooding mess of a husband she expected. It was perfect. The pop and hiss of the wood was as soothing as the dance of the flames.

I took off my trench coat and sunk into our brown leather sectional sofa, the same one that had hosted my orange-peeling sessions during *American Idol*. The fire quickly chased away the chill from seven hours on the frozen tarmac. The self-pity was a little trickier to dislodge.

Stina treated it with a bowl of chicken stew, two large pieces of challah toast dripping with butter, and a glass of red wine. It didn't take as long as I would've thought. By my second bowl of stew, watching Barack Obama walking down Pennsylvania Avenue to the White House, I could feel myself lighten. While everyone was swept up with Obama and the many challenges greeting the start of his presidency, I was thinking of Bush, if not identifying with him. Here we both were, getting ready to simplify our lives.

I had nothing left to wrestle to the ground. There was no more confusion to understand, no more bitterness to process. It was time to move on. Settling in with Stina and the kids under blankets in front of a fire, I sank deeper into the couch. In the short term, I'd be back doing the kind of journalism I most enjoyed. In the long term, I hadn't a clue. In between, there was a marathon to run.

The pale olive-green easy chair in my bedroom wasn't much to look at, but it got the job done. In fact, by the beginning of 2009 it had become my most favored possession. I spent hours planted in it, developing an almost embarrassing dependency on my bedroom chair.

When Stina first bought it, I'd been put off more by its feel than by its color, which was remarkable only because the particular shade of green, which the manufacturer insisted upon calling "sage," was wholly repellent. "Mid-flu mucus" would have been much more accurate. But the feel of the chair was far worse, like trying to cozy into cardboard. I begged her to send it back the first time I sat in it.

Stina told me to give it time. A week later, after dinner, I asked her to come upstairs with me. In the bedroom I made a big show of trying to sit down in the chair, pointing out that after seven straight nights of trying to plop into it after work, the cushions were still so stiff I could barely dent them.

"Honey, please? Can't we just send it back?"

She looked down at the carpet. After nearly twenty years together, I knew immediately that the chair would never be returned.

She loved it and was sure that eventually I would as well. As the one who'd have to arrange for the company to come pick it up, she was prepared to wait me out.

So the chair sat in our bedroom for the next several months accumulating dirty clothes that needed to be washed or clean clothes that needed to be folded. When there was no more laundry to be done, piles of books took the place of piles of clothes. Some nights I'd wedge my laptop in between the books, or perhaps add a stack of CDs I wanted to download to our computer. I might throw my work bag on the chair when I got home from the bureau, or my gym bag on it after working out. Over time, all these did what I could not—they broke in the cushions. Once the chair was softened up, I started to spend hours sitting in it after work, often with a book and a cup of tea. Not that my chair provided me with a solitary retreat. It was more a front-row seat.

Our bedroom was on the second floor, just to the left of the staircase leading downstairs. The way Stina had positioned the chair in our room provided me with a perfect view of the top of the staircase and of all the action in the house at night. The kids would head from their rooms on the second and third floors to the kitchen downstairs for a snack and back up again, or to the dining room table, where they often did their homework. They couldn't make a move without my being aware of it, and I'd often stop them at our bedroom doorway for a progress report or beckon them in for a hug.

Emma, halfway through seventh grade, sought report cards full of As to anchor herself as the strong social winds of adolescence started to pick up. Her sterling bat mitzvah performance paired neatly with her straight As to provide a nice confidence boost.

About to turn eleven, William was a kid with a dry wit and a gift for making friends. Confident where his sister was diffident, he had a drawer full of T-shirts that reflected his slightly offbeat sense of humor. "Giraffes United Against Ceiling Fans" was my favorite. "It's All Fun and Games Until the Flying Monkeys Attack" was a close second. Will practiced his trombone cheerfully, though only after being harassed repeatedly. He'd developed an effective roundhouse kick in Tae Kwon Do. And he brought home report cards that included plenty of As as well as an occasional light slap on the wrist in the comments section: "Will needs to limit his socializing with his neighbors."

He was a warm and loving little guy, but his tendency to keep his deepest thoughts to himself plagued me. What Stina saw as his private nature, I read as a consequence of my having been gone too much.

At five, Bobby had settled comfortably into kindergarten, much to our relief. We'd had no idea whether he would be able to fashion enough routine out of his day to be comfortable. He was our little rule-follower. More than the other two, Bobby needed to know what was expected of him. If he understood what he needed to do—as well as when, where, and how he needed to do it—he was fine. Otherwise, he became an intimidated, agitated, overwrought mess, turning his palms up, shrugging his shoulders in confusion, his face streaked with anxiety and dissolving to tears. Toilet training had nearly broken us. But so far, it was so good, with Bobby hopping on his bus each morning and back off nearly every afternoon with smiles and bright spirits.

Stina had chosen the colors for our bedroom, where I'd sit each night in the green chair, charting the comings and goings of the kids. The walls were a tawny yellow, with an orange master bathroom. The throw pillows and blankets on our bed were soothing mustards, greens, and browns. Stina loved the colors of fall. "They're so tranquil," she'd said often. "Makes me feel like we sleep in a forest."

Stina wanted our bedroom to be a sanctuary, a place of respite from the stresses of daily life. We'd lived in the Chevy Chase house for two and a half years, but I hadn't noticed how fully she had met her objective until now. When I rushed off in the morning to the White House or collapsed in front of the TV when I got home, my focus had been elsewhere. But sinking into the broken-in cushions of my ugly chair, surrounded by the sounds of our kids and the tranquil colors of an autumnal forest, I was captive to the atmosphere Stina had created. For all the behind-the-scenes access I had to the

A-list White House life in Washington, the hours I spent in my green chair were my happiest there.

Sitting in my room the night after the Obama inauguration, my head in a golf magazine, I heard a muffled thump. I looked up to see Will in our doorway, sweatpants and T-shirt, socks but no sneakers. With his arm extended straight up, fingers outstretched, he was jumping, trying to touch the top of the doorframe. He didn't wait for me to ask what he was doing before volunteering an explanation.

"Dad, you know what Mr. Palmer told me today?" He paused to jump twice more, getting nowhere close to hitting the frame. "He told me I was looking good. We started the basketball unit today." Will stopped and caught his breath. "Mr. Palmer says I have a nice shot."

Team sports weren't his thing. Like nearly every other suburban kid, he'd played soccer in first and second grades. Then we moved to Washington, in time for Will to start third grade and experience his first asshole coach. He'd been at that point where natural talent was starting to emerge in a select few. While he clearly wasn't among the chosen, his easygoing personality would've made him the perfect candidate for "just having fun out there." But once this minor-league Great Santini ripped Will a new one for being out of position in a defensive scheme the Brazilian national team would've found too complex to implement, it was over for him. Watching from the sidelines, I wanted to kill the coach. Not for yelling at my kid as much as for snuffing out a spark in him. I could see it go, the tears flowing from the eyes of my confused son, like a chimney damper shutting off the flow of air to a flame that was already flickering. Will was done with team sports.

I kept telling myself that was fine, just fine. My standard paternal line had always been that I cared only about my kids' developing a passion. It didn't matter to me where they trained their focus—sports, drama, music, reading, Chinese, robotics—as long as they discovered the magic of intense connection. Still, baseball and basketball had provided me with my first experiences with passion and given me a way to stay in touch with my father. During the years he was withdrawing in so many other ways, a shared box score over English muffins brought us closer for a few minutes each morning.

Watching Will jump to touch my bedroom doorframe, I realized I hadn't fully given up on having some of that for myself. Yes, yes, yes. Of course I'd "honor his nature." Wasn't that the mark of the modern evolved father? He liked computers, video games, and science-fiction novels, but perhaps there was still room for cracking open the sports section and analyzing the standings together, father and son. My dream didn't have to die just yet.

Will had gone downstairs by the time Stina popped her head in the door. I told her about his jumping in the doorway. She raised her eyebrows hopefully. "I'm going to see if I can get some Wizards tickets," I declared, referring to Washington's NBA team. "And could you maybe keep your ears open if anyone has Georgetown tickets they're trying to get rid of? Or Maryland. American. George Washington," I continued, rattling off the college teams that played nearby. "Doesn't matter. I just want to get him to a game."

The next morning, January 22, I got to work and saw an e-mail telling me the executive producer of *CBS Sunday Morning* had bought my pitch to profile Craig Robinson, the head basketball coach at Oregon State University, who had a compelling backstory. A two-time Ivy League player of the year at Princeton, Robinson had gone on to a successful finance career in Chicago, making a ton of money. Raised in a working-class family that had scrapped it out on the South Side of Chicago, he'd been pulling down a high-six-figure income—and had all the homes, cars, and vacations that came with it. He was living the dream. Well, he was living a dream. But not his.

Coach Rob's heart wasn't in finance. It belonged to basketball. He may have been the richest guy in the room, but he wasn't the happiest. All the more rare, he knew it. So he took a 90 percent pay cut to get back into college coaching. Nine years later, he had taken over the Oregon State University program, a former national power that had become the cellar-dweller in the Pac-10 Conference. It was especially galling to Beavers fans that OSU had been regularly overshadowed and outplayed by its hated rival, the University of Oregon, in games so intense they were referred to as "the Civil War." Heading into his first Civil War game against Oregon, Coach Rob was beginning to make strides in his mission to return OSU to its former glory. This was a terrific story about a man who'd made an intriguing midcourse correction once he realized the suit he'd been wearing for the previous decade no longer fit.

Oh—and he was Michelle Obama's older brother.

I was thrilled. For the first time since leaving the White House, I'd be shooting a story that excited and intrigued me—flying to Oregon to hang out with a major college basketball team, go to their biggest game of the year, and then tell millions of people about the experience. It was one of those professional experiences that left me feeling as if I should've been paying CBS, not the other way around. I came home that night and excitedly described the whole thing to Stina, not just the story I was about to cover but how it was a model for my future professional happiness.

"Honey," I said to Stina that night, from the comfort of my green chair, "think about it. If this is what I get to do, if these are the stories I get to tell, then leaving the White House is going to be the best thing that ever happened to me." She nodded, tacking back to our jumping boy.

"Wouldn't it be great if you could take Will with you?" she asked. Having listened to my repeated laments of not being there enough for Will, she'd been expecting a reaction other than the blank expression on my face. She pressed on. "Weren't you just talking about trying to get some tickets to a game? Spark a flame? Wouldn't taking him with you on this trip be even better?"

I shot her down reflexively. "Stina, you're going to just have to trust me on this," I said a touch too quickly. "It wouldn't work." The idea of flying my kid cross-country to go on a shoot with me left me highly uncomfortable. It struck me as vaguely unprofessional, something done by B-listers who weren't properly focused on their responsibilities. The last thing I wanted was Coach Robinson wondering what kind of clown had shown up with his fifth-grader in tow. Instinctively, my concerns about my professional image trumped my fears that I wasn't spending enough time with Will.

Off the top of my head I started listing reasons why it wouldn't work. Will would miss school, he'd be a distraction, he'd make my travel more difficult, he'd be in the way. Irritated, Stina shrugged her shoulders and walked out of the room. I went back to my magazine.

The next day was Friday, January 23. I got up at 5:00 and headed out into the darkness for a run. Over the past few weeks, every couple of runs, I'd been mixing in a 5-mile loop with my standard 3.7-mile tour of downtown Bethesda. So far I'd been unable to complete the longer loop without stopping to walk, but I was getting close. As I walked the half a block from our front porch to the corner where I started all my runs, I cleared the time from my last run off my watch and started to rotate my arms from the shoulder blades to loosen my upper body. I tightened the waistband on my sweatpants, wondering if this would be the day I'd run the entire five miles without stopping.

It wouldn't be. Forty minutes in, a little more than a mile from home, I felt a slight twinge in my left calf. Monica had been militant about what to do at the first and smallest sign of a problem. If I felt something, anything, even the slightest, barely noticeable pain, she'd ordered me to stop running immediately, stretch, and walk it in from there. It had happened only twice since I'd started to run again in December. Each time her instructions worked perfectly.

This time was no different. I stopped and stretched and walked it in. Climbing my front steps, I felt fine. I was a little disappointed I couldn't make it all five miles, but other than that, it was a standard end-of-the-week run. Except there was never anything standard about January 23. This one made it nine years since my father died.

In the shower, the hot water rolling off my back as I pushed off the back wall and continued to stretch my calf, I realized I hadn't been to the cemetery in more than a year. This was the kind of thing I thought about every January 23, taking inventory of his presence in my life, how much it had faded or intensified during the past year.

The steam in the shower loosened my leg muscles. Within a few minutes there wasn't a trace of pain in my calf. Relieved, my mind wandered to the state of the landscaping around my father's headstone.

He'd bought a big plot at Elmwood Cemetery, just around the corner from our family synagogue. It was a peaceful graveyard, nestled in a working-class immigrant neighborhood of New Brunswick. Depending on the time of day and the direction of the breezes, you might hear kids playing soccer in an adjacent park or perhaps the traffic on the main artery that bordered the cemetery's east side.

My dad never thought he'd beat all four of my grandparents into the ground. Since his was the first grave dug, we hadn't known what to expect when it came to the grass growing in. During the first few years, my mother would often call the caretaker to complain that the grass wasn't taking root quickly enough. She was disturbed by the perfect outline of his coffin formed by the rectangle of brown dirt dotted with tufts of grass blades. It made perfect sense to me—my father wasn't a guy who was going to be easily absorbed back into the earth without some sort of protest. But my mother hated it, as if she needed to see grass, not dirt, before she could move on.

I came out of the shower and asked Stina if we could put Elmwood on our itinerary for our next trip to New Jersey. Something about hobbling down those stairs just after Election Day and coming face-to-face with my father's exhilaration at the marathon finish line had left me needing to visit.

Over the years, I'd stared at that photo dozens of times. But only in the past few months had I started to understand it. It should have been clear cleaning out his office after he died, packing up his wall of framed certificates, medals, and plaques, where it was literally on display. Not just memorabilia from this New York Marathon, but a certificate of achievement from the 1978 Edison Recreation Department Run-A-Thon (ten miles in 77:41), another for the 1982 Princeton Half Marathon (1:47:37.4, for 816 out of 2008 finishers), and his finish-line photo and medal for the 1985 New Jersey Waterfront Marathon (3:57:32 at the age of forty-nine). And just in case anyone thought he was slipping as he closed in on fifty, the next frame held the certification of his finish in the 1987 Marine Corps Marathon, where he once again came in under 3:30, clocking a 3:29:41 at the age of fifty-one.

It should have been clear then, but it wasn't. That was his joy. For him, the accomplishment was the time, the achievement chronicled precisely to a tenth of a second. Each medal and plaque was a tangible piece of evidence illustrating that in his understanding of success, destination beat journey. He had managed to do what I patently had not, apply his rules of life to the rules of running. That definition worked well for him. For me, it was ass-backward.

Heading down Connecticut Avenue on the ninth anniversary of his death, I realized that I'd rigged the game against myself. I was seeking happiness by following a set of rules inherited from my father, only I was attempting to do him one better. Never mind that I couldn't—he was simply a much better runner—I'd never asked whether those rules worked for me. Hell, they hadn't even worked for him.

By the time I pulled into the garage across from the bureau, I was thinking about the World's Fair, and my father's strong arms pulling me out of the Small World boat. I parked, walked across the street to my office, picked up the phone, dialed the CBS travel agent, and asked her to book another ticket to Oregon.

The following weekend, Will and I headed off to see Coach Robinson. As we climbed into our rented white Chevy Blazer at the airport in Portland, I heard Will's deadpan from the other side of the SUV. "Man's car for a man's trip," he said as he opened the passenger door. I started to giggle.

Looking at each other across the armrest, we bumped knuckles. Over the years, I'd tried to pass down my father's lesson about the importance of a good handshake on that day we went to Yankee Stadium when I was a kid. Will had just done me one better.

He fiddled with the radio as we headed south down I-5 until he found an all-1970s station. Driving into the dull gray sky of a Pacific Northwest winter afternoon, belting out "Bohemian Rhapsody" with Will at the top of my lungs, I felt twinges of Scrooge waking up on Christmas Day. It hadn't been too late.

The next morning, we got up early for Coach Robinson's pre-dawn practice. Will was the perfect partner. Unlike just about every day at home, he hopped out of bed without a word of complaint to take his morning shower. At practice, he gave everyone he met a firm handshake just as I'd instructed, remembering to squeeze firmly, look them squarely in the eyes, and clearly say his name. The knuckle bump in the Blazer had been just for me.

Every time I had to leave him alone to focus on the story, he'd pull out a book, stick his nose in it, and quietly stay out of the way. He was starting to make me feel like an idiot, revealing with his perfect behavior that whatever reasons I'd come up with about why it wouldn't work to bring him were utter horseshit. I didn't look like a clown bringing my fifth-grader. I looked like a dad who knew exactly what he was doing, a man with a plan of his own.

During the main interview with Coach Robinson, in a quiet VIP room at the top of the football stadium, I asked Will to sit in a chair at a long conference table to the left of where the cameras were set up. I wanted him out of the way as I conducted the interview, but still close enough to see everything. He wasn't in my direct line of sight, but in the middle of the interview, out of the corner of my eye, I saw him stand up. I wondered what he was doing, but I wasn't about to stop the interview just as Coach Robinson was getting to the good stuff, telling me how he took Barack Obama to a playground pickup game in Chicago two decades ago to see what kind of game his sister's new boyfriend had. And I certainly wasn't going to stop it to find out what the hell my ten-year-old was up to.

Careful to stay out of camera range, Will walked over to the corner where we'd piled our jackets and started to delicately sift through the pile. I wasn't amused. As the thought started to creep into my head—"See, I knew this wasn't a good idea"—and my irritation began to spike, my son found his down jacket in the pile, pushed it to his face, and sneezed, muffling the sound so it wouldn't disrupt the interview.

The next day, as the clock ticked down the final seconds of a close game with Oregon, the crowd inside Gill Coliseum started to go bleacher-shaking nuts. The public-relations folks had been great, giving a press pass to Will as well. They were the golden tickets that gave us the run of the place. As Oregon State dribbled down the court to take the last shot, we were standing at the edge of the tunnel that led to their locker room, just off the corner of their court, no more than fifteen feet from the action.

I put Will in front of me, wanting to have both arms on his shoulders in case the fans stormed the court and I needed to move him quickly away from the mob. I looked down at him. He was biting the inside of his right cheek, sliding his pursed lips around to the left side of his face. I knew that move.

I'd just turned seven when my father and I visited Yankee Stadium one winter day in 1970, back when the team still held an off-season open house for fans. Our next-door neighbor, Mr. Filippine, had snagged the invitation. A jolly man with a big heart and a pronounced stutter, he didn't have any kids. So he invited my father and me.

The Yankees gave their guests a tour of the clubhouse and had a couple of second-tier players stand in front of their lockers for autographs and pictures. The team president, Mike Burke, greeted everyone with a handshake. Right before we left, my dad wandered over to a large white canvas cart in the middle of the locker room. It was the kind you'd see piled high with dirty shirts at an industrial laundry. This one was filled with bats. Real bats that belonged to real New York Yankees. My dad grabbed one and handed it to me.

"Get in your stance, Jimmy. Let me take a picture." Still wearing my blue Mighty Mac winter coat, with its large T-shaped metal zipper pulled halfway up my chest, I got into my best batter-up position. In the middle of the New York Yankees clubhouse, holding a New York Yankees bat, I stood in the adoring gaze of my father, with my arms back and fists together slightly over my right shoulder, holding the bat at a forty-five degree angle, ready to swing for the fences. He snapped the picture, catching me biting the inside of my right cheek, which I could reach because I'd slid my pursed lips around to the left side of my face. It was the only way I could contain my overwhelming joy.

Now my son had his own too-much-to-handle moment unfolding. Coach Rob's team came down the court and, right in front of us, nailed a basket with three seconds left to win the game. With security guards holding back the erupting crowd, all of us—coaches, players, Will, and I—were swept into the locker room, where the players started dancing and chanting in celebration. One of the players, an exuberant, gangly nineteen-year-old named Kevin McShane, trained his wide, goofy smile on Will and demanded, "High five, little man." Will slapped hands with him, and I turned my head. I wasn't sure about the propriety of a reporter bringing his boy into a locker room. But I certainly knew the reporter shouldn't be seen crying.

It was a few minutes before daybreak on a late-February morning when I got to the base of the hill on Brookville Road, dark enough for cars to still need their headlights but light enough so their beams threw off shadows against the ground when they hit something solid. I'd just passed a row of stores—a small grocery, a pharmacy, a barbershop, a dry cleaner, and finally the high-end home-decorating shop that was our village's cradle of snobbery, exuding a distinctly unwelcoming air the only time Stina had ever stepped foot inside. Still, it served an important purpose on my morning runs, marking the mental starting line for the last hill of most of my loops.

Despite the frigid temperatures, I felt great as I ran along that last stretch, infused with the power of momentum. I'd been able to sustain more than two solid months of training since I started back the week after Emma's bat mitzvah. The idea that I could get myself into the kind of shape required to finish a marathon, for so long too preposterous to contemplate, had started to hold a glimmer of possibility.

Since it was so early, I was running in the lane for oncoming traffic. I preferred that whenever possible. The smoother pavement meant fewer chances to trip than running on sidewalks, with their occasional jutting slabs. I wasn't worried about cars driving in my direction. Brookville was a two-lane road, with a speed limit of twenty-five miles per hour. I'd have had plenty of time to move back onto the sidewalk if I saw any lights in the distance moving toward me. And as I started to climb the last hill, all was unbroken gray-blue dawn. There wasn't a car in sight.

It was a fairly sharp incline, a couple of hundred yards long, which finally leveled off into two short blocks that signaled the end of the run. The temperature was in the high teens, but I was layered with a short-sleeve shirt designed to wick away sweat and a new turtleneck and cold-weather top combination made from some cutting-edge, high-tech insulating material. I'd added a warm wool hat and a pair of running gloves with Day-Glo green stripes. I could feel the cold on my face, but it was no match for the joy of having the frozen streets to myself.

It had been another pain-free run. Monica's stretching regimen had produced such a long, uninterrupted string of no-problem running that I'd gradually stopped worrying about calf pain and shin swelling at all. They seemed to be as much a part of my past as the twenty pounds I had dropped. I picked up the pace as I moved up the hill.

I heard a car coming up behind me. Since I was on the far side of the other lane of traffic, I didn't feel the need to move back onto the sidewalk. I could sense the beam from the headlights as it hit my back, casting my shadow out in front of me and projecting it up the hill. I looked up, taken by the way the shadow elongated my body and smoothed out my stride, presenting a pleasantly distorted version of myself that was taller, more graceful, and much more appealing. I got lost for a moment watching my shadow-self eat up the challenging hill in long, loping strides.

My reverie was punctured by a series of quick, rhythmic slaps on the sidewalk behind me. I turned to look over my left shoulder and saw a much faster runner approaching quickly. Just as I'd done all those months ago on the Outer Banks when that young mother zoomed past me with her stroller, I tried to make eye contact and nod hello to the only other person sharing this stretch of empty road. And just like that mother in North Carolina, he looked right past me.

He was short, with a stocky build, covered in a couple of layers of Patagonia on top and wearing black running tights. Figuring he didn't see me in the dim light, I tried again. I turned my head back toward him and nodded again, this time adding an audible "Good morning." My voice was on the softer side but certainly loud enough for him to hear.

No response. His eyes never moved to acknowledge the greeting, remaining fixed directly in front of him. I read him as intense more than rude, so focused that he hadn't heard a thing.

At first I thought I detected a slight grunt back at me, but quickly realized he was just breathing hard coming up the hill. He looked to be somewhere in his mid-thirties. I smiled as he blew past me, this fellow so focused on what lay ahead that he missed the guy ten feet away trying to bid him a good morning. I smiled to myself, thinking about what the next few years might have in store for him, when he started to try to reconcile what the vision for his life he formed in his twenties had actually yielded in his forties. Silently I wished him good luck. He had no idea what was heading his way.

January and February had injected me with a much-needed booster shot of optimism, a sense of possibility that maybe, just maybe, I'd finally figured out what was required to sustain my training. It wasn't fun to leave my warm bed in the morning, and certainly wasn't easy, but it also wasn't something I had to convince myself to do. The sense of control and progress provided by my daily morning run brought me a dependable measure of happiness I was unwilling to do without. Still, while I thought I was now on my way, I'd been down this road before. I couldn't be sure.

During the first week in February, when I was with Will in Oregon for the Coach Robinson piece, I'd missed three days in a row.

There was simply no way I could leave him alone in a hotel room while I went for a run. This was the first serious challenge to the momentum I'd been building since starting back again in December. On the flight home, I felt a twinge of panic. Well, a twinge in the same way a tsunami is a ripple. Was I about to sink back into my damaging pattern of running for a month, hitting some obstacle, then looking up after several weeks of inactivity to realize I'd done it again? I could sense a familiar shadow hovering. I decided to disperse it with an immediate show of stiff resolve.

I got home and reeled off five days in a row, a crucial reminder that I was in charge of my training. Momentum wasn't something created passively when the planets aligned correctly. I created it every day that I dragged myself out of bed, laced up my shoes, stretched, and went for a run. I had an obligation to produce that for myself every day that I could. If I hadn't misunderstood the Bob Axelrod rule to "never say no," I'd certainly misapplied it.

"Never say no"? I'd limited the practice to my career decisions, thinking those were the most important I'd face. I had some simpler ones in front of me now—roll over or get up, sleep or run—but they were even more crucial. I needed to refine my thinking. The only person I should never say no to was myself.

The realization was well timed, because I was entirely out of excuses. My newest loop, a five-miler with seven separate hills, reminded me of that every time I ran it. The fourth hill was the killer, a sharp quarter-mile incline up a section of Connecticut Avenue that served as one of Washington's main arteries out to the suburbs. Coming up the hill, six lanes of traffic ran back and forth to my right, while the squat buildings of a 1970s apartment complex sat to my left. A library and a firehouse greeted me at the top, where the hill flattened out.

Each time I got to this section of Connecticut, as the sidewalk grade steepened, I struggled. Halfway up the slope, the part of me that wanted so badly to stop would start to debate the rest of me. Lungs burning and legs aching, I'd have to fight off the idea that it was okay to walk. I'd run the loop half a dozen times since January and hadn't given in yet. The Wednesday after returning from Oregon was no exception. As I approached it, my body posed the familiar question: "Do I have to keep going?" I didn't linger on it; there was no real consideration of walking up the hill this one time. I chased the thought away the same way I always did, by pumping my legs. In less than a minute, I was at the top of the hill, relieved to know that indeed, this hadn't been the first time I yielded to the temptation. Relieved, but not surprised.

It's where my thinking had been heading. I couldn't blame a bad calf for not running. Monica's stretching regimen had taken care of that. I couldn't blame my demanding job—I was no longer at the White House. I wasn't eating poorly. I wasn't drinking too much. I wasn't having any trouble sleeping. There was my elegant binary— do or don't, my choice—staring me in the face. There was nothing left to do but somehow get myself to the top of the hill. And I did.

I ran five out of seven days the first week of February and followed that up with five out of seven the next week. By the middle of the third week of February, continuing to run with the same frequency, I'd safely driven off my fears of falling into damaging old patterns.

Getting up on Thursday morning of that third week of February, I looked at my runner's watch. It was the nineteenth. It had been one year since I'd stood on that platform in Houston, one year since I'd watched Barack Obama stride across the stage, one year since I'd realized my spirit was broken, my body bloated, and my once sure-footed journey was becoming a stumble down the wrong path. It had been one year since I'd read Dave's e-mail in the Toyota Center, one year since I'd committed myself to getting in good-enough shape to run a marathon.

One year later, I liked what I saw when I looked in the mirror. I weighed 195 pounds, 21 less than I did when I started. I was able to run five miles without stopping, in under ten minutes a mile. After three false starts, I'd harnessed enough momentum to sustain a training schedule of five runs a week. I'd found out the hard way that doing work I didn't love wasn't the best route to a promotion. I was a better husband and a more present father. A year later Danny Leong's suits fit almost perfectly. If anything, they were a little loose.

When Dave had sent that e-mail a year ago, I'd looked at my dad's marathon times and reflexively started to calculate whether I could run the 26.2 miles faster than he had at the same age. It was no different from what I'd done for years whenever I got a raise, plugging my new salary into a website that converted it into a dollar amount for 1976, or 1983, or any other year I chose to let me see if I was making more than he had at my age. But as I'd learned in the past year, plotting my course by his compass, aspiring to make more money than him or to run a faster marathon was a lousy route to greater happiness. In fact, racing his ghost generally worked against it.

I hadn't stopped measuring myself. How far, how fast—it was still my metric of choice, the best way to chart my progress while whipping myself into shape. But I was convinced there was a difference: I'd stopped using his yardstick as mine. And as spring rolled around, my training started to provide the same kinds of clear, unmistakable signs of renewal as the tulips popping through the mulch in the beds next to our front steps.

I started slowly in March, hampered by a busy travel schedule and a late-winter snowstorm that limited me to just nine runs during the first eighteen days of the month. I woke up on the nineteenth wanting a reality check on my fitness. I decided to try my newish five-mile loop, the one with seven hills. Three miles in, I was sailing along so smoothly I lost track of where I was. I didn't notice I'd tackled the long hill, the one in front of the library and fire station, until I was at the top of it. Even then I didn't feel the least bit drained. I kept pushing all the way home, looking down at my black-and-silver Timex runner's watch. The numbers read 48:11—my best time for the loop so far by 23 seconds.

The ensuing endorphin rush was a bonus—producing the kind of glow I'd thought available only in a nineteenth-century Chinese opium den—as I marked my new best time in my journal.

The next day, I knocked off my touchstone 3.7-miler through Bethesda a minute and a half faster than my previous best time for it. This was starting to feel like some sort of breakthrough, the pay-off for the pain.

My legs had more bounce and spring, a resilience I owed to Monica. She'd been after me to join a gym, wanting me to reduce the pounding on my legs from the asphalt while still developing my aerobic capacity. Instead of five or six runs a week on the pavement, she wanted to see three or four, supplemented by a couple of sessions on the treadmill or the elliptical machine. In February, I'd given in and joined the Washington Sports Club. Once again, Monica had been right.

On Saturday, April 4, the day before we headed off to Orlando for spring break, I woke up to a cold and blustery day in Washington. Bolstered by how far and how fast I'd been running recently, I'd planned to see just how far I could go. I had an idea of a loop that was six miles plus, but wanting to be precise, I'd measured it again in my car the night before.

The wind was howling directly into my face, almost standing me up straight, hitting me most forcefully on the hills. Each time I hit one I leaned forward to try to cut through it. The new route included the longest, steepest hill yet. I'd driven it before, on the way to get takeout from our favorite Chinese restaurant, and had wondered what it would be like to run, but I never pictured climbing it head-long into a twenty-mile-per-hour wind.

I hit the hill and didn't stop. I felt a deeper fatigue in my upper thighs than my usual loops produced, and I was breathing heavier, but I kept putting one foot in front of the other, surprising myself by how quickly I conquered it. It wasn't easy, but it never felt insurmountable.

At the top I still had two miles to go, but they were flat. The hard part was over. The brutal wind was now at my back. Just under twenty minutes later, running right down the middle of our dead-end street, I broke the tape at the imaginary finish line extending from my front steps. I'd done it. I'd run 6.2 miles. And I'd done it in less than an hour: 58:07 to be exact.

This was my longest run since we'd lived in Washington, and for many years before that in Montclair. I showered, changed into sweats, and collapsed in a happy heap on our couch, deep in the hold of the familiar glow. My progress was measurable, dependable. I wasn't going to beat my dad, but neither was this marathon going to beat me.

I fell into a deep nap. Stina woke me an hour later, since we'd promised the kids we'd start our spring break the right way, going out for breakfast. We headed to the Tastee Diner in Silver Spring, a 1940s classic with a red-and-white awning, a dozen red vinyl spinning stools mounted on steel posts in front of the counter, and a shiny stainless-steel cupboard holding three rows of homemade cakes and cream pies.

We found a parking spot half a mile from the restaurant. The temperature had dropped since my run and the wind had picked up even more. I looked down at Bobby as we walked. He was wearing jeans and a denim jacket over a hooded, long-sleeve black-and-white striped shirt. It wasn't nearly enough in the biting wind. He was shivering.

I scooped him up and cuddled him to my chest as we walked. When he hadn't stopped shivering a couple of minutes later, I unzipped my brown Patagonia fleece top. One month shy of six, Bobby was still small enough for me to hold him tight to my body, while I pulled both halves of the front of my fleece around him and re-zipped it over him, creating the full kangaroo-pouch effect.

Bobby had been wrestling with one of his periodic bouts of intense anxiety. A few days earlier, his best pal, Daniel, had thrown up on him during their bus ride to school. The aides said Bobby had handled the whole thing like a champ, making it easy for everyone by not crying or complaining. He simply slipped into the generic spare change of clothes the school nurse kept for such emergencies and went about his day like a brave little man.

No one even bothered to call Stina, because Bobby seemed so matter-of-fact about the whole deal. But underneath, the ill-fitting pants and shirt had heated Bobby's cauldron of fretful anxiety to a full boil. Ever since the great bus-vomit trauma, he hadn't stopped chattering to Stina and me about the perpetual state of vigilance now required of us. "Dad, Mommy promised she would give the nurse some of my clothes to keep at school. Daniel could throw up on me again. I don't want to wear the clothes in the nurse's office."

But as we walked, Bobby ensconced in my fleece, having slid his arms snugly up the sleeves along the tops of my arms, his mood changed. He went quiet for half a block, nestling his head into my chest. Then he leaned back against the zippered fleece, craning his head from the neck to say what he'd obviously just been turning over in his mind. "You know, Dad," he said with his trademark matter-of-fact delivery of some precocious observation, "when I'm a dad, I think I'll do this with my kids. They'll ask me where I learned it. I'll tell them my dad used to do it."

A waitress led us to a long rectangular table at the back, in the diner's modern addition. Sitting with Stina to my left, Will next to her, Bobby across from me, next to Emma and her best friend, Anna, I felt warm and weather-beaten. The waitress set two large glasses of water in front of me, along with the grapefruit half and bowl of oatmeal I'd ordered. I leaned over to Stina and softly repeated the same two words I'd whispered when we'd stepped onto the bimah on Emma's bat mitzvah day: "Freeze it."

I kept up my training momentum during our week in Florida, waking early and running before our day trips to Disney and Sea-World. I'd been concerned, knowing I didn't have an encouraging track record when it came to exercising on vacations. But this time, I ran five out of seven days, including forty minutes on Friday, which would have been my father's seventy-third birthday. We flew home on Saturday, and I ended the week on Sunday the way I started it eight days earlier—with another 6.2-mile run.

This time there was no blustery wind, just warmer temperatures and a gentle breeze. I passed the steps in front of my house a minute and a half faster than I had the week before our vacation. Only this time I didn't stop, hooking a left around the block and continuing until the numbers on my watch said 1:00:00. For the first time in seven months, I'd run an hour straight.

I was on a roll. Nothing left me feeling more confident than a new personal best for how far or how fast I was able to run. A few weeks after spring break, in early May, I tackled that 6.2-mile loop again. I didn't exactly scamper up the nasty hill, but I got to the top feeling as if I hadn't exactly tangled with Everest, either. I continued toward home. Once again, as I broke the imaginary tape at the finish line in front of my house, I kept going, circling around a couple of blocks before heading back to my front steps.

My watch read 1:06:20 when I stopped. I walked into the house, still huffing hard for air, grabbed my keys, and hopped in my car to measure the extra distance I'd run. I pumped my fist with each tenth of a mile the odometer clicked off. One-tenth. Two-tenths. Three-tenths. I kept pumping until I reached nine-tenths of a mile, which meant I'd run 7.1 miles total—my first time over seven. I kept testing my body, and in my runner's journal I kept recording passing grades.

I needed something powerful and positive at that moment. When I'd wrapped up my post–White House contract with CBS the previous summer, we'd agreed I'd move back to New York as soon as possible after the inauguration. But neither side had counted on the economic crisis that would make selling a house just about impossible.

When Stina and I moved to Chevy Chase three years earlier, we'd bought a hundred-year-old farmhouse. With its beautiful deck over-looking a peaceful backyard that deer ran through and a gorgeous wraparound front porch, we figured it was as safe an investment as anything else. We'd taken great care of it, painting it inside and out, laying new carpets and floors, and renovating the attic to create two bedrooms for the boys.

For years, the way real estate had worked in Chevy Chase was no different than in Montclair, or in dozens of other zip codes around the country during the housing bubble. The house went on the market on a Wednesday, the seller's agent showed it to buyers' agents on Thursday, had an open house that weekend, collected multiple offers on Monday, and had it sold by Tuesday. The only question was how much the home would fetch over the asking price. Not anymore.

We'd put our home on the market the previous October. Forget selling it five days later; we hadn't sold it five months later. Or six months. Or seven months. My bosses were understanding, telling me to take the time we needed to find a buyer, even if that meant working out of Washington longer than either they or I had planned. I'd come to accept the lessons of both Paulson's pinkie and Coach Robinson's midcourse correction. I wasn't a CBS A-lister on an escalator going up, but there was a place for me producing the sorts of stories I loved. The place was in New York, however, and I had to get there.

By the time we cut the price enough to sell it in May, we'd taken a huge bath and lost all our equity. I suppose there were plenty of moons to howl at—ourselves for not renting in the first place when we came to Washington and buying too much house instead, our fast-talking real estate agent who seemed a little late to understand that the market had fallen apart, the Wall Street geniuses who had generated the subprime mortgage collapse that froze the housing market—but I couldn't quite work up much of a sustaining rage.

Yes, it was a loss well into six figures. But if we'd never come to Washington, I would've never bottomed out. If I'd never bottomed out, I would've never had the incentive to examine my approach to life. I would've continued chasing power and prestige in a town that held nothing for me, until I veered so far off course, I might never have found my way back onto the proper path. I could almost convince myself that the bath we took selling the house was the tuition for a big life lesson.

Besides, we had found a perfect place back in Montclair, a nineteenth-century stone carriage house on a dead-end street. The lot had been carved out years earlier from a number of large, heavily wooded adjoining backyards. We'd walked into the house on an early-spring day and opened the sliding glass doors that led down a couple of steps into a screened-in porch, where we sat on a cushioned wicker love seat. The light breeze blowing gently across the lawn was strong enough at the treetops to make the oak branches sway, shifting the patterns on the sun-dappled walls as they did. We felt as if we'd stumbled onto a woodsman's cottage nestled in a small clearing in an enchanted forest. Stina and I looked at each other and realized we were home.

Yes, we were selling our house in Washington at a monster loss, but we were buying the coziest home we'd ever set foot in for an equally depressed price in Montclair. I could finally tell my bosses I'd be coming back to New York at the end of June.

With the last major distraction created by our move to Washington three years earlier now cleared up, I focused on ramping up my training for the marathon that was closing in on six months away. While I knew my time would be well over my father's 3:29:58, there was the simpler matter of what, in fact, it would be. I'd built a solid base, able to now run comfortably for an hour or more a couple of times each week, plus several other thirty- to forty-five-minute loops. But I needed to start pushing myself well beyond what I'd come to think of as my limits. In mid-May, I knocked out an eight-mile run as part of a twenty-eight-mile week. Still, I needed ten-mile runs and thirty-mile weeks. And I needed to start producing them soon.

The first Sunday in June, I headed out on a 6.2-miler. In my head, before I started, I'd mapped out a way to extend it several miles, depending on how I was feeling. The way I'd figured it, the loop maxed out close to ten miles, maybe a little more.

I felt surprisingly strong as I passed the 6.2 mark and kept going, finishing the entire loop I'd sketched out but never measured. I hit my stopwatch and looked down to see 1:33:28. I couldn't believe it. I'd just run more than an hour and a half. At nine-minute miles—which I'd been clocking regularly—that would mean I'd run ten miles.

I walked up the front steps and giddily kicked open the front door, wanting desperately to let loose with "Stina, guess what? I ran ten miles!" But just before I opened my mouth, I was seized by both caution and nagging doubt. After all, it was a makeshift route I'd never run before. I wasn't entirely sure. Before I broke my arm patting myself on the back, I thought I should measure the loop.

I hopped in the car to trace the route. Coming up the last hill, where that super-fit runner in his thirties had blown by me without returning my hello on that frigid morning in February, I started to get a sinking feeling. My odometer read 9.6. I'd run those last few blocks dozens of times. I knew I had somewhere between three-tenths and four-tenths of a mile left. It was going to be close. I didn't want to acknowledge what my gut was telling me—that I was going to come up just short. But I knew it. I slowed the car, as if by driving slower I might be able to coax that last important tenth to turn on my odometer before I got to the finish. I was desperate for this to be a ten-mile run.

I passed the corner where I'd ended my run. I looked down on my odometer. Nope. Just as I'd expected, I'd come up short: 9.9 miles. I let out a good old-fashioned Bob Axelrod "Goddamn it!" as I smacked the center of the steering wheel with the outside end of my balled-up fist.

I had just finished my longest run in half a dozen years. My post-run weigh-in had me at 191.5 pounds, nearly 25 pounds lighter than when I'd started this whole process fifteen months ago. On the mental-toughness front, I'd been dog tired at the eight-mile mark, but I hadn't quit. I'd gutted it out. Yet I couldn't shake the disappointment. Somewhere around six miles I'd started fantasizing about writing "RAN TEN MILES" in big, bold letters in my running journal. And now, as good as I felt about everything I'd just done, I couldn't.

Pissed off as I was, I had no time to wallow. In four hours, Stina and I would be hosting a dozen of Bobby's kindergarten classmates for his sixth birthday party. Between our three children, this would be the twenty-eighth birthday party we'd thrown. The other twenty-seven, at various roller rinks, dance studios, and laser-tag battlegrounds, had taught us that nothing beat low-key when it came to marking another year. Stina had found a small theater company that was putting on a delightful production of one of Bobby's favorite bedtime stories, Strega Nona. There was a small room off to the side for pizza and cupcakes. Parents would drop their kids off at one and pick them up at three. Perfect.

While historically I'd never been an ogre at the kids' parties, I'd never been fully engaged, either. Facing the tyranny of the over-sugared five-year-olds, the chorus of frantic screams for juice boxes and ice cream, I'd always held back some small part of myself. I'm sure I came across as somewhat vacant, but it seemed essential to preserve some small measure of sanity amid the chaos. I was always smiling behind the video camera as Stina brought out one of her homemade cakes in the shape of Barbie or Pac-Man, and my affect was nothing as pronounced as that of my father, who'd famously exploded into a paint-peeling cry of "Bloodsuckers!" at one gathering of frenzied children, but it wouldn't have been terribly difficult to place me as a guy who felt that his kids' birthday parties were as much to be endured as enjoyed.

Not this time. As I greeted Bobby's playmates, my endorphins still steadily pumping out their mellow bliss, I found myself on a pleasant stroll through the usual birthday-party minefield. The room filled with the typical racket produced by a pack of kindergartners in tight quarters, requiring full-throated shouts at each kid to see whether they wanted apple juice or chocolate milk. We ran out of chocolate ice cream and barely avoided a vanilla-only riot. The un-charged battery on our video camera gave us about ninety seconds of footage before shutting down. The kids lollygagged when we tried to herd them into the theater, threatening to delay the start of the show. And yet I negotiated it all calmly with the look of a smack junkie three minutes after tying off, my eyes glazed with a delicious fatigue.

When Bobby's friend Doug, a sweet and slight little boy, was spooked by the loud volume and dramatic entrance of the scary witch thirty seconds into the play, I gently put my arm around him. Watching his face, I knew where this was going and guided him safely to the lobby, where we hung out for the remaining forty-five minutes of the play. Doug seemed torn as we watched the production on a monitor. There was no way he wanted to be in the theater, but he didn't want to deal with the embarrassment of not being able to handle it, either.

"Buddy, we did the right thing getting out of there," I reassured him, as we sat next to each other on brown metal folding chairs. "That witch was scary!" Doug nodded agreement, exuding a six-year-old's gratitude. Complicit in a mutual acknowledgment that we'd done the right thing, Doug relaxed into restored happiness. For my part, I stretched my legs and rethought my run. Who ran 9.9 miles only to obsess about the one-tenth not run?

There in the lobby of a children's theater, in the company of a six-year-old stranger, I could sense the clouds parting. How far, how fast? No, that simply wasn't the point—no matter whose yardstick I used, my dad's or my own.

Yes, I measured my progress with a stopwatch and a runner's journal, of course I did. Distance and speed were crucial metrics, they let me know I was getting fit, but they weren't the accomplishments I valued most. It was the quieter mind that descended on me during a run. That's what I was after. The joy of watching my shadowed, younger self race up a hill, the pleasure of less-labored breathing walking up the stairs at the office. The greater capacity I felt as a father and husband. It was the grounded feeling of calm I had stretching out my legs while the chaos of a six-year-old's birthday party raged all around me. That was it. A good run was like Bobby's birthday party. There was plenty to endure. But there was joy available as well. More than I'd ever imagined. It wasn't even especially well hidden. It was laced through the entire experience, if you only knew where to look.

The next weekend, we drove up to Long Beach Island. Peter, Leah, and Oz were in from San Francisco for a week to visit my mom. As my father had discovered more than thirty years earlier, Long Beach Island was ideal for a long run—flat, straight, and marked every mile.

I got up early that Sunday morning, eager to run before the breezes quickened. Peter hadn't been running much since he'd joined a swimming club and started doing laps around San Francisco Bay, but he wanted to run the first couple of miles with me. It was exactly five miles from my mom's house to the lighthouse toward the near end of the island. We started out in the opposite direction, ran a mile, then turned around. When we got back to my mom's corner, two miles into the run, Petey dropped off, yelled "Good luck," and sent me on my way.

The five miles to the lighthouse plus the two I'd already knocked out would make seven miles total. The only surprise for me was how uneventful it was ticking them off. I checked my watch as I ran through the shadow cast by the Barnegat Lighthouse: 1:03:15—nine minutes a mile, almost to the second. Not bad.

Still feeling surprisingly strong as I came up on the nine-mile mark, I started to negotiate with myself about how far I'd go. Ten miles wasn't going to be an issue, not the way I felt through miles seven, eight, and nine. Passing the ten-mile mark gave me a boost. Coming up a tenth of a mile short the week before was now just a funny story I'd tell about my training one day.

I hadn't given any thought to what I'd do once I made it past the ten-mile mark, mostly because I wasn't convinced I would. I suppose I figured if I did, I'd be so drained that I'd immediately stop running and start walking; that is, if I didn't collapse first. Which is why the most surprising part of passing the road sign that signaled ten miles was how fresh I felt. No part of me wanted to stop.

When I got to eleven still feeling strong, I set my sights on my mom's house. A mile later, I passed the corner of East Atlantic Avenue and Long Beach Boulevard, where I'd started with Peter 1:49:50 earlier.

I slowed down and let my disbelief evaporate in the face of the numbers on my runner's watch. Twelve miles. I'd just run twelve miles, the longest distance since my senior year in high school—twenty-eight years ago. Nothing, not even my reflex to place the run in some sort of glass-half-empty context—twelve miles wasn't even half a marathon—was about to rob me of the deep satisfaction washing over me.

I felt as if I was floating down I-95 as we headed back to Washington, holding hands with Stina and singing along with Journey's "Don't Stop Believing," the Plain White T's "Hey There Delilah," and whatever else the kids selected off their iPods. I had two weeks left in Washington to tie up some loose ends before heading back to New Jersey for good.

I kept running strings of numbers though my head. "Stina, check this out," I said across the front seat. "I'm doing twelve-mile runs. I'm knocking out thirty-mile-plus training weeks." I was doing a horrendous job of masking how self-impressed I was. "I'm under ten minutes a mile for twelve miles. Well under. Can you believe this, girl?"

She started to answer. "Jimmy, this is wonderful. I mean think about it. A couple of months ago you were just worried—"

I cut her off.

"Everything's right on track. Five months to go and I am right on track. What a process."

As if I had it all figured out.

I've long known my daughter, Emma, is much smarter than I am, ever since she interrupted my impassioned lecture to her and William about the importance of an optimistic outlook in life.

"So listen up, kids," I was holding forth somewhat self-righteously, building to the big teachable moment I probably forced on them too often. "Your glass needs to be half full, not half empty."

Emma didn't miss a beat. "But, Daddy," she interrupted, "what if your glass is half full of a liquid you don't like?" She was seven.

Another one of Emma's precocious pearls of wisdom guided our move from Washington back to Montclair and our new home. Not that I got it at the time.

Three years earlier, when we'd moved to Washington, we tried to establish some routines and rituals to help make the new city ours. One we'd come up with almost right off the bat was a family walk through the local Audubon nature preserve. We tried to get out there at least once every couple of weekends.

On this particular Sunday several months into our move, Emma and Will had gone running ahead of Stina and me, to lead the way down the path. I had Bobby, who was three at the time, on my shoulders, my hands gripping the backs of his lower legs. His little calves, each one a tight plum of muscle, fit perfectly into my palms. As he usually did when he rode on my shoulders back then, he'd crossed his arms at the wrists, forming a triangle with his forearms and chest that he pressed gently onto the top of my head like a three-corner hat. I couldn't see his face, but I always liked to picture him intensely focused with just a hint of a smile, like a rancher on his favorite horse, ambling through the back forty on a particularly beautiful day.

From our first nature walk, the path at the Audubon sanctuary was one of our favorite spots in Washington. Half a mile long, it started at the top of a small hill by an old mansion and wound down through thick woods to a small, brackish pond encircled by a raised walkway constructed of worn, rust-colored decking. It was late autumn and the shadows were starting to grow longer as the temperature dropped. I figured we had about forty minutes of sunlight left.

The route back to the car took us through a narrow slice of meadow, where we'd often see deer. Sure enough, there were four—a couple of grown does, a fawn that looked four or five months old, and, standing off on his own, a buck with a decent rack of antlers.

With the sun slipping behind the tops of the tallest trees and the scent of peat, earthy and damp, heavy in the woods, we started across the meadow, passing through small pockets of even-cooler air. It was the time of day in the time of year when the earth seemed to be yawning before settling in for a deep sleep.

We were three months into the school year. I was fully immersed at the White House, drinking from the fire hose and barely keeping myself from drowning. Already it was clear that my new job wasn't going to be any more family-friendly than my old one, despite what I'd promised Stina. The kids were still trying to settle into life at Chevy Chase Elementary School. Will, an intrepid social connector, was having an easier go of it than Emma, who was more cautious wading into the social pool and had yet to make any new friends. When Will regaled us at dinner with the details of his latest pal, Emma listened glumly.

Our car, a six-year-old dark-red SUV, was parked in a lot next to the mansion where we'd started the walk. Stina, Bobby, and I got back first. I cupped my hands around my mouth and shouted back down toward Emma and Will, who were lollygagging their way up the hill, testing the mellow mood the nature walk always created for Stina and me.

"Hey, guys," I yelled, "come on. Let's get going." Emma was scowling, scrunching up her nose to create the same three sharp creases on the bridge that had signaled anger and frustration ever since she'd been a toddler. I herded everyone into the backseat for the ride home. Bobby slid in first, crawling along the top of the bench seat to get to his booster. Will got in next, reaching across Bobby's seat to help him buckle up. Emma was last to get in, angrily pulling the door hard so it slammed shut just a little too loudly. I sat on my instinct to snap around with a stern glare to let her know she was out of line.

As I looked in the rearview mirror and saw her beautiful, sullen face, I was glad I'd chosen honey instead of vinegar.

"Come on, Beanie," I said softly, using the nickname I'd given her in the delivery room when she was not yet an hour old. It was my most dependable method of sending a shot of tenderness her way. I tried to meet her eyes in the mirror. "Hold it together until we get home."

"Dad, we're not going home," she shot back with a surprising edge. "We're going to our house. Chevy Chase is where our house is. Montclair is our home."

We moved back home to Montclair the second week in July, the eighth time in twenty years Stina and I had set up a new home together. But this was different. Each of the other times, I'd measured success by how fast we moved out. A new house meant a new position in a new city—all unmistakable evidence of my continued climb up the career ladder. As the moving trucks pulled away from our new home, I was floored to realize how profoundly unhappy that constant impermanence had left me. I'd never had a house before, or a life for that matter, where success was defined by staying put. I had both now.

It was more than the location—a five-minute walk to a vibrant village full of shops, restaurants, a bank, a post office, a movie theater, and a train to Manhattan. It was more than our simple but elegant dining room, with its own fireplace, where thirty seconds after stepping into it for the first time, we envisioned hosting Thanksgivings for years to come. It was more than the soothing sense of sanctuary I enjoyed each time I walked in the door after work and headed to the screened-in porch with Stina, to share a glass of wine in the gentle pine-scented breeze blowing lazily across our backyard.

This was deeper than location, or architecture, or even place. This was a matter of fit. Over the years, I'd flown into so many different airports to come home. Looking down at the lights of a city below as we circled had always provided an incorruptible real-time gut check about my feelings for where I was living. Landing in New Orleans filled me with intrigue, landing in Raleigh felt safe and rooted, and landing in Syracuse always gripped me with a cold ambivalence. I'd never landed in Miami without feeling a buzz, thrilled to think of it as home. I'd never landed in Dallas without wanting to poke a rusty screwdriver through my eye.

This wasn't about the cache of the city, some sort of cool-by-association status conferred by living in a hip place. Raleigh had no more style than Dallas. But long after I'd moved away from there, landing at Raleigh-Durham International Airport felt like a homecoming, while I still didn't even like to change planes at DFW. It wasn't a measure of how my life was going at a particular time, how well I was—or wasn't—keeping the balls of my marriage, family, and career up in the air at the same time. I'd loved New Orleans right out of school when I was rudderless and confused. And not unlike Emma, I'd never warmed to Washington, even in the beginning when I swore I was on a launchpad for fame and fortune. How I felt when I landed at a given airport was an intangible measure of the resonance between the city and my soul.

My feelings about our new home were an unforeseen benefit derived from my curbed career ambitions. Rather than thinking about what my next house would look like, which was standard operating procedure when each new home was understood to be a prelude to the next step up, I was gripped by the desire to play my cards right so that I'd never have to leave this one with its made-to-measure fit. Waking with the sun streaming through large, sliding glass doors in our bedroom that opened onto a stone patio bordered by several flower beds and a small lawn, I placed a feeling I'd never had before— not in the house where I'd grown up, nor in any of the places I'd lived by myself after college, nor in any of the homes Stina and I had set up together. Given the chance to choose, I wanted to die in this house. I certainly hoped I'd have a new kitchen and master bath by then, but I wanted my body carted out of this front door. It was entirely new, and more than a bit strange, to know for the first time where I wanted to die, but stranger still was how deeply settled it left me.

All my new running loops in Montclair started on Upper Mountain Avenue, a busy two-lane road that ran north and south along a series of hills that formed the town's western border. A mile south on Upper Mountain, Berkeley Place, running east to west, offered a broad, unobstructed view of the New York City skyline fifteen miles away. Each morning, looking to my left for a few seconds at daybreak, I would see ribbons of pinks and purples light the sky over Manhattan as the sun emerged behind the sharp-angled skyscrapers, a vivid reminder of exactly where I was. And each dawn, I was reminded that exactly where I was, was exactly where I wanted to be.

My running picked up in Montclair where I'd left off in Washington the previous week, going just under eleven miles on the Fourth of July, which sent me off to Montclair's holiday parade filled with optimism. That made three times in the past three weeks I'd run eleven miles or more. Running for an hour and a half was a demanding workout, but no longer an insurmountable challenge. With less than four months to go before the race, I wasn't exactly as fit as I'd hoped to be—I would've preferred to have a fifteen-miler under my belt by this point—but I knew I was in solid shape to start my final, critical training push.

During the third week of July, I ran 4.1 miles on Monday, took Tuesday off, ran 4.2 on Wednesday, 6.9 on Thursday, 4.1 on Friday, and after another day off on Saturday, ran 11.3 on Sunday. That made 30.6 for the week, my first 30-mile training week since I'd started.

This put me well beyond any kind of training I'd done in high school. I was out of my depth and knew it. I perused a couple of marathon training sites on the Web looking for some approaches to the last few months of training, asked Peter how he'd handled the run-up to marathons, and started reaching out to anyone else I knew who'd done it before.

My buddy Billy answered the call with generous enthusiasm. A twinkle-eyed, switched-on trial lawyer, he thought nothing of running seven miles in the morning, then smoking two cigars while walking eighteen holes of golf in the afternoon. Still in great shape twenty-five years after his high school lacrosse career ended, he'd run the New York Marathon a couple of times.

Billy was an advocate by nature. And he'd taken me on as his client. The week I'd left Washington in late June, he e-mailed me. "Circle August 1st on your calendar. We're going 13." He knew from his own experience the crucial step I'd take, physically and mentally, once I knew I could run half the distance of a marathon.

Billy lived in western New Jersey, his home surrounded by miles of gorgeous running trails that cut through thick forests where Revolutionary War battles had been fought. They were perfect: soft, rolling, and heavily shaded.

"We're doing this in two loops," he told me. "Seven miles on one set of trails. Six more on another. We'll pass the house in the middle. You can get some water and take a leak."

Billy's suggestions to lower my arms and let loose a bit more on the downhills seemed to help, as did his gentle insistence that I lose the heat-trapping black wool baseball hat I'd worn on a hot August day. ("You're an idiot. Take that thing off.") But there was no tip to overcome my biggest challenge—Billy naturally ran about a minute and a half faster per mile than me. Compassionately, he tried to slow the pace to something more my speed, but even his slower gears forced me to push hard just to keep up with him. When Billy told me we'd just finished our third mile, I felt as I usually did after six. I couldn't imagine how I'd make thirteen.

Somewhere near the middle of mile four, I came as close to stopping in the middle of a run as I had at any time since my painful, swollen calves had rendered my legs useless and driven me to the orthopedist nine months earlier. It was futile. The trails were great and my partner was supportive. I just couldn't keep up.

I pushed on, mostly out of embarrassment, shortening my immediate focus from how I could possibly run another eight miles, to simply the next mile in front of me. The trails weren't marked, but Billy told me we were moving at a pace of somewhere near 8:30 per mile. So when I looked down at my watch, and saw 38:25, 38:26, 38:27, I made a deal with myself. I wouldn't even consider walking again until my watch ticked past 42:30, which would've put me somewhere near five miles.

"Less than two miles to the house," Billy said after a few more minutes had gone by, sounding as if he was reclining in a lounge chair by his pool. I knew I could hold on for another fifteen minutes. I banished from my head the idea of another six-mile loop after that and pushed on.

"You okay?" he asked after another five minutes, at the bottom of a long hill. "We don't even have a mile."

"I'm good," I pushed out in response. I was fairly certain he'd exaggerated, and shortened the actual distance remaining in order to boost my spirits. I appreciated the gesture, but I realized it meant I must've looked like hell.

"All right. I'm going to pick it up. Top of the hill, you'll see where you are. A left and a right and you're in my driveway. Meet you there." He took off, which was fine with me. I was left alone to lumber.

Straggling into his driveway, I could see him already sucking down a Gatorade. His wife, Stacey, had brought out towels, drinks, and bananas, which his six-year-old, Henry, held out helpfully. I'd finished the first loop in a little more than 58 minutes, less than 8:30 a mile and much faster than most of my training runs.

Once I caught my breath I felt surprisingly good. Maybe it was the endorphins, but my legs still had some zip. Standing in his driveway, I started to grow slightly curious. Did I have another six in me?

"We were moving at a pretty good pace," Billy said as we headed off for the back half. "We'll take it a little easier. This loop isn't nearly as hard," he added, offering up a carrot of encouragement.

I tucked in behind him, and using Billy as a pacesetter I knocked off the last six with no trouble. In fact, the longer we went the stronger I got. Rather than checking my watch obsessively, I found myself trying something novel for a training run—enjoying my surroundings. Miles eight to eleven were a smooth glide through a series of meadows and gentle rolling hills that ended at a fountain overlooking a complex of lacrosse fields. Billy hadn't included this water break in his description of the run, so it came as an unexpected bonus. With a drink of water and a chance to collect myself, we now had two miles to go. I hung on surprisingly well as we scurried up a final, nasty hill and finished off miles twelve and thirteen. Including the mid-run break and the second, shorter water break, my watch said 2:01:19.

I'd just finished the longest run of my life. Two hours plus.

"Let's go. Backyard." Billy was twenty yards in front of me, heading for his pool. I hit the water and came up slowly. Sitting on the concrete steps in the shallow end, up to my neck in a languid serenity, I felt the satisfaction consume me. It was official. I had a witness. I could run half a marathon.

After Billy first floated August 1 for my thirteen-miler, I'd planned an even bigger challenge for two weeks later, when Stina and I were taking the kids to Long Beach Island for a week. As I'd known since I was a kid, the island was eighteen miles long. I'd had friends who regularly biked from one end to the other, even a few who'd run it. On my father's wall of achievement in his office, he'd hung a framed certificate for finishing the October 1987 Long Beach Island eighteen-mile road race (2:12:16, 190 out of 1,150 finishers). But while I'd always been intrigued about the idea of getting from one end to the other on my own, I'd never had a reason to try. Now I did.

If I could make it the length of Long Beach Island two and a half months before the marathon, I'd be right on schedule, if not a little bit ahead. Running the island would definitely be stepping it up a notch—not a mile or two farther than I'd ever run, but five miles longer than the personal best I'd just set—but I wanted to give it a try.

I roused Stina at 5:00 a.m. on the Tuesday of our vacation week. My mother's house was exactly five miles from the Barnegat Light-house at the northern tip of the island. Stina drove me the thirteen miles from my mother's house to the southern end of the island, planning to pick me up at the lighthouse a few hours later. She dropped me off in a municipal parking lot as the first rays of sun were peeling away the last layers of predawn darkness.

"See you at the lighthouse at 9:15," I said optimistically, as I leaned across the front seat to give her a kiss and then got out of the car. The gnats were up before the sun, chewing on my legs as I stretched against the wood fencing that separated the parking lot from the beach. It was a little before six o'clock. I figured I'd stretch for another fifteen minutes. If I ran the eighteen miles in ten-minute miles, it would take me three hours to get there.

I hadn't remembered to bring the running belt my brother berated me into buying after my first twelve-miler back in June. He'd been right. The belt let me carry a bottle of water from which I could sip as needed, as well as packets of energy gels, gooey boosts of caffeine, sugar, and carbohydrates that I'd started eating on long runs at his recommendation as well. But hanging in my closet back in Montclair, the belt wasn't going to do me any good this morning. I did have the twenty dollars I shoved into the small pocket of my running shorts so I could stop for water at a 7-Eleven a little more than halfway into the run.

I started off slowly, hoping to conserve energy. The southern half of Long Beach Island was more commercial than the northern. Most of the traditional summer businesses and tourist traps had developed on that end in a shoulder-to-shoulder series of small towns I was about to run through, the backdrop for so many childhood memories.

A couple of miles into my run down the boulevard, I passed Centre Street in Beach Haven and looked left down the block for a glimpse of the Holiday Snack Bar, the old-time hamburger stand that served the thick slabs of yellow cake iced with the impossibly fluffy chocolate frosting my father had commanded us to order thirty-five years earlier because "it shouldn't be a total loss."

By the time the memory-lane loop in my head got to my father polishing off his cake, then draining a glass of the coldest milk this side of an Alaskan dairy, I was seven blocks north. Perfect timing, since dinner at the Snack Bar had always preceded our annual trip to Hartman's Amusement Park, which had been located at Seventh and Long Beach Boulevard.

Hartman's had been gone for a quarter century, replaced by a newer park, but that didn't matter. Running by, I could smell my father's Bay Rum cologne as he buckled me into a miniature Mustang convertible for a spin around the kiddie-go-kart track that featured perfectly rendered, life-size cardboard cutouts of Batman and Robin, the Joker, and the Penguin all drawn with precise comic-book detail.

A raised strip of metal ran down the middle of the track to prevent the car from running off it and into a fence. But even at six, I would still make sure to never let my eyes hang on Batman too long when I went around the curve where he stood. I knew that was how accidents happened. And I was always disappointed when I'd unintentionally let the car drift too far right or left and the metal block would automatically correct it, keeping me on the track but degrading my fantasy that I was actually patrolling Gotham City.

Continuing north up the island, my ride around the track at Hartman's ended just as I approached the Spray Beach Yacht Club. That's where my mom bought a small sailboat for us without first asking my father—one of my earliest acquaintances with rebellion.

Ten more blocks, looking left to the bay, I saw Howard's Seafood Restaurant and Pop-Pop Aaron taking us all out to dinner. Howard's was a bit fancy as restaurants went on Long Beach Island. "Just get whatever you want, dear." It was Pop-Pop's voice, sweet and kind, reassuring my cousin Sugie, who'd just indicated an interest in Howard's famous French Fried Lobster—the house specialty, chunks of breaded, deep-fried lobster, was among the priciest selections on the menu.

Next was the M and M Steam Bar, where I'd eaten some of my first steamed clams, across the street from Marvel's grocery store, where as a kid I'd waited at dawn with my dad for their homemade doughnuts.

As I made my way north from Peahala Park to Brant Beach, then Ship Bottom, I saw the church where my sister and I watched awe-struck as an old man was loaded into an ambulance. We were eight and six at most but knew things weren't looking good for the man on the gurney. A few blocks later, I ran past a miniature golf course that long ago had a hole requiring a steady shot through the Lone Ranger's legs. Soon after, I came upon a deli that had been one of the few businesses open year-round when I was a kid. I had a flash of my dad and me eating corned-beef sandwiches one winter day in the early 1970s when he took me along for an off-season drive to check on the house.

The memories were a perfect distraction. A hit parade of happy moments, providing a boost every time I loaded one into my mind. Who needed the energy gels? I hadn't even noticed how far north I'd run until I passed Stutz Candies, a few blocks from the causeway that bisected the island.

Stutz made me well up. On the weekend of my father's sixtieth birthday, Pop-Pop Aaron and I had been dispatched down the island on a last-minute mission to buy cocktail napkins. My mother had told us the color, shape, and pattern of the napkins she wanted but didn't know a specific store where we could find them. That would be up to us.

We'd struck out everywhere we had tried. Stutz was our last chance. We pulled in—"C'mon, Pop-Pop, let's give this place a shot." When the plump woman behind the register told us they didn't sell napkins, ensuring we'd return home as empty-handed failures, I saw a small, knowing smile break out on my grandfather's face.

"Jimmy, we are going to catch hell," he announced as we got back in the car, anticipating Nana Helen meeting us with that click of disappointment she produced by rapidly and repeatedly snapping her tongue off the roof of her mouth and shaking her head sorrow-fully. But my grandfather seemed amused at the prospect of a chid-ing, delighted to be bonded with his grandson in the brotherhood of scolded men.

Just down the block from Stutz was a strip of stores that had housed the Sneak Box a generation ago, the discounter where my dad bought our sneakers for us. I was just settling into a recollection of my father picking out a pair of red Converse All-Stars for me when I saw the 7-Eleven coming up across the street. I'd run a little more than nine miles in just under an hour and a half, chewing over a new set of warm memories every couple of blocks. My mind had wan-dered as it pleased, with no direction from me. I was so lost in my thoughts that I hadn't once bothered to check my pace.

Without any water on the first half of the run, I was parched as I headed inside, grabbing a twenty-ounce wide-mouth bottle of orange-flavored Gatorade and a twenty-ounce bottle of water out of the refrigerated case. I picked up a banana at the counter, headed back outside, and snarfed it all down, wanting to get back on the road as soon as possible. The early-morning cool had burned off and the temperature was rising. I could feel a full-throttle muggy mid-August New Jersey beach day starting to emerge.

I got halfway down the next block before I realized my mistake. I'd drained about two-thirds of each bottle. I felt pregnant. And if I was looking for more blissful memories to keep me company as I moved into the second half of the run, I was on the wrong end of the island. The north end was mostly residential. There would be no memories of red-pepper relish to distract me or my father's cologne to boost me. I'd have to gut it out.

I could feel the fatigue build as I passed mile markers ten, eleven, and twelve. Slogging along, I was in a battle with my urge to stop and walk, but still in command. The fatigue didn't feel any different from what any long run produced. Two narrow bands of muscle running diagonally from my hip bones down through my groin were starting to strain, making it a bit more painful to keep one foot following the other. But coming upon the familiar stretch of the Long Beach Boulevard leading to East Atlantic Avenue, my mother's block, I felt as if I had more than enough fuel in my tank to power through.

The marker for mile thirteen was planted in the sandy soil ten yards before her corner. I had five more miles to go. Seeing it, I thought back to the exuberance of approaching the same corner two months earlier, although from the opposite direction. That day back in June, I'd run twelve miles for the first time, thrilled to be redefining my limits. Now I was battling the disappointment of coming up against them. Again.

It was approaching 8:30 as I neared East Atlantic. I was picturing the kids just getting out of their beds when suddenly I stunned myself. With no warning, or forethought, I simply stopped and began to walk. As heavy as my legs felt, as painful as it was becoming to lift my feet, I hadn't been making any deals with myself. Not once had I thought "If you just make it to Mom's, you can stop." It was a complete surprise.

I'd been jogging along more slowly than I'd expected, but that was the pace I figured I needed to run all the way to finish, not because I was about to quit. The wiring in my brain simply short-circuited, dropping the trapdoor of my gas tank, draining it of whatever I had left. I walked along the boulevard with my hands on my hips, bewildered as I tried to digest what had just happened, that I'd actually stopped running. The warm memories of the south end of the island gave way to a familiar spasm of self-loathing—"I'm not fit enough, not dedicated enough, not good enough"—here on the north. I kept walking, wondering what about running past my mom's home had sapped me of my resolve.

A mile later, I ducked into a small deli, bought another bottle of water, took a couple of swigs, and started to jog again. I fell into the old but familiar pattern, alternating five minutes of running with five minutes' walking, just as I had eight months ago when I started training again after Emma's bat mitzvah. I kept up the cycle of five minutes' running, five minutes' walking for the next forty-five minutes, until the lighthouse was a little more than half a mile away. Then I ran all the way to the end, where I saw our car parked in the lighthouse lot.

Stina and Bobby were exploring the base of the lighthouse when I saw them. The moment she saw me, Stina started running in my direction, cheering "You did it. You did it." I wasn't quite so sure.

On the one hand, I'd run thirteen miles without stopping for the second time in a little more than two weeks. I'd also walked and run another five, making it from one end of the island to the other for the first time in my life. It had been hotter than I expected, and much more humid than I thought I could handle. I didn't have my water belt to properly hydrate. All told, I'd walked and run—but mostly run—for 3:16:45 straight. By those measures, I had a lot to feel positive about.

But of course, there was the other hand. And that was the one I used to berate myself. The clarity I'd gained at Bobby's birthday party wasn't some lightbulb switched on once to provide perpetual illumination and never to burn out. I'd set out to accomplish something specific and quantifiable, and I hadn't done it. My running the last few months had been an uninterrupted exercise in expanding my capacity. I hadn't come up short in quite a while. I'd long since moved past self-doubt. This was dragging me right back to it.

I was still unsure about what to make of my eighteen-miler five days later, when I headed back to work. But I didn't have a chance to spend much time brooding about it. On my second day back, Ted Kennedy died in the middle of the night and I drove to Boston for the next five days of all-consuming coverage. I managed just one run, 4.4 miles through South Boston. Driving back home on Saturday night, August 29, my anxiety starting to spike over the missed training, I decided to try to bust out a long run the next day. I simply needed to cut off any lingering doubt. Anything longer than thirteen miles would do.

I came up short again, unable to make it a step beyond eleven miles. I started to panic. Here I was, looking at a calendar that said September 1, two months from Marathon Sunday, and I still couldn't run more than half the distance. Yes, I'd done thirteen. But not a step more. Two months away and I was only halfway there. Twice in the past two weeks I had tried to go longer. Twice I could not.

My legs felt good. My lungs weren't an issue, either. My breathing was strong and steady. I called Peter looking for some advice, if not reassurance. He pointed out that I hadn't been sleeping very much, especially with round-the-clock Kennedy coverage. He was a big believer in the basics—eating right, sleeping well—and told me to take a few days off, making sure to stretch and sleep above all else. We agreed to hold off making any grand assessments of my fitness until I was well rested. Then I'd shoot for a forty-mile training week, including a run of longer than thirteen miles. I put the long run down on the calendar for Labor Day, a week away.

I took the next two days off, then ran five of the next seven. I took a later train to work so I could sleep a little longer and stretched twice a day. If I failed again on Labor Day, I wasn't going to be able to blame inadequate preparation.

I'd mapped out a 7.3-mile loop through Montclair that included one long downhill and two short but steep inclines. Twice around would make 14.6 miles, a perfect distance to build confidence. I set out down Upper Mountain Avenue with a full bottle of water attached to my belt. I'd left a second bottle at the foot of our street sign, this one supplemented with electrolyte-replacement powder. I also carried two energy gels in the zipper pocket of my belt.

The earliest hints of autumn had started to appear in a string of gorgeous, one-for-all September days. The slightly lower temperatures and diminished humidity chased away at least two dimensions of struggle that had accompanied nearly all of my runs in August.

I didn't want to jinx myself, but as I came up the long slope that finished off the loop for the second time, I felt terrific. Maybe it was the extra rest or the proper hydration. Maybe the promise of future memories in Montclair was more powerful fuel than those of the past on Long Beach Island. Or maybe I simply couldn't have worked as hard as I had for as long as I had without eventually seeing some striking payoff. All I knew was I had no interest in stopping, and my body wasn't suggesting I needed to.

I continued on another smaller loop around the neighborhood

that I'd previously measured out at 2.1 miles. I realized as I finished the smaller loop that I was completing nothing short of the longest, strongest run of my life: 16.7 miles in 2:31:02.

All the way up a small hill to our block, I just kept murmuring "Wow, wow, wow" to myself. Stina met me inside our front door with a look of concern and a mystified "What happened to you?" She pointed at my chest. I looked down. My white running shirt had two narrow threads of red running from my chest to my waist. I'd been warned about this, but never thought I would run long enough to chafe my nipples raw. Sure enough, they were bleeding. I smiled deliriously at my two red badges of honor. "Stigmata," I offered up with a laugh.

I'd been despondent and started to think I simply didn't have what it took. Now, in one two-and-a-half-hour run, I'd answered all the questions I had allowed to plague me for more than a month, obliterating the doubt building in me since I'd crapped out in front of my mother's house on Long Beach Island. In the shower, I crossed my arms and cupped my palms over each side of my chest. While I'd long expected my training regimen to leave me feeling better, I never guessed I'd find pure bliss. Or at least not standing under a shower-head desperately blocking jets of hot water lest they sear my bleeding nipples.

Six days later, I bookended my 16.7-mile run with a 15-miler. Adding in the week's three other runs, I'd totaled 45 miles, my first 40-mile week ever. Two weeks later, I knocked off 11 miles on a Tuesday before work, ran 15 miles five days later with Billy along the Jersey side of the Hudson River, threw in a couple of 7-milers and a pair of 4-milers. In the last full week of September, I had totaled 48 miles.

The marathon was now five weeks away. I had one last long run ahead of me. Nearly everyone I knew who'd run a marathon told me I needed to get at least one 20-mile run under my belt no later than three weeks before the big day. Go 20, they told me, and the cheering crowds and race-day adrenaline would carry me for the remaining six. I planned the last long one for Sunday, October 11. That would give me three weeks to recover and taper, a process of running progressively shorter distances to get my legs as fresh as possible for November 1.

The two 40-mile-plus training weeks put me in the perfect mind-set. I was now able to run as long as I needed to, as often as I needed to. When I got on the scale after my 15-miler along the Hudson, I weighed 186 pounds. That was an even 30 pounds less than I weighed when I'd busted through Danny Leong's suit 19 months ago. There was no other way to look at it. I was in the best shape of my adult life.

Everything was firing right. Five of my oldest friends were planning to come to Montclair the following weekend. Friday night we were going to see Bruce Springsteen during his final set of shows at Giants Stadium before they knocked it down to make room for a new one. Stina and I had bought tickets to take the kids the next night as well. I couldn't think of anything more inspirational to kick off my last push to the marathon starting line than back-to-back Springsteen shows at Giants Stadium. I would wake up Sunday morning, October 4, after the second Springsteen show, fit, inspired, and ready to go with exactly four weeks to the marathon. At least that was the plan.

After nineteen months of training, running hundreds of miles in freezing cold and sweltering heat; after ripping my pants just by trying them on; after being passed by mothers pushing strollers; after surviving swollen calves, a crushed ego, and the loss of my professional bearings; after making peace with my dead father; after redefining accomplishment and repeatedly redrawing the vision for my life; after dodging mortar shells in Afghanistan, bullets in Iraq, and vodka in Texas; after trading Hank Paulson's mangled pinkie for Barack Obama's brother-in-law; after crashing hard and digging deep to make a painful midcourse correction; after losing thirty pounds—after all of this, I'd started to feel as if I'd figured a few things out and was ready to live as a wiser, happier, more satisfied man.

But first, I needed to be catheterized.

It began innocently enough in the parking lot of Giants Stadium on the first Friday night of October, where Mikey, Eddie, Paul, Neil, Dave, and I, friends for more than thirty years, were meeting to kick off another of our "guys' weekends." Our reunions were tame by any standard: forty-eight hours of stepping back to our collective adolescence, which had been sweet, conformist, and fairly boring. We stuffed ourselves with junk food, rented *Blazing Saddles*, and retold stories about our eccentric tenth-grade chemistry teacher, Mr. Smith, who, legend had it, once drove to a ball game in Philadelphia, forgot he had parked in the lot at Veterans Stadium, took the train home, and reported his car stolen to the police the next morning. The vice of choice for our weekends was Magic Shell, a kind of chocolate syrup that hardened into a crust instantly upon contact with ice cream.

None of us had been rabid Springsteen fans when we were growing up. While you couldn't be a teenager in New Jersey in the late 1970s without knowing plenty of kids who worshipped the articulator of their adolescent alienation and pulled a lyric from "Jungleland" for their yearbook quotes, that hadn't been any of us. Paul had fallen under the spell at Rutgers. He'd drive an hour and fifteen minutes from his campus to the Stone Pony, the club on the Jersey shore where Springsteen would often appear unannounced, and watch him play from so close that he'd get sprayed with the Boss's sweat. After catching one of these impromptu concerts in Asbury Park, the Jersey beach town where Springsteen got started, Paul always had the rapturous look of a pilgrim just back from Lourdes. It took the rest of us a few more years to catch up, but eventually we all got there in varying degrees of intensity. Arriving at another common destination, this one thirty years after we'd first discovered so many other crucial parts of life together, was a big part of the fun.

As his tour wound down, Bruce had taken to performing entire albums during his concert. On our night, we got *Darkness on the Edge of Town*. The songs of struggle, hope, and resignation didn't make for my favorite album, but that didn't take a thing away from the evening. I'd never been into the poetry of Springsteen as much as the joy his riffs and rhythms were able to draw out from deep within me. I was a cheap date; all he had to do was play "Tenth Avenue Freeze-Out" and "Rosalita" and I was sure to go home grinning.

As always, the part of "Tenth Avenue Freeze-Out" when "the big man joined the band" knocked me out. Bruce, in a gray button-down shirt and black vest, wearing some sort of wrist brace on his right arm, stood on one side of the stage, looking to Clarence on the other. Clarence took his hands off his sax for a second, lifting his arms into the air, then waving them back and forth, signaling thousands of "little pretties" to do the same.

On the floor of Giants Stadium, where we were standing about forty yards from the stage, I threw my arm around Dave and turned us both to look at the huge crowd behind us, eighty thousand pairs of arms moving together on an unseasonably warm and humid night. I pointed at the upper deck. "Holy shit, buddy—look at that, can you belie—" It was as far as I got. A bolt of emotion stripped my voice from me.

Wagner's *Ring* cycle did it for some. Verdi's *Rigoletto* did it for others. But not in the swamps of Jersey. Bruce, the company of my oldest friends, my health, and the ecstatic crowd packing Giants Stadium, that's what knocked me out. I'd been with the same group six years ago in Hershey, when Stina fell and I didn't go to her. Bottoming out during that guys' weekend, I was all the way back for this one. In fact, I'd come even further than that. It was all too much. I couldn't finish my sentence, caught up in a poignant, perfect moment.

After the show, we drove the ten miles back to Montclair, sitting up until a little past two and talking over Rolling Rocks, three kinds of chips, and half a dozen different flavors of ice cream. One of our rituals was everyone sleeping in the same room, air mattresses all pushed together in our best approximation of twelve-year-old boys on a sleepover. Everyone but me. At least this time.

I knew they'd keep talking, laughing, and farting for another hour or two. So after I got them situated in the basement TV room, I headed back upstairs to my bedroom, a small concession to my training. I hated to miss a minute with the guys, but Petey had been hounding me to get as much sleep as possible in the homestretch.

The plan was for the guys to hang out all Saturday morning and leave after lunch. Mikey, Eddie, and Neil would head off to Asbury Park to continue mainlining Bruce with a trip to the Stone Pony, while Dave and Paul had to split early to get back to their homes.

I planned to run seven miles, then head right back to the Meadow-lands that night with Stina, Emma, and Will for my Springsteen encore. The kids had never seen Bruce. They'd need at least one Giants Stadium concert to be able to claim an authentic Jersey childhood after they were grown.

When Stina woke me at eight to tell me the guys were up, my T-shirt was completely drenched and my forehead beaded with perspiration. I didn't think twice about that, since I'd changed into sweats to hang out after the concert and was so tired when we'd called it a night that I'd slid under the covers fully clothed. That explained the clammy layer of sweat, or so I thought. Of course, that didn't account for the dull ache in my right side and lower back.

I headed to the kitchen to make coffee. While the pot was brewing, I grabbed some plates to set the kitchen table. Suddenly the dull ache became a sharp stitch in my right side, beneath my ribs, like someone was poking at my kidney with an ice pick. The whole area felt distended. I went to the bathroom hoping that after the gross consumption of junk food the prior evening, I was simply having a weapons-grade gas attack.

No such luck. In fact, the pain only got worse. Coming back to the kitchen, the sharp stitch intensified into something more closely approximating a small steel ball barbed with razor blades flagellating the entire right side of my body. The next thing I knew I was down on my hands and knees, arching my back toward the ceiling, the only position that would grant me even the smallest measure of relief. If my appendix hadn't been removed twenty years earlier, the diagnosis would've been a piece of cake. But it had. So, down on all fours under the kitchen table, moaning in pain, I was left to wonder what the hell was wrong with me.

Stina wanted to take me to the emergency room, an idea I instantly dismissed. Never mind not wanting to ruin the rest of the time with the guys; nothing was going to get in the way of taking the kids to see Bruce later that day. Then I started throwing up.

Mikey, a dermatologist, called his brother Richie, a urologist, who took somewhere between three and five seconds to diagnose a case of kidney stones. Richie told Mikey I should go to the emergency room right away. After four hours of ever-escalating pain, having sweated through three different shirts and now throwing up every fifteen minutes, I was no longer arguing.

We had a choice of two emergency rooms. One was a couple of miles away at a small, local hospital housed in a tired, slightly run-down set of buildings; the other was a sparkling, modern facility at a larger, fancier hospital half an hour away. We were in the car for half a block, trying to figure out which one to choose, when we hit a pothole. "Mountainside," I screamed, demanding that Stina make a beeline for the closer one. I couldn't handle another thirty seconds of jostling, much less another thirty minutes.

Stina drove right up to the ER entrance. I hobbled in and saw it was quiet. The admitting nurse was just wrapping up with the only other patient there. Although she looked as if she'd be done any second, I couldn't sit and wait. Hopping from foot to foot was the only way I could keep the pain remotely bearable. And even that was starting to lose its effectiveness. I needed opiates. And I needed them immediately.

The nurse finished with her patient, took one look at me, and said, "Kidney stones."

"How do you know that?" I shot back while continuing to hop from foot to foot, astonished by her instant diagnosis.

"You're doing the dance, honey."

"I'm not arguing," I said, trying to flash her a smile. "I'm buying anything you're selling. Just get me a big needle full of something. This is killing me." I'd instinctively started to channel my father and rule number one of handling a dire situation—charm the hell out of the person in charge. Maybe it wasn't the way to go in every circumstance, but it seemed to work well in an emergency.

I detected a slight but distinct connection as she started to enter my basic information into her computer. "Okay, honey, we're gonna take care of you, and we're definitely gonna take care of that pain. Now tell me, dear, what's been going on the last couple of hours?" I'd gotten through.

I described the sweat, the nausea, and the pain.

"Any other problems?" she asked.

"No, I'm a very healthy man," I said, grimacing, as I shifted my weight back and forth.

"I can see that," she answered deadpan, playing along.

"No, really," I continued. "I was the picture of health until I woke up this morning. I was at the Springsteen concert last night."

"So was I, honey!" she said excitedly, her face brightening even more. I'd collected three "honeys" and a "dear" in my first four exchanges with her. "Great show, wasn't it? But I wish we'd got some other album. I'm not a big *Darkness* fan. What can you do?"

I loved New Jersey. About to pass out from a killer case of kidney stones, I first had to analyze the set list from last night's Springsteen show with the admitting nurse.

"We gotta get some vitals," she said, suddenly all business. She put her finger on my wrist to take my pulse. "Hey. That's a forty-eight. Are you an athlete?"

Aside from Bruce, the only other force strong enough to distract me from the agony was vanity. My body was shaking, my teeth were chattering, and I was about to throw up again from the pain. But I could still process a burst of pride that the nurse thought I had the pulse of an athlete.

"I'm a runner," I gasped through gritted teeth. "I'm supposed to run the New York Marathon in four weeks."

"All right, honey, we'll get you taken care of. Don't worry about a thing."

She turned me over to Michelle, an ER nurse. A tall, thin Jersey girl in her mid-thirties, Michelle was a no-bullshit straight shooter who defined compassion as hitting you right between the eyes with everything you needed to know. Or in this case, between the legs. She didn't take more than ninety seconds to make her initial assessment.

"When's the last time you urinated?" she asked.

"I don't know. Several hours ago, at least," I answered.

"Okay, we're going to catheterize you," she responded in a tone that sounded quite untroubled considering what she was proposing.

"Let's do it," I said immediately. If anything was going to reduce the pain—a set of medieval thumbscrews would've been a step up at this point—I was all in. Even if it was the one thing all men fear most.

Michelle handled the whole thing with cool professionalism, if not a bit of gallows humor to dull the pain. "*Yeeeowwwwwww!*" I screamed as she began the process. Stina turned away. The relief was immediate. The urine started flowing, relieving the pressure just as Michelle thought it would.

"Thank you, Michelle. Thank you. Thank you."

"Um, sweetheart," she countered. "I just stuck a needle up your dick, and you're thanking me?"

"Good point," I answered, looking for Stina's eyes, just to make sure I'd heard that right. She was smiling, knowing as I did that we'd just heard one of the stunningly great lines of our lives.

Michelle gave me some morphine while I waited for a CT scan, knowing it might be a while until they could fit me in. I enjoyed the haze for a couple of hours until they finally wheeled me down the hall, a loopy grin plastered on my face. The timing couldn't have been worse. The morphine started to wear off just as the orderly was helping me slide into a long metal tube, unmasking a crippling pain and rendering me a shaking, chattering mess. I pathetically tried to control it with a half-assed approximation of what little I could remember from the Lamaze classes Stina and I had taken fourteen years earlier.

It was futile. But fortunately, we were able to get the scan done on the first pass. Immediately they shot me up with more morphine while I waited for someone to read the images. The needle took the edge off everything, including the realization that the Springsteen concert with my kids wasn't going to happen. They wheeled me back to my curtained-off cubicle in the ER, where Michelle told me all this trauma was being inflicted by a three-millimeter stone working its way through my kidney.

I drifted off to sleep thinking about my last trip to the ER, nineteen years earlier, with appendicitis. My dad had been running the show that night, grilling every doctor and nurse who got within twenty feet of my bed. I was in horrible pain then, too, but felt enormously safe listening to my father go up one side of the anesthesiologist and down the other when the poor guy told us putting me out would be a "normal procedure."

"I make my living when 'normal procedures' have abnormal outcomes—so why don't you just explain to me what you plan on doing to my son. In small words."

All these years later, I held Stina's hand as I fell off, yammering incoherently about how much I wished my dad was there to grill the anesthesiologist.

I woke up as the sun was setting, my anxiety spiking as the reality of what was happening started to settle in. The pain was under control. I now had a little pump for medication. Whenever I started to feel discomfort build, I pressed a button and administered a dose of heavy-duty painkillers. But once the pain was under control, my panic began to spin chaotically out of control. The last place I expected to wake up just four weeks from the marathon was in a hospital room. I started to realize I could miss days of training, possibly weeks. This was time I didn't have to lose.

Dr. James Saidi, the on-call urologist, came into my room and spelled it out for me. A slim man with olive skin and a Mediterranean two-shaves-a-day beard, Dr. Saidi had a serious bearing that read as sure, confident, and exceedingly competent—just what I wanted in any doctor in general but in a urologist in particular. He seemed to be a few years younger than me, his grave demeanor leavened by the smile he flashed when listening at bedside. It contained the barest hint of whimsy.

Dr. Saidi spelled out my two options. The first was to let the stone pass naturally. He promised they'd keep me doped up with painkillers until it did. Judging from the CT scan, he thought I was looking at no more than a couple of days. But he couldn't make any guarantees.

The alternative was a surgical procedure. But once I heard the words "penis," "stent," and "threading instruments," I stopped listening. The catheter had been more than enough fun for the time being.

Actually, it was a no-brainer, even without the threading instruments. If the stone passed naturally, I'd be back on my feet and running as soon as a day or two later. The surgical procedure, on the other hand, would require five or six days without any running on the back end. How could I afford to miss an entire week with only a month left to go? The only problem with choosing to wait and let the stone pass on its own was the possibility that it wouldn't. Then I'd still need to have the procedure, and still be out of commission for five or six days—only I would've delayed getting started while I waited around for the stone to pass.

We decided to give the stone until noon Monday to pass on its own, and then have Dr. Saidi perform the procedure—stent, threading instruments, and all. That way, while I knew I'd lose some time healing, I could guarantee being back on the road by the following weekend. The worst-case scenario would still leave me three weeks until the race. It wasn't ideal, but still better than nothing.

Stina and I were now riveted on a quart-size clear-plastic urine receptacle. With the catheter removed, I got out of the hospital bed every couple of hours, steadied myself against the metal rail, and filled up the receptacle as best I could. While I collapsed back into bed, Stina would take the receptacle to the bathroom and filter it, hoping to find a tiny stone.

With no indication that the stone was moving, I was discharged Sunday afternoon to wait it out at home, armed with prescriptions for Percocet and Ketorolac, two heavy-duty painkillers. I got home, climbed into my bed, and immediately started shaking in pain. My teeth were chattering so badly I thought I was going to lose a filling, and again I broke out in a drenching sweat. I popped my meds and settled in for what I hoped wouldn't be too long before I found a kidney stone in my piss receptacle.

Thanks to a prescription for Flomax, I filled the container half a dozen more times Sunday night and Monday morning. Each time we came up empty. Once or twice we saw something floating that we thought might be a stone, but when we filtered it and put it in a plastic bag to bring to the doctor, it dissolved, my hope dissolving with it.

The procedure was set for Monday afternoon. Late Monday morning, I got out of bed to head over to the hospital, pausing one last time to fill the receptacle. Stina saw something bloody; it was similar to the other false alarms that had dissolved, but a touch more solid. Small and brownish-white, it looked like a large grain of sand. But after so many false alarms, she just filtered it, put it in a plastic bag, and said, "Let's go, we're late."

We tried to present it to the woman registering us at the same-day surgery center. She told us to "show it to the doctor." She sent us up a floor to the admitting nurse. We pulled out our small baggie there and tried to get her to take a look. "Show it to the doctor," said the admitting nurse. We were taken to a cubicle, where I was given a gown and a brief description from a nurse anesthetist about how they'd put me under. When Stina dangled the baggie with the stone in it to her, the nurse said, "You can show it to the doctor, but I'll be back in a minute to start your IV."

Finally, as they were ready to take me to the operating room, Dr. Saidi strolled in to say hello. "Any last questions?" he asked. Stina handed him the baggie. He looked at it, worked it between his fingers a few times through the plastic bag, and immediately pronounced, "This is it. Forget it. We're done."

I was astonished. "Hang on a second," I said, still unsure that I'd heard what I'd heard. "No procedure, doctor?"

"No procedure," he repeated, the whimsical smile widening.

I'd bet right. Just like that, the great kidney stone fiasco was over. Or so we thought.

When we got home, I swept up all the painkillers on my bedside table and threw them out. I figured I'd give myself another day for my body to flush the drugs from my system and start running again on Wednesday, wanting to get back on the road as soon as possible. In the meantime, I told Stina, I was going back to work the next day.

That was still the plan the next morning, even though I woke up in a junkie's strung-out flop sweat. I headed off to work, but by midmorning I realized I'd made a mistake. The grip of a paralyzing despair was tightening around me. I sat at my desk, staring at nothing, feeling an encroaching blackness settle over me.

No doubt fueled by withdrawal, along with my inability to concentrate on work, I got nailed by a case of withering self-doubt. Having long ago made peace with never beating my dad, I was now certain I wouldn't even make it to the starting line. Everything I'd worked for in the past nineteen months seemed to be evaporating. I was helpless, overtaken by a crushing sense of failure. It was everything I could do to keep from dissolving into a weeping mess.

A little after noon, I told the bureau chief that I had to go home. I was able to drive, finding the focus required to deal with midtown Manhattan traffic to be a welcome diversion from the consuming despondency. Once home, I climbed cautiously into bed and started to sob. I was completely wigged out, with no idea what was going on, except that I felt as if I was in the middle of a full-scale breakdown. Everything was black. I was sure that the marathon was out.

The next day, Wednesday, I didn't even try to go to work. I was crying steadily, like a teenage girl with a hormone imbalance. I got out of bed, got dressed, and walked Bobby to his bus, then burst into tears seeing him climb cheerfully up the steps. It was his confident air, poised to attack another day, which sent me over the edge. Stina met me when I came back.

"How'd he get off, Jimmy?"

"Oh, Stina, it was so beautiful. I mean, there he was, completely in control, nothing was going to intimi—" I stopped mid-sentence and dropped my face into my right hand, overcome. When Stina asked me if I wanted a bagel, I wept. When my mom called to check on me, I started bawling. When Dave e-mailed to ask how my hospital stay had been, I lost it as I started typing about the exquisite care provided by the nursing staff in the ER.

It was the painkillers. Rather, it was my trying to wean myself off the painkillers. They belonged to the devil. I'd been on them for only a couple of days, but they already had their insidious hooks in me. I was consumed by hopelessness, convinced I'd never recover in time to run the marathon. I was sure my walls were falling in on themselves just three and a half weeks from the starting line.

"Why me?" I wailed to Stina. "Why now?"

The proof of performance for my entire reclamation project, a year and a half in the making, had been scuttled by one three-millimeter kidney stone. And there wasn't a single goddamned thing I could do about it. Somewhere deep inside my drug-induced misery was yet another caveat to the rules of life the process of training for a marathon had been yielding. "The one person you could never say no to was yourself"? Actually, sometimes your body took that one out of your hands as well.

I went back to bed and lay down. I was caught between an all-consuming lethargy, which had me under the covers tucked in the fetal position on my side hoping I'd fall asleep, and full panic, which had my eyelids pinned wide open. I lay there for half an hour. Any hope of regaining control of the situation depended on my dragging my ass out of bed, putting on my shoes, and going for a run. I had to get up, just had to. And I couldn't.

My eyes stared blankly into my closet. All my suits were hanging there in front of me, but what I saw were amorphous patches of gray and blue. Five or six seconds passed between blinks. I made a deal with myself.

Two miles. Just get up and walk or run or crawl. That's all I was asking—two miles. Run two miles and at least I could keep the possibility alive of rallying enough during the next few weeks to run the marathon.

It took me almost twenty-two minutes, nearly eleven minutes a mile. I felt sluggish and bloated, as if I was dragging a piano behind me. My back ached and my legs felt like anvils. I didn't remember any of it, my mind still shrouded in a blank fog. But I made it.

After I got back and showered, I went with Stina to run some errands in the shopping district closest to our home. We walked, three-quarters of a mile at the most. I was exhausted. She went into the post office to mail a couple of packages. I stayed outside, leaning against a pair of mailboxes to keep me from collapsing onto the

sidewalk. A kind-looking woman who appeared to be in her late fifties approached. She hesitated, waiting until I saw her and moved
aside to make room for her to get by. She dropped her letters in the
box, and as she turned to go, she stopped and looked at me. Just the
sight of me, wan and feeble, had raised the red flag. "Are you all
right?" she asked with the compassion of Florence Nightingale tending to the Crimean War wounded.

The marathon was twenty-five days away.

I was slightly less despairing the next day and was able to get out
for another run. Still foggy and web-headed, I struggled on, knowing I had only a week and a half of real running left before I'd begin
tapering. I doubled my distance from the day before.

The further away I got from the painkillers, the more a clear-
headed sense of normalcy returned. I was steadily getting better, but
it was hellish. For the first time in my life, I understood why someone
might choose to kill himself rather than live every day feeling trapped
like that.

On Friday, I slogged through 7.3 miles, so compromised I could
barely lift my feet the last half a mile. Catching my foot on a seam in
the sidewalk, I wiped out at the foot of the last hill, falling directly
onto the slabs of cement in front of me. My hands were scraped and
bruised, but it could have been much worse—I'd just missed slamming my head on the sidewalk as I tumbled into a somersault. I
gathered myself and jogged up the hill home, shaken at my infirmity.
On the one hand, I was back to more than seven miles, regaining
strength and endurance each day. On the other hand—actually there
was no other hand. I felt horrible.

Before the kidney stone attack, I'd planned the single most important run of my entire training regimen—the twenty-miler—for Sunday. Of course, when I'd laid out the last weeks of my training schedule,
I hadn't planned to be laid up the entire week before. Now it seemed
laughable; there was no way in hell I was ready for a twenty-mile run.
But I decided to give it a whirl. I wanted to see how far I could go. If
nothing else, I'd get a good reading on just how much the kidney stone
had taken out of me. I made myself a simple promise: I'd try.

I didn't know if I could run my usual seven-mile loop once, let alone three times. I got through the first loop, just barely breaking a sweat. I was moving at a slow pace. Time meant nothing to me. The only thing that mattered was staying in motion for as long as possible. I came through the second loop feeling surprisingly fresh, continuing right into the third on a wave of optimism that perhaps I was bouncing back more quickly than I'd imagined possible.

The weather was perfect for a long run: temperatures in the low sixties, light wind, and a good cloud cover to keep the sun from beating down directly on me. I was continuing to feel good as I approached the halfway mark of the third loop. Then, with no warning, I suddenly realized my tank was empty. I started to walk, exactly as I had when I'd passed the beach house on my eighteen-miler in August.

I walked the rest of the loop and then immediately got in my car to measure how far I'd gone. The odometer measured three and a half miles into the third loop, which, combined with two loops of seven miles each, meant I'd crapped out at 17.5 miles.

I couldn't figure out whether I should be pleased or not. It clearly wasn't bad, especially considering that I'd been in the hospital at this time a week ago. It was longer than I'd ever run. But it still wasn't the twenty-miler that would have erased all doubt. I'd come up more than eight miles short of marathon distance. My only hope was that my body was still in the process of recovering from both the kidney stone and painkiller withdrawal. I was feeling stronger every day, but I wasn't fully there yet. What I didn't know was whether I had enough time to regain the ground I'd lost.

I ran relatively low mileage the next week, with the exception of a last fifteen-mile run on Saturday that went smoothly enough. That would be my last long run before the marathon. I had two weeks to go, but the time for building endurance was over. If I didn't have the capacity I'd need, it was too late now. This was the body I'd be taking with me to the starting line.

As I began my two weeks of tapering, it was clear I'd been through something traumatic. Even light four-mile runs, designed just to loosen my muscles, left me badly winded, so different from just a few weeks earlier. Perhaps it was the tension and anxiety, but the left side of my lower back began to twitch and spasm uncontrollably. It got so bad I thought I was getting another kidney stone to balance out the one that had nailed my right side.

The last week leading up to the big day was filled with muscle relaxants, massages, stretching, and baths. My back loosened up somewhat, but as I climbed into bed the night before the marathon, I was worried—unsure whether I had trained hard enough, but knowing there was nothing I could do if I hadn't. I felt as if I was limping into the big day, fighting off a sneaking suspicion that somehow I'd blown it.

In bed, I checked my BlackBerry one last time. There was a message from my friend Jo Gwin Shelby. She'd been in her late thirties when I'd taught school with her in New Orleans nearly twenty-five years earlier, a lean, muscular Southern beauty who ran marathons and rode her bike a hundred miles at a shot. Now she was in a wheelchair, with late-stage Lou Gehrig's disease. So when I saw her name and opened the message—"Go Jim Go"—I felt as if I'd just won the inspiration lottery, knowing how much it had taken for her to type out those three words with cutting-edge technology that allowed her to stare at a keyboard and have her eyes do what her hands no longer could.

Stina was in the other room watching TV with the kids. I called for her to come. Without a word I put my BlackBerry in her hand to read Jo Gwin's message.

In the darkness of our bedroom, Stina sat on the edge of the bed and gently put her hand on the side of my face. "Jimmy," she said, "I guess in life you never know when you're going to get kidney stones or your back's going to go out or you're going to get ALS. So grab the happiness when you can. You just never know." She leaned over and kissed me good night. "Get some sleep. And whatever else happens, you're going to have fun out there tomorrow."

S tuck in traffic three-quarters of a mile from the runner's staging area, I just couldn't take it anymore. I'd tried to mask my
building anxiety, but Stina could easily see the stress spread
across my face as I raised my eyebrows, squeezed the bridge of my
nose between my left thumb and index finger, puffed both cheeks
full, and blew a narrow stream of air hard through a small opening
in my pursed lips toward the windshield. I thought I'd left myself
plenty of time to get to the staging area from Montclair, some thirty
miles away, even factoring in New York Marathon traffic. But clearly,
I hadn't.

It was 9:15 on Sunday, November 1, 2009. The marathon was
scheduled to start in less than an hour. The last thing I wanted was to
be rushed. My mind was racing—I still needed to stretch, change my
socks and shirt, and hit the Porta-John. I was also hoping for a few
minutes to clear my head and get ready for the final steps—both literal
and symbolic—of my journey that had started twenty months ago.

"Jimmy, why don't you go," Stina instructed me gently. "You
should probably get out and start walking."

I looked at her, too agitated to share any kind of meaningful moment, and nodded my agreement. I put the car into park, unbuckled my seat belt, leaned across the armrest, and gave Stina a kiss goodbye. She held my face. "Good luck, Jimmy boy. You're gonna do great." I welled up and smiled, unable to say a thing.

I popped out of the car and opened the back door to lean in and kiss the kids goodbye. The moment I slammed it shut, I heard, "Hey, Jim." It took me a second to place the voice. It was my buddy Billy, who'd taken me on my first thirteen-miler on the trails near his home three months earlier. Of course. There were 44,177 people running the race, and here was the only other guy I knew personally who was signed up to run. I took it as an unmistakable sign of good karma that he just happened to be walking down the sidewalk where I'd pulled over my car at the exact time I was getting out of it.

We walked briskly toward the starting line, hopped up and chatting nervously. After passing through a metal detector, we split up. All 44, 177 runners couldn't start at once. The organizers divided the field according to how fast runners expected to go. Billy's wave of faster runners started at 9:50. Mine would cross the starting line twenty minutes later. We gave each other man hugs and separated into our respective corrals.

It was a good day to run: overcast, temperatures in the low fifties with a slight breeze. Everything I'd read instructed runners to wear the rattiest pair of sweatpants they owned to stay warm, and then discard them right before the start. I had on an ancient pair of black sweats that fit the bill. I lubed up, sliding Vaseline between my toes, on my chest, and all around my old-school jockstrap. I still had a few minutes left. I slowly stretched out each leg a few more times and took several long breaths. In the distance I could see the faster runners already heading across the Verrazano. This was getting exciting.

Through a megaphone, I heard the instructions for the runners in my group to start making their way down a slight hill toward the starting line. "Welcome to the 2009 New York City Marathon." The announcer greeted us in a voice full of energy and optimism. "Get ready. Five more minutes and you're on your way."

While I was no longer racing my dad, I was keenly aware that I was running in his footsteps. No doubt, this was my marathon, not his. I was running in my way, for my reasons. But I felt his presence simply in knowing I was getting ready to tackle one of the challenges he had always adored. I hadn't felt this close to him since delivering a couple of Cokes and a pack of Goldenberg's Peanut Chews to him in his hospital bed nine days before he died.

I took a deep breath and tried to relax. Everyone I knew who'd run the marathon had warned me not to get sucked into the exuberance. I'd heard all sorts of cautionary horror stories from people who'd repeatedly reminded themselves to go out slowly, only to get caught up in the moment, sprint out much faster than they could handle, and pay a steep price later in the race.

The announcer counted off four minutes, then three, then two, then one. Thirty seconds later, the sounds of Frank Sinatra singing "New York, New York" blasted through the air. Here I was, battling to control my emotions, and the race organizers clearly weren't playing fair. The crowd starting singing along with Frank until suddenly, thirty seconds into the song, they broke into a roaring cheer. A hundred yards ahead of me, the front of the pack had crossed the starting line.

I covered my face with my hands and blew out a couple of breaths to steady myself while I waited for our part of the pack to begin moving. While I needed to concentrate, if for no other reason than to monitor my pace, I wanted to take a moment to drink in the undiluted joy. I'd made it to the starting line!

Still, I had to contend with a slight but distinct heaviness. It was no more complicated than the intimidating challenge that stretched out in front of me, the final 26.2 miles of a journey so long in the making. Nearly nine miles longer than I'd ever run in my life. Yes, I'd made it to the starting line. But the starting line wasn't the finish line.

No, I didn't care about my time. But I didn't want to be the guy limping over the line in the dark eight hours later. I had one goal, simple but meaningful—I wanted to, and needed to, run the whole way. I didn't want to walk, not a step. Confronting all the challenges of the past year and a half had left me with one bumper-sticker life lesson: don't stop. But as I approached the starting line, I honestly didn't know whether I could run the next 26.2 miles without stopping.

The race organizers provided each runner with a computer chip embedded in a loop of plastic. I slipped the loop through my left sneaker, and my time at every mile would be posted on a Web page so any of my friends and relatives could follow my progress. Huge digital clocks positioned at every mile marker would keep us all apprised of our times as well. Neither I nor anyone who cared about me would have any trouble knowing exactly how far or how fast. Perhaps it was superstition, but I also wanted to start my own watch, the one that had been with me for every mile I'd run in the past twenty months. As I crossed the starting line, I pressed the button on the side of my Timex. I was off.

All the warnings were dead-on. The urge to pick up the pace required constant vigilance to resist. I made a conscious effort to go slow, checking in with myself every thirty seconds or so to make sure I hadn't subtly started to accelerate. "Slow down, you'll go farther" had never been more important. I kept repeating it to myself up the first long incline of the bridge.

The light breeze at the starting line had turned into a fairly stiff wind at the crest of the Verrazano, the highest point on the course. A few hundred yards before the first mile marker, I passed half a dozen guys on my right who'd already stopped. Lined up shoulder to shoulder, they were pissing off the south side of the bridge. It must've been some sort of primal territory-marking exercise, since they'd just left a staging area with nine thousand Porta-Johns. Mercifully, the wind was at their backs.

Other runners were flying by me as we approached the one-mile mark, idiots whooshing just to the right or left. A few clipped my shoulders and arms in their rush, as if they didn't have the next twenty-five miles to sort out their position.

I thought of what the salesman at the running store told me the previous day, when I'd bought new shorts for race day. "Whatever pace you've been training at, run the first five miles a minute a mile slower than that. If you've been running sevens, run eights. If you've been running eights, run nines." I'd been running nine-minute miles the last few months of my training. I saw the clock for my first mile split— 10:06, 10:07, 10:08—perfect. I was barely breathing hard at all.

We started our gradual descent toward Brooklyn. Standing at the bottom of the bridge, atop a concrete embankment, was a welcoming party—a dozen people screaming encouragement. It looked like a couple of families: the women, plump and seated in folding lawn chairs; the men in work jackets, holding coffee mugs. The kids, girls and boys all under ten, wore hoodies with their pajama bottoms. Not one of the people standing there cheering looked like a member of the New York Road Runners Club.

All of them were sitting or standing under a hand-drawn banner that said GO RUNNERS. Two of the girls held up either side of a brown cardboard sign with YOU CAN DO IT drawn in the neatest lettering a seven-year-old could manage. The one girl closest to the runners held her half of the sign with her left hand, reaching her right out for high fives. Framing the whole scene was another sign about five feet behind the group. This one was official, put up by the borough: YO—WELCOME TO BROOKLYN.

I made the sharp left turn onto Ninety-second Street. Standing on the sidewalk in front of the Fresca Bakery, next to a parking lot protected with rolls of razor wire, was another guy I never would've pegged to be a big fan of marathon runners. But there, in a grease-stained sweatshirt and ragged gray chinos, he stood, holding up his sign, written in the voice of the runners. Three simple lines: I AM STRONG. I WILL FINISH. I HAVE NO FUCKING LIMITS. I wasn't so much wondering where these people had come from—it was their neighborhood, after all; we were the intruders—as why they were out on the street cheering so enthusiastically and how they knew exactly what to say.

Three blocks later, I turned right onto Fourth Avenue. Whoever described it as a five-and-a-half-mile standing ovation undersold it. The faces of those cheering changed as we ran down one of Brooklyn's classic boulevards, past the bakeries, nail salons, apartment buildings, and halal butchers of Dyker Heights, Bay Ridge, Sunset Park, Carroll Gardens, Park Slope, Prospect Heights, and Boerum Hill. The names on the storefronts morphed from Italian to Arab to Asian to Latino to Jewish. But no matter where we were, or who was on the sidewalk cheering, all 44,177 of us were greeted with the same sustaining buttress of encouragement; none of us was running alone.

Standing three deep in front of bodegas and gas stations, the people of Fourth Avenue held signs of support high above their heads. Plenty were meant to encourage anyone running by. There was TODAY YOU ARE ALL KENYANS, and others custom-designed for a Jake or a Nancy, a Rosa or a Luke. Some marketing whiz at Dunkin' Donuts had been handing out rectangles of white cardboard, blank except for the corporate logo in the corner, perfect for writing a succinct message of support. Half a dozen blocks after turning onto Fourth Avenue, I ran past three in a row. The first said GO PENNY. Right next to it: YOU CAN DO IT. The third, held by a man with a mischievous, unrepentant smile, was the exclamation point: RUN BITCH RUN.

Every few blocks, the sound of a different band reached out to carry us along. It was almost like a musical bucket brigade. Four ZZ Top look-alikes blaring Southern rock from in between gas pumps at a convenience store passed us on to a middle-aged Van Morrison wannabe blasting "Brown Eyed Girl," who handed us over to an all-Korean brass band playing "America the Beautiful," who delivered us to a gospel choir shaking the heavens from the front of a funeral home. In one three-block stretch, two different bands worked their way through "I Saw Her Standing There," linked by a corner with no band at all, just a loudspeaker blasting Carlos Santana and Rob Thomas doing "Smooth."

It was difficult to tell who was getting more out of the exchange, the runners or the rooters. Near the end of my trip up Fourth Avenue, at the intersection with Bergen Street, two elderly black women stood, in housecoats, next to a black man of similar age, stooped, thin, and drawn, with a scraggly ten-day beard. All three were clearly suffused with the spirit of the day. They held out what they could for the runners. The woman had a roll of paper towels she was holding from the bottom in her upturned left palm, thumb hooked under the cardboard tube to balance it. She tore off single sheets at a time to offer sweaty runners as they passed by. The old man had one eight-ounce plastic cup half filled with water, pinching it at the rim between his thumb and index finger and holding it out to no one in particular, just hoping someone would take it.

I ran through the eight-mile checkpoint, turning right onto Lafayette Avenue, surprised by how fresh I felt. It was more than just race-day adrenaline. It was the energy given off by an entire block of race-watchers at Lafayette and Clermont, halfway to mile marker nine. Arrayed on the front steps of their brownstones, they bellowed along to "YMCA" as the original blasted from a couple of monster speakers. An Indian chief and a navy sailor in full Village People regalia led the neighborhood chorus through the arm motions. At least one runner peeled out of formation to temporarily join the crowd.

One block later at Lafayette and Vanderbilt, looking up the street to see if I could eyeball the next water station, I saw the head of a runner who looked as if he was surrounded by a security team. Curious, I picked up my pace and pulled closer, next to one of the five surrounding runners whose shirts said "Support Team." I craned my neck slightly to see who was in the middle, the object of support. All I could see was his back, and a runner's shirt with the name "Ben" lettered on it, along with a couple of phrases I couldn't make out. As I worked my way down to his legs I suddenly got it. Ben was bounding along on two prosthetic legs, a double amputee.

The air filled with the loudest cheers of the day from the crowds: "Go, Ben. Come on, Ben." I stayed exactly where I was, drafting in the reinvigorating energy of Ben and his peloton. Trouble was, Ben was running too fast for me. I was pushing too hard to keep up with him and had to fall back. I was unable to keep up with a double amputee, and loving it.

I hit the eleven-mile mark in Williamsburg feeling terrific—my breathing wasn't the least bit labored and my legs felt strong. Of course, half a second later I realized being eleven miles in meant I still had fifteen to go. A fifteen-mile run on top of what I'd already done? The idea seemed laughable. I would have chewed on the over-whelming nature of that for a while longer, except my attention was snagged by a couple of Hasidic Jews trying to time a lull in the run-ners' traffic for a sprint across Bedford Avenue.

I passed a synagogue. Men in their black hats and *payis* were coming and going, trying hard to pretend it was any ordinary day. It must have required extraordinary concentration, however, because normal days didn't feature a reggae singer in dreads banging away at his electric keyboard, offering up a joyful version of "Could You Be Loved" just to the right of the shul's front door.

After a couple more miles that twisted through Williamsburg and Greenpoint, I saw the Pulaski Bridge in front of me—the half-way point. I couldn't believe who was standing at the foot of the bridge. My man in the gray chinos had skipped ahead eleven miles to greet us again with his plainspoken inspiration scribbled on a sign he held over his head: I AM STRONG. I WILL FINISH. I HAVE NO FUCKING LIMITS. I pushed out a "thank you" as loudly as I could, but he didn't hear me. Of course not. He was too busy screaming encouragement as runners passed the 13.1-mile marker. I was halfway home. The clock ticked 2:14:19.

Consumed by everything playing out along the route, I hadn't paid any attention to my time beyond monitoring my splits enough to know I was running at a pace of roughly ten minutes a mile. Dou-bling my split for the first half, I'd be in the neighborhood of a 4:30 marathon, though there was hardly any guarantee I could sustain the pace of the first half through the second half. Twenty months earlier, the whole idea was to beat my father's time. If I kept up this pace, I wouldn't even be within an hour of it. Having just mainlined the energy of Brooklyn, feeling strong, without the slightest fear of stopping, I couldn't have cared less.

The first challenge of the second half started with the Queens-boro Bridge, which came just after the fifteen-mile marker. The half-mile incline to the crest of the bridge was widely known to be the big killer hill of the race. As I came around Crescent Street to

Queens Boulevard, I immediately understood why. The route took runners up the bridge's lower span, which was dark, dank, and steep. For the first time, I saw runners in groups of two and three deciding to walk. I reached into my pocket, grabbed my third energy gel, and humped it up and over the bridge.

The exit ramp dumped the runners onto Manhattan's East Side. First Avenue was just what every runner needed coming off the Queensboro, cheering throngs packed five and six deep behind blue police barricades, just like at the Macy's Thanksgiving Day parade. Their yelling echoed through the canyon of buildings on First Avenue to create a wall of sound, a powerful boost that bucked us up and spurred us on.

I'd made plans with Stina to rendezvous eleven blocks north of the bridge, at East Seventieth. She was meeting me there with the kids, my mom, Dave, and his son, Theo. Just before the seventeen-mile mark, they'd be waiting with hugs, kisses, Fig Newtons, and a big bottle of water supplemented with electrolyte-replacement powder.

Emma was the first to see me approaching, abandoning her teen-ager's deep-seated fear of embarrassing herself by looking like a kid and screaming *"Daaaaaaady!"* like a five-year-old surprised with a new Barbie. She threw her arms around my neck as I approached, pulling me toward her and over the top of the barricade. "Easy, Beanie," I said through my smile, while I met Stina's eyes. She looked thrilled, telling me I was earlier than she expected—the perfect greeting. I kept my legs moving while she gently patted the sides of my face, gave me a kiss, and sent me on my way.

The Fig Newtons provided just the jolt of carbohydrates and sugar I needed. I thought I was in good shape as I reached seventeen miles, figuring I had another mile and a half on First Avenue before I'd hit 110th Street and turn left. I had less than ten miles to go.

The crowds started to thin as we made our way toward upper Manhattan. There weren't as many signs of support. The cheering wasn't nearly as loud. That was okay, I told myself. I would soon turn off First Avenue and take the very first steps in the direction of the finish line in Central Park. We'd still have more than seven miles to go, but it would be another perfectly timed emotional lift. I counted off each street. I hit Ninetieth, then Ninety-fifth, then 100th. All I had to do was hold on for a few more blocks and begin the symbolic start home.

Which is why I was so confused when I looked up at 109th Street expecting to see the pack in front of me turning left, and watched as everyone continued to run straight up First Avenue instead.

I wasn't sure why I'd thought we'd be turning at 110th. I'd read the map before the race. I saw that the route took us straight up First Avenue to the bridge into the Bronx. There was clearly no left turn off First. Yet somehow during the first eighteen miles, the idea of running no farther than 110th Street had gotten stuck in my thick, disoriented skull.

My confusion quickly turned to dejection. I now had no idea how much farther I had to go up First Avenue at a point when I really needed to know exactly where I was headed. I passed the nineteen-mile marker, and my calves began to cramp for the first time. I'm sure glycogen depletion would've been the scientific explanation. But at that moment, it seemed to me much more likely that my endurance was being sapped by loneliness and dread.

Finally, seventeen blocks later, I reached the top of First Avenue and the Willis Avenue Bridge, which would take us over the Harlem River. Apparently the engineers had never been told that thousands of runners would be using the bridge one day each year, and that it might be nice not to torture them, seeing as they'd be nearly twenty miles into a marathon when they ran over it. The bridge featured sections of metal grating instead of pavement. The grating was made of strips of steel running lengthwise and across, forming one-inch squares. Each corner of each square, where the metal strips intersected, was raised and pointed. A carpet had been laid over the grating, but it wasn't nearly enough. Each time my foot landed, several of the raised points bore into the ball of my foot, leaving me feeling as crippled as Ratso Rizzo, the con man played by Dustin Hoffman who'd limped across the Willis Avenue Bridge in *Midnight Cowboy*.

Coming off the bridge and turning hard left, we were now in the Bronx, a destination not traditionally known for lifting anyone's spirits. Passing the twenty-mile checkpoint, I'd now gone two and a half miles farther than I'd ever run before. But I was still 6.2 miles from the finish line. We couldn't have been in the Bronx for much more than a mile before crossing the Madison Avenue Bridge back over the Harlem River. It took me a moment to place the sense of déjà vu I had running back into Manhattan. The short bridge shook the memory loose. Eight years ago, I'd walked across the same bridge to get to the CBS Broadcast Center on 9/11, when I'd been sure I'd missed the opportunity of a lifetime.

The route took us a block over to Fifth Avenue and the start of a three-mile slog due south to where we would enter the park. I followed Fifth Avenue as it jutted around Marcus Garvey Park in Harlem, past mile marker twenty-two, and smack into the one facet of running a marathon I'd anticipated with a combination of curiosity and fear all day: the wall.

Everyone had warned me. There would come a point of utter depletion—physical, mental, and emotional—when I would wonder whether I'd be able to finish. As my field of vision started to narrow, giving me the sense of looking through a sea captain's spyglass, I realized I was there. I started to tune out everything happening around me, feeling my spirit receding deep within. The sounds of the street grew soft and muffled. I couldn't hear much but the slapping of other runners' shoes on the street, and even that was dull and diffuse, as though filtered through cotton.

Time started to bend. On the way up First Avenue, it had seemed as if every few minutes I chewed up another group of streets—the Seventies, Eighties, and Nineties all went flying by. Now, heading back down Fifth Avenue, even though I was running at a nearly identical pace, everything seemed to be taking much longer, as if I were on a treadmill. I looked up to get my bearings. I was at 118th Street. I ran for what felt like ten minutes. I looked up again. I was at 116th Street. I'd gone two blocks.

I tried to eat another energy gel, but my body didn't want any more sugar bursts. I felt nauseous trying to get it down. The thought of Gatorade made me gag. I grabbed some water at mile marker twenty-three. My lungs were fine, but my legs were starting to turn to stone as I pushed my way down Fifth Avenue.

I was getting loopy, a perfectly timed onset of fraying faculties designed to round the sharp edges of the distress building in my body. In the midst of my building delirium, three faces traded appearances in my mind. There was Jo Gwin, whispering "Go, Jim, go." Then Peter faded in, reminding me, "Slow down, you'll go farther." Finally, I saw my father, who said nothing. He didn't need to. I got a boost just from having him with me as I realized I was now running alongside Central Park on my right. He was smiling. I was going to make it.

I had just three miles left, about half an hour of running. And a big chunk of that would be downhill. Any doubts about finishing were wiped away by Stina and the kids. After our rendezvous at First Avenue and Seventieth, she'd headed straight to the park, posting up halfway between mile markers twenty-four and twenty-five. The second I saw her jumping up and down and clapping, I raised my arms high. Dave couldn't contain himself, jumping in alongside me for seventy-five yards in his jeans and old Asics, holding up his phone and recording a few seconds of us talking.

When I passed mile marker twenty-five and saw the Plaza Hotel right in front of me, I knew we were about to dump out onto Central Park South for a final few blocks on the streets of New York City. I'd pictured getting to this point for months. A mile away from the finish line, I'd figured, would be when I would start to take it all in, a final stretch of poignant reflection of what I was about to accomplish.

Instead, I had to swerve to avoid a couple of EMTs taking a runner away on a stretcher. All I saw were the guy's yellow shorts and his reddish-blond beard, but I got a good enough look at his face to know that he was younger than me. This was no time for premature celebrations. I needed to bear down and get it done. I saw a sign marking the final eight hundred meters. I was half a mile from the finish line.

I ducked back into Central Park at Columbus Circle, heading down a gradual decline and then turning left toward the finish. Another sign popped out on the right: two hundred meters to go. While I'd thought about this moment at least once on nearly every run I'd taken in the past twenty months, now that I was here in the homestretch, most of me was just blankly putting one foot in front of the other. The small part of my brain still able to hold a thought conjured again the grinning face of my father. Here, at the end, I just wanted to be with my dad.

Coming up one last, small hill, I saw the finish line. I started to mumble. "We good?" I asked softly. "We okay?" After all this time I needed to be sure my father knew. I wanted no doubt for either of us. Everything that needed to be cleaned up had been. He had run his race the best he knew how; I finally knew how to run mine.

I crossed the line answering my own question. "We're good now, Dad."

I hit the stop button on my watch: 4:30:00.6. The first I'd thought about my time since the half-marathon marker. I had run nearly the same time for the second half of the marathon as I had for the first. But the numbers were meaningless. My mind was cloudy and dull, able to hold exactly one thought: "I didn't stop."

I took a couple of halting steps. Someone handed me a rectangular space blanket adorned with the logos of the race's corporate sponsors. I wrapped it around me; for the first time in four and a half hours, I'd started to feel cold. Another volunteer met my eye as she handed me a bronze-colored medal on an orange ribbon, my prize for finishing. A third volunteer gave me a bag with a bottle of water and a bagel, which I gobbled down immediately. I was famished. Then we were all herded along a path for another three-quarters of a mile to a park exit.

Physically, I couldn't do anything more than shuffle along with the wave, though my mind started to sharpen after finishing the bagel. I thought about where I'd been four weeks ago, in the hospital. "I didn't stop." I thought about where I'd been twenty months ago, on the platform in Houston. "I didn't stop." I thought about Stina, the kids, and my father. "I didn't stop." I'd done something the right way, the way I defined it, and exactly as I'd envisioned it. "I didn't stop." I broke into a deep, satisfied, exhausted smile. I was strong. I'd finished. I had no fucking limits. "I didn't stop." Not a bad approach for the long run I'd just completed, or for the one that lay ahead.

ACKNOWLEDGMENTS

My wife, Christina, was steadfast, encouraging, and sure—every step of the way. Her wisdom and vision have always provided a path to a richer, more contented life. I am grateful beyond words that she proved patient during the course correction I needed to make to put myself back on that path and heading toward a lasting, and shared, sense of happiness. Emma, Will, and Bobby Axelrod put up with too much of their father's absence without a word of complaint. Their trips to the green chair, where I sat typing as they headed off to bed, were nourishing and sustaining.

My mother, Joan Axelrod, brought enormous generosity to this project, never blanching from my telling parts of our family's story that she reasonably would've preferred to remain private; my brother Peter and his wife, Leah, were there for me in every conceivable way; my sister, Lisa, helped me clarify and sharpen many memories, and her husband, Michael, helped whenever legal questions arose; and my brother Teddy graciously applied his skill as a master photographer to help complete the book's jacket. I owe my entire family a debt for their willingness to bless this book with the good karma of collaboration.

ACKNOWLEDGMENTS

Simply put, there would be no book without the support of David Moughalian, Michael and Edward Ioffreda, Neil Olderman, Paul Sbrilli, David Mauro, Chris Desisto, Kevin Rendino, Phil Appel, Glenn Salzman, Billy Pinilis, Josh Dvorin, Richard Levinson, Barnett Hoffman, Robert Quackenboss, Christine Zmigrodski, Roberta Chrzan, Susan Newman, Mark Frost, J. R. Moehringer, Michael Bamberger, Rebecca Skloot, Ann Arensberg, Tom Rosenstiel, John Gomperts, Anthony Bossis, Sarah Hunninghake, Mark Wetmore, Bernard Goldberg, Larry Doyle, Bill Plante, Mark Knoller, Andy Wolff, Ward Sloane, Kate Rydell, Maureen Maher, Randall Joyce, Andy Stevenson, Byron Pitts, Terry Hunt, Mitch Weitzner, Larry and Brenda Boggess, Chloe Arensberg, Jo Gwin Shelby, Carol Leff, Doug Husid, Linda Mason, Glenn Altschuler, Kevin Morris, Davy Thomas, Charlie Thomas, and Jon Greene.

Mo Goins had the compassion to make sure I was all right during the invasion of Iraq and, even more important, after I was home. He is simply the bravest man I've ever met.

Mario de Carvalho and Geoff Thorpe-Willett are two men who will have their own unique places in my soul for the rest of my life. What I went through with them on our way to Baghdad belongs to the visceral, not the articulable. There is no way to thank them, only to thank God I was with them.

Finally, there are two men who deserve special thanks. My agent, David Black, is a dream maker. He is honest, encouraging, and big-hearted. One of the safe places to wait out the many storms of life is tucked safely under his wing. My deepest gratitude to him and everyone at the David Black Agency.

There is no way to adequately thank my editor, Thomas LeBien, and his team at Farrar, Straus and Giroux: Dan Crissman, Abby Kagan, Lisa Silverman, Brian Gittis, Ryan Chapman, and Amanda Schoonmaker. I would've thought after a hundred thousand words that I wouldn't have any trouble adding two more. But "thank you" doesn't begin to cover things when it comes to Thomas. The crossing of our paths has been one of the great strokes of good fortune in my life.

CPSIA inform
Printed in the
LVOW12s173

419464L

80809 057528